SMASHING
jQuery

PUBLISHER'S ACKNOWLEDGMENTS

Some of the people who helped bring this book to market include the following:

Editorial and Production
VP Consumer and Technology Publishing Director: Michelle Leete
Associate Director—Book Content Management: Martin Tribe
Associate Publisher: Chris Webb
Publishing Assistant: Ellie Scott
Development Editor: Linda Morris
Technical Editors: Andrew Croxall, Dennis Cohen
Copy Editor: Linda Morris

Marketing
Senior Marketing Manager: Louise Breinholt
Marketing Executive: Kate Parrett

Composition Services
Compositor: Wiley Indianapolis Composition Services
Proof Reader: Susan Hobbs
Indexer: Potomac Indexing, LLC

SMASHING
jQuery

Jake Rutter

A John Wiley and Sons, Ltd, Publication

About the Author

Jake Rutter is a user interface designer and front-end developer with a keen interest in writing jQuery for Web site applications. Jake is currently the senior Web designer and developer for Direct Wines, a company that sells wine online and offline, where he manages the front-end for four e-commerce Web sites. He is very enthusiastic about working with Web technology and is always pushing himself to learn something new in an industry that is ever-changing.

In his spare time, he runs a blog at `onerutter.com`, where he posts tutorials on jQuery, PHP, Magento, WordPress, CSS, and HTML. Jake lives in Connecticut with his wife and two dogs.

Author's Acknowledgments

Many thanks to my project team: Chris Webb, for giving me the opportunity to write this awesome book; Linda Morris, my project editor, for correcting my schoolboy errors; and Andrew Croxall and Dennis Cohen, my technical editors, for ensuring that my code and explanations were correct.

Also, I cannot forget to thank my wife for supporting and helping me through the process of writing a book. I wouldn't have been able to get through this challenge without her. To my parents for teaching me that hard work really pays off and prepares you when you try to achieve what you used to think was impossible. Thanks to my current and past employers for giving me the opportunity to work with open-source projects such as jQuery to push the limits of the Web.

Most importantly, an enormous thanks to John Resig and the jQuery team and community for creating a remarkable library that has brought me great career opportunities and the ability to create amazing Web applications with less code.

Contents

PART I: INTRODUCING JQUERY AND JAVASCRIPT   **3**

Chapter 1: Introducing jQuery   **5**

Discovering JavaScript Libraries   6

Realizing the benefits of using a JavaScript
library versus the traditional approach   6

Getting to know the main library players   7

The jQuery advantage   9

Chapter 2: Getting Started with jQuery   **19**

Setting Up Your Development Environment   20

Using Firebug in Firefox   21

Downloading the jQuery Library   27

Including the jQuery Library in Your Web Page   30

Understanding the jQuery Wrapper   31

Running code outside of document ready handler   34

Preventing conflicts with other libraries   34

Using JavaScript with jQuery   35

PART II: LEARNING THE JQUERY FUNDAMENTALS   **37**

Chapter 3: Using Selectors, Filters, and CSS: jQuery at Its Core   **39**

Working with DOM Elements using jQuery Selectors   40

Selecting page elements by using CSS selectors   41

Filtering DOM Elements Using jQuery Selector Filters   52

Applying basic filter definitions   52

Creating zebra-striped tables using the even and odd filter   53

Styling the first and last items in a list or collection of elements   55

Filtering elements that contain a specific element   56

Filtering elements that do not contain any elements or text   57

Filtering elements that contain text   59

Selecting Elements in the DOM by Their Attributes   60

Selecting links that contain a specific Web site address   61

Selecting all elements that end with a specific word   62

Manipulating your HTML and CSS with jQuery   63

Adding, removing, cloning, and replacing DOM elements
and content   64
Working with CSS and jQuery   69

Chapter   4: Working with Events   **71**
Understanding Events in jQuery   72
Working with Document and Window Events   72
Detecting complete loading of the DOM with the ready() event   73
Preloading images with the load() event   73
Showing an alert as a user leaves a page   76
Displaying a backup image using the error event   77
Getting Started with Event Delegation   77
Using bind to attach an event handler to an element   78
Using live to attach an event handler to an element   79
Using delegate to attach an event handler to an element   80
Capturing Mouse Events   81
Adding and removing content to or from a
page with a mouse click   82
Understanding how the double-click event works   85
Creating a tooltip that shows content during the hover event   85
Creating basic Add to Cart functionality
with mousedown and mouseup events   89
Creating a rollover effect on a button with images   93
Capturing Form Events   94
Adding a border to a form field when the user adds focus   94
Showing a message after a user leaves an input field   95
Capturing Keyboard Events   95

Chapter   5: Making Your Web Site Come Alive with Effects   **99**
Discovering What jQuery Effects Can Do   100
Showing and Hiding Elements Using Show and Hide   101
Setting a message to appear only once on site
using the show method and cookies   103
Toggling between show and hide   104
Sliding Elements Up and Down   106
Displaying Alternate Search Options with the slidetoggle Method   107
Fading Elements   109
Building a Basic Image Gallery with a Fade Transition   110
Adding Delay to Create a Timed Animation   114
Chaining Multiple Effects Together   115
Creating a News Feed Ticker with Multiple Effects   116
Creating Advanced Animations   119
Building an image gallery with text captions
using advanced animations   120
Additional easing effects using the jQuery easing plug-in   127

PART III: APPLYING JQUERY TO YOUR WEB SITE   **129**

Chapter 6: Improving Navigation: Menus, Tabs, and Accordions   **131**
Setting All Links on a Page to Open in a New Window   132
Setting an Active Item in Your Navigation Menu   133
Creating a Basic Drop-Down Menu   135
    Using advanced effects to the basic drop-down menu
    using animate   141
Creating an Accordion Menu   142
Creating Tabbed Content   147

Chapter 7: Creating Interactive and Exciting Tables   **155**
Styling the Data in Tables with CSS   156
    Adding alternating row colors using filters   157
    Adding a simple hover effect to rows   157
    Adding an advanced hover effect to rows   159
Manipulating the Data in Tables   161
    Adding a message after the first/last rows of the table   162
    Removing a row using a filter selector   164
    Adding a row after a row based on its index value   165
    Removing a row based on its index value   166
    Adding a message after rows with specific content   166
    Removing a row based on its content   166
Setting Up Table Pagination with jQuery   166
Creating Advanced Tables Using jQuery Plug-ins   172
    Sorting rows using the tablesorter plug-in   173
    Changing default sort order   175
    Creating sexy charts with tabular data using Visualize   176
    Creating a bar chart   177

Chapter 8: Creating Advanced Forms with jQuery   **181**
Focusing on an Input Box After Page Load   182
Disabling and Enabling Form Elements   182
Highlighting Current Fields in Forms   183
Creating Default Text within Input Fields   186
Limiting Character Counts on Input Fields   188
Creating a Check All Check Boxes Link   190
Getting the Value of an Input Box   191
Retrieving the Value of a Select Option   193
Adding Simple E-Mail Validation to a Form   194
Copying the Contents of One Field into Another   198
Enhancing Forms with Plug-Ins   201
    Incorporating qTip into your Web site   201
    Creating a basic form field qTip using the title attribute   203
    Using the jQuery validate plug-in to validate your forms   203
    Adding Simple validation to a contact form   204
    Adding advanced validation rules and messages
    to a contact form   208

PART IV: EXPLORING ADVANCED JQUERY   **211**

Chapter 9: Working with Dynamic Data and Ajax   **213**
- Discovering Ajax   214
- Loading Dynamic Content from a Web page   215
  - Loading all of the content   216
  - Handling errors if the content you load is missing   217
  - Loading sections of the content   219
- Submitting Forms Using Get and Post   221
  - Using POST to submit contact forms without page reload   223
- Working with XML Data   227
- Parsing Internal XML Data and Creating HTML   229
- Working with JSON Data   231
- Retrieving Internal JSON Data and Creating HTML   234
- Creating a Delicious User Widget by Receiving JSONP Data from API Requests   235
- Creating a Yelp Top Reviews Widget
- Using JSONP via the Yelp API   241
  - Getting Approved for a Yelp API Key   243
  - Using the Yelp API to Show Reviews Based on Telephone Numbers   243

Chapter 10: Creating and Using jQuery Plug-Ins   **251**
- Getting to Know Plug-Ins   252
- Incorporating a jQuery Plug-In into Your Web Site   253
- Incorporating jQuery UI into Your Web Site   253
  - Downloading jQuery UI   255
  - Adding jQuery UI to your site   255
  - Understanding how jQuery UI widgets work   256
  - Customizing the design of jQuery UI   256
  - Creating a UI theme with ThemeRoller   258
  - Using jQuery UI themes   261
  - Incorporating jQuery UI features into your Web site   261
- Incorporating Popular jQuery Plug-Ins into Your Web Site   269
  - Using jQuery tools   269
  - Fancybox   272
- Writing Your First jQuery Plug-In   274
  - Sketching out the plug-in   275
  - Understanding the plug-in structure   276
  - Setting the options for the plug-in   276
  - Creating the plug-in   277
- How to Distribute a jQuery Plug-In   284
  - Packaging your jQuery plug-in for distribution   284
  - Submitting your plug-in to Web sites   285

Chapter 11: Developing for the Mobile Web with jQuery   **287**

Building for the Mobile Web Using jQuery   288

Mobile Browsers   288

Understanding CSS3   289

Understanding HTML5   290

Getting set up to start mobile Web design   291

Working with the Apple iPhone Safari mobile browser   293

Working with the Google Android browser   293

Displaying content based on which smartphone your users have   295

Developing mobile Web sites and applications with jQuery   296

Introducing jQuery Mobile Preview   296

Mobile Frameworks   296

Working with Appcelerator Titanium Mobile   296

Working with the jQTouch plug-in   298

Chapter 12: Finding jQuery Resources   **301**

Watching jQuery Grow   302

Using the jQuery Web Site   303

Working with jQuery API documentation   303

Finding jQuery tutorials   304

Attending a jQuery meetup or conference   304

Submitting bugs to the bug tracker   306

Getting involved in the jQuery forum   308

Other Web Design and Development Resources   308

INDEX   **309**

XI

Introduction

jQuery has become a part of my everyday routine in Web design and development, so when Wiley approached me about writing a book on jQuery, I was thrilled. jQuery has opened up a world of possibility for Web design. Through this book, I hope to show others how using jQuery can really speed up your development time and allow you to write interactive components that you thought were impossible without serious programming knowledge.

Think of this book as both an introduction and cookbook of jQuery examples with real-world solutions that you can use in your everyday working environment. *Smashing jQuery* is divided into four parts, which I detail here.

PART 1: INTRODUCING JQUERY AND JAVASCRIPT

The first part of the book introduces you to jQuery from a beginner's perspective by discussing JavaScript libraries and how they have become an important part of every Web designer and developer's daily toolbox. The benefits of using jQuery are explained in-depth, giving you a full understanding of why jQuery has become so popular. I also touch on the importance of using progressive enhancement. After I lay the foundation for why you should be using jQuery, I dive right into how to get jQuery set up and ready to use on your Web site.

PART 2: LEARNING THE JQUERY FUNDAMENTALS

The second part of the book walks you step-by-step through all of the jQuery fundamentals such as using selectors and working with events and effects. The selectors in jQuery are extremely powerful, which is why I have dedicated an entire chapter to guiding you through all of the different kinds of selectors, giving examples of their usage. Events and effects are also covered in Part 2, to give you a solid foundation for building your own Web site application and user interface components.

PART 3: APPLYING JQUERY TO YOUR WEB SITE

The third part of this book focuses on how you can apply the jQuery concepts I discuss earlier in the book to your Web site or application. (Part 2 offers examples but not full tutorials such as how to create your own accordion menu or tabbed navigation.) Part 3 also covers using jQuery to improve form validation on your Web site.

PART 4: EXPLORING ADVANCED JQUERY

There comes a point in every jQuery developer's career when they want to move on to more advanced topics such as working with and creating plug-ins, writing jQuery to handle Ajax requests, or working with jQuery mobile apps. Part 4 delves into these advanced topics. Plus, I include a chapter that outlines all of the jQuery resources that are available online.

WHO THIS BOOK IS FOR

This book was written for Web designers and front-end developers who are just starting out with jQuery. You may have installed and set up a plug-in, but your aren't really familiar with how to write your own jQuery. Maybe you've heard the buzz online about jQuery and are looking for someone to show you how to use jQuery to improve your Web site. Readers should have a solid background in HTML and CSS and a basic understanding of JavaScript.

ABOUT THIS BOOK

Code and URLs in this book use a special font that looks like this: www.jquery.com. Code listings have been colorized similar to how IDEs and text editors use syntax coloring to help to distinguish between elements of the syntax, such as methods, properties, comments, and so on. New terms appear in an italic font. Text that you should type is in a **bold** font. All of the examples in the book are shown using the Firefox Web browser, but all examples are compatible with Microsoft Internet Explorer 6+, Mozilla Firefox 2.0+, Apple Safari 3.0+, Opera 9.0+, and Google Chrome. The code presented in the book's examples is available for download at www.wiley.com/go/smashingjquery.

INTRODUCING JQUERY AND JAVASCRIPT

Chapter 1: Introducing jQuery

Chapter 2: Getting Started with jQuery

1

INTRODUCING JQUERY

JQUERY IS A JAVASCRIPT LIBRARY created to help Web designers and developers write and extend JavaScript interactions quickly and concisely using a defined set of methods wrapped around the native JavaScript functions. jQuery does not offer any new functionality, but it takes existing hard-to-understand-and-write JavaScript APIs (application programming interfaces) and makes them available to a wider audience through easy-to-understand-and-write jQuery syntax.

In this chapter, I guide you through the benefits of using a JavaScript library, show you the different libraries that are commonly grouped into the same category as jQuery, and give you a good background on the features of jQuery and why it's a great library.

DISCOVERING JAVASCRIPT LIBRARIES

JavaScript libraries allow Web designers and developers to extend Web page interactivity and usability by employing a framework of commonly used JavaScript functions built using native JavaScript primitives.

Think of libraries as frameworks or blueprints with a set of rules and guidelines to help you build your Web site. JavaScript libraries make writing JavaScript much easier for Web designers and developers — they are a starting point. Many popular libraries such as Prototype, MooTools, Dojo, YUI, and the main focus of this book, jQuery, are used widely on the Web today. Each library has a specific feature set, with jQuery owning the DOM (Document Object Model) manipulation space.

The Document Object Model is the actual HTML code that represents a Web page, structured like a tree, with each branch being a node tied together in a hierarchical sense. Each node can be accessed most commonly through CSS and also through JavaScript using selectors. The DOM is the API (application programming interface) for how Web designers and developers can manipulate the Web page using methods created by the HTML standards committee. HTML 5 offers a new set of APIs for interacting with the DOM and creating a richer Internet experience for users. After a Web page is fully loaded, the DOM is ready to be interacted with.

A JavaScript framework allows a Web designer or developer to extend the DOM by adding a JavaScript include (`library.js`) to a page and then using special functions set up within the library.

REALIZING THE BENEFITS OF USING A JAVASCRIPT LIBRARY VERSUS THE TRADITIONAL APPROACH

The greatest benefit of using a JavaScript library is being able to tap into a huge assortment of functions to extend your Web pages beyond dull, non-interactive content.

JavaScript libraries can offer ways for Web designers and developers to work with effects, animations, events, Ajax, and interactive user interface widgets for faster and rapid Web development. Designers and developers are not limited to those functions provided by the library. You can also write your own.

The beauty of JavaScript libraries for Web designers who understand the DOM is that manipulating the DOM with a library becomes inherently easier than manipulating it by using the limited API of JavaScript.

In order to get the same features by writing your own JavaScript, you would have to spend countless hours and long nights programming, testing, and bug fixing, which would probably result in massive amounts of code. JavaScript libraries help greatly in this area by reducing the amount of code it takes you to do something that might normally be four times as big if it was done with native JavaScript.

Avoiding repetition is another benefit of using JavaScript libraries. As you start writing JavaScript functions to do similar tasks, you end up with a lot of very similar code — by using a library, you can eliminate that repetition.

GETTING TO KNOW THE MAIN LIBRARY PLAYERS

When you select a framework, you have about 20 JavaScript libraries to choose from, with five of those libraries being the main players. These five main players — YUI, Prototype, MooTools, Dojo, and the topic of this book, jQuery — have risen up above the rest because of their ease of use and the enormous audiences they have. The main differentiators between most of these libraries include size and browser support.

The five libraries I discuss are open source, which means that anyone can contribute to the source code that makes up these libraries. Microsoft software, for example, is not open source — it is propriety software owned by Microsoft. Microsoft employs its own programmers to develop it. Microsoft then sells their software for a licensing fee. The licensing fee allows you to use the software, usually for a set period of time, and gives you access to support from Microsoft if you have problems.

Open source software is different. Anyone can download the source code and contribute changes to it — which makes for better code because it's all created on a volunteer basis with a goal of writing better software, not making money. Because you are not paying a licensing fee, you are free to do whatever you please with the library. The open source community on the Web is huge, with millions of users contributing through blogs and forums, and it's now quite easy for designers and developers to find support when they need it.

One important thing to keep in mind is that when you are learning a JavaScript library, you are learning to read and write in what feels like another language — it is another interpretation of the JavaScript language.

YUI

The YUI (Yahoo! User Interface) JavaScript library was created by the Yahoo! Developer Network in 2005 and is under the BSD (Berkeley Software Distribution) license. The BSD license allows software to be distributed as permissive-free software, which has the least amount of restrictions for distribution purposes compared to other similar licensing options such as GNU General Public Licenses. YUI is fully supported on Internet Explorer 6 and later versions, Firefox 3 and later, Safari 3 and later, and Opera 10 and later.

The total file size of the YUI library is 31 KB.

To give you an idea of what YUI code looks like, here is some sample JavaScript code showing how to implement a click event using YUI. There are two parts to the `click` event here: the function that is called when the click occurs and the actual `click` event itself. The code is not that elegant and uses a lot of YUI-specific syntax.

```
function handleClick(e) {
  Y.log(e);
}
YUI().use('node-base', function(Y) {
  Y.on("click", handleClick, "#foo");
});
```

Prototype

Prototype, a JavaScript library created by Sam Stevenson, became popular because it was the first JS framework to be bundled with the also-popular rapid development-programming framework called Ruby on Rails. Because it's incorporated in Ruby on Rails, I have always felt that it wasn't meant for Web designers, but more for hardcore Web developers to use in conjunction with Ruby on Rails.

The Prototype library is a base library with Ajax functionality, which becomes more feature-rich with the addition of Scriptaculous. Scriptaculous offers effects and user interface elements and only works in conjunction with Prototype. The major downside to this library is the size: Both .js files total up to 278 KB.

The documentation for the Prototype and Scriptaculous libraries can be hard to understand for inexperienced front-end developers. As with other libraries, a community of supporters exists, but Prototype can still be hard to learn because of some of its more complicated syntax. To give you an idea of what Prototype code looks like, here is some sample JavaScript code showing how Prototype handles a `click` event. The `click` event is very similar to setting up a `click` event in jQuery, but looks can be deceiving — many of the other methods in Prototype are actually more difficult and look less like jQuery:

```
$("foo").observe("click", function() {
  alert('Clicked!');
});
```

MooTools

MooTools was first released in 2006, and is a similar JavaScript library to Prototype — the syntax is aimed at intermediate to advanced Web designers and developers. The MooTools JavaScript library allows designers and developers work with an object-oriented framework to extend the JavaScript API and provide interactivity on the Web pages. MooTools is for those looking for a library similar to pure JavaScript.

Here is some sample code showing how MooTools handles `click` events:

```
$('foo').addEvent('click', function() {}));
```

Dojo

Dojo was first released in 2004 as a JavaScript framework for creating cross-browser compatible Web applications and for adding seamless interactivity to Web sites. Dojo's syntax can be quite confusing; it feels much more like writing native JavaScript and is aimed at experienced front-end developers, making it harder for beginners to use and understand.

Here is some sample code showing how Dojo handles `click` events:

```
fooNode = dojo.byId("foo");
fooConnections = [];
fooConnections.push(dojo.connect(fooNode, 'onclick', foo));
```

As you can see from all of the preceding examples, JavaScript libraries can have pretty confusing syntax. Now take a look at an example of how jQuery handles `click` events:

```
$('#foo').click(function() {
  //click event
});
```

THE JQUERY ADVANTAGE

jQuery comes with a lot of advantages. You can see by comparing it to the previous syntax examples that jQuery is the most concise and easy to understand. That's the advantage of jQuery — it just gets it done. No fluff, no confusing code, and you don't need to be a back-end programmer to write it, but that's not to say that jQuery doesn't have an advanced side.

Figure 1-1 shows the jQuery homepage at `http://jquery.com`.

Figure 1-1: The jQuery Web site

A Brief History of jQuery

jQuery was created in 2006 by John Resig as an alternative to more complicated JavaScript libraries. jQuery enables Web designers and developers to write simpler JavaScript that still enables them to perform advanced JavaScript functions on their Web sites.

jQuery is awesome because no hardcore programming knowledge is required to perform DOM manipulation. jQuery does have some advanced areas that require prior JavaScript knowledge, such as working with the Ajax methods in forms to get and post content, as reviewed in Chapter 9, creating custom jQuery plug-ins, as reviewed in Chapter 11, and working with mobile Web sites, as reviewed in Chapter 10.

Most designers and developers whom I know use, or have used, jQuery at some point in the past four years. When I ask why, they usually answer, "Is there anything easier?" Its ease of use attracts so many people to use jQuery; you don't need a master's degree in computer science to make a form submit via Ajax.

You may be wondering what sort of things you can do with the jQuery library. The answer is, everything you can do with the native JavaScript API. I dive deeper into what you can do with jQuery throughout the book, but here is just a quick overview of the main features of jQuery:

- Events that include mouse, keyboard, form and user interactions
- Effects that include show/hide, sliding, fading, and custom animations
- Animation that allows you to make things move by utilizing CSS and native effects
- Ajax methods to interface with server-side form processing using XML and JSON
- Extensibility to create your own plug-ins that extend the jQuery API core
- DOM manipulation
- Cascading Style Sheet (CSS) manipulation
- Utilities that provide browser detection and easier interfaces for common JavaScript functions

Who uses jQuery

Web designers and developers are the main users of jQuery. I've seen jQuery used on a wide range of sites: everything from small-town mom and pop Web sites to full-blown enterprise sites. Because jQuery is free, all kinds of designers and developers use it. It brings the benefits of JavaScript to Web designers who may not know a thing about programming, but want to add cool effects to their Web site.

jQuery became more popular when Google and Microsoft started to offer hosted solutions. A hosted solution is when a file is hosted from a Web server — in this case, through a CDN (content delivery network) — to offer increased performance from those Web sites that use the file. This move by Google and Microsoft indicated that jQuery would be a preferred library and a major player within the open source JavaScript library community. Google,

BBC, Dell, Bank of America, Major League Baseball, NBC, and Netflix are part of the growing number of companies who are using jQuery on their Web sites. Netflix, a Web site that offers movie rentals to customers through direct mail and online channels, has been using advanced JavaScript to drive the user interface for a number of years. Figure 1-2 shows a menu creating using jQuery that appears as you hover over a movie title, allowing the user to view more information without leaving the page.

Figure 1-2: The Netflix Web site

Seeing How jQuery Works with Web Pages

jQuery is easy to set up. Just as with other JavaScript libraries, you include the JavaScript library at the top of your page between the `<head>` `</head>` tags. Here's how to include the jQuery JavaScript library in your site:

```
<!doctype html>
<html>
  <head>
    <script type="text/javascript" src="jquery-1.4.2.js"></script>
    <script type="text/javascript"></script>
  </head>
  <body>
    <a href="http://jquery.com/">jQuery</a>
  </body>
</html>
```

After you've added the jQuery library to your page, you write JavaScript code using the jQuery API (application programming interface) to access different parts of your page through the DOM (Document Object Model), which most Web designers and developers should be familiar with. If you are a Web designer, you work with it on a daily basis but may not even be aware of it.

You can also use jQuery to add and remove HTML from your page and respond to actions users perform on your page, such as clicking a link or filling in a form. You can also create animations and use Ajax to send and load content through Web services without having to refresh the page.

Exploring the Advantages of jQuery

Web sites have become much more than just text, images, and links to other pages. Internet users expect greatness from a Web site and the bar is constantly being raised by Web sites and companies such as Facebook, Google, Microsoft, Twitter, and Foursquare, to name a few. The technology is constantly changing, and using jQuery helps you keep up with the fast pace. jQuery is a library that promotes rapid development of Web sites or applications and allows you to focus on user interaction and interface design without having to write long, bloated code.

Writing jQuery is easier than writing JavaScript code because you are following an API. If you are proficient in writing HTML and CSS, you can understand and write jQuery because most jQuery functionality is based on interactivity within the HTML and CSS.

Open Source

JavaScript libraries are supported by the open source community and are well tested and updated. The open source community a huge support network. Web designers and developers are continually creating tutorials, books, and plug-ins to help and extend the jQuery library.

Great Documentation

By far, one of the greatest benefits of jQuery is its documentation, which is what makes a great library. The team behind jQuery has spent a great deal of their time documenting how the library works and how to navigate around their API. The jQuery documentation site has tutorials complete with code examples, plus a huge community of supporters across the Web. Figure 1-3 shows the Documentation section of the jQuery Web site.

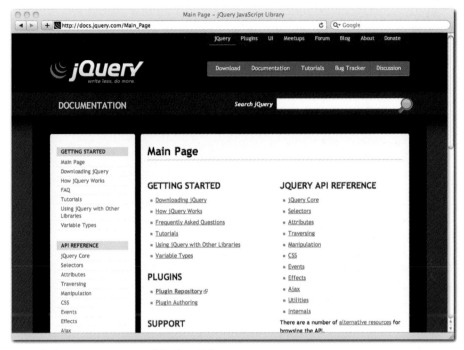

Figure 1-3: The Documentation section of the jQuery Web site

The community of developers and programmers that has created the jQuery library are constantly improving and releasing new versions. jQuery was first released 2006 as v1.0. Since then, the code has been updated 23 times, which brings us to the current release, v1.4.2. jQuery is continuously being improved, which is one of the reasons it has become so popular. Libraries that aren't updated as often are not as popular.

As updates occur, the documentation is updated for methods that have become deprecated (slated for removal in the next release) and to ensure that the library will be backward-compatible — that is, that it works with older versions. When a library is updated to a new version, the process of upgrading is painless — you just drop the new JavaScript library on your server. In addition, you should usually look over the changelog, a section that outlines each release and the changes that have been made to the library, to see if any methods you are using have become deprecated.

jQuery is released under the MIT License or the GNU General Public License (GPL), version 2. This basically means that it's free, and as long as you give credit to the author within the jQuery plug-in itself, you are free to use the code as you wish.

Same JavaScript with Less Code

jQuery is JavaScript: Everything you can do in JavaScript, you can also do in jQuery. The possibilities are endless. What I love about jQuery is that it gives you a base you can build on, but you're not limited by what jQuery offers. When you're using jQuery, you have three options when coding:

- Use the extensive jQuery API
- Use or create a jQuery plug-in
- Write regular JavaScript

Another attractive benefit of jQuery is the brevity of the code. If I want to change the background color in plain JavaScript, the code looks like this:

```
document.getElementById('mydiv').style.backgroundColor = 'red';
```

By using the powerful selection engine, jQuery needs only one shorter line to achieve the same outcome:

```
$('#mydiv').css('background-color','red');
```

The syntax is easier to understand than JavaScript and was created with Web designers in mind. When you compare this syntax to other libraries such as Prototype or YUI, you can see why jQuery has become the choice for many Web professionals. The selector engine is the most prominent and loved feature of the jQuery library. It allows you to use CSS2 selectors, which makes it incredibly easy for Web designers with CSS knowledge to pick up.

Chaining

One of jQuery's greatest features is chaining, which allows you to chain multiple methods one after the other. This helps to keep your amount of code smaller and therefore improves the speed with which your jQuery code is retrieved from the Web server and executed.

Here's an example of jQuery code that uses chaining:

```
$('#foo').addClass('active').prev().removeClass('active');
```

Here's an example that doesn't use chaining:

```
$('#foo').addClass('active');
$('#foo').next().removeClass('.active');
```

The example that uses chaining is a cleaner and more concise way to write jQuery. I use chaining in my code examples throughout the book.

Cross-Browser Compatibility

With the recent updates to Safari, Firefox, Internet Explorer, Google Chrome, and Opera, creating pages that work across all of the major browsers is the top priority. Browser wars have become a part of every Web designer's daily struggle.

When you use jQuery, you can rest assured that it's cross-browser compatible with all the popular browsers, such as Internet Explorer 6.0+, Mozilla Firefox 2+, Safari 3.0+, Opera 9.0+, and Google Chrome.

Often, a major issue with JavaScript is that you need to create different code to support multiple browsers. Some Web designers and developers choose to create alternate browser-specific style sheets to support CSS in different browsers, mainly Internet Explorer versus the rest. The same issue often occurs with JavaScript. The following code represents how to set up an Ajax request that works in multiple browsers:

```
If(window.XMLHttpRequest)
  {
  xhr = new XMLHttpRequest(); //Code for Firefox/Safari
  }
  else
    if(window.ActiveXObject) //Active X Version
    {
      xhr = new ActiveXObject("Microsft.XMLHTTP"); // For IE
}
```

Using plain JavaScript, you have to write two different functions, test those functions, and fix any bugs. It's quite a lot to manage, not to mention the repetition that occurs when you have to write several functions to do the same thing to support multiple browsers, instead of one script that supports them all, such as in jQuery.

By contrast, the following piece of code shows just how easy an Ajax request is in jQuery:

```
$.ajax();
```

CSS3-Compliant

All modern browsers support CSS1 and CSS2 (the first two versions of Cascading Style Sheets), and most Web designers and developers these days use CSS2. CSS3 is in development and offers enhanced features such as embedded fonts, rounded corners, advanced background images, and colors, text effects, and transitions. Only a handful of browsers currently support the full CSS3 spec as of July 2010 — Firefox 4, Internet Explorer 9, Opera 9, and Safari 4. Some older versions of these browsers do support certain features of CSS3.

jQuery has CSS3 support for new selectors only. What does that mean? One of the new features of CSS3 is additional attribute selectors, which are an improvement from the attribute selectors included in CSS2 and are similar to the attribute selectors in jQuery. These selectors allow you to style content based on its attributes, so you can filter based on specific values found in the attributes. Check out the following sample code:

```
p[title=*foo] {background:black;color:white}
<p class="text" title="food is good foo you">This is my sample text</p>
```

Practicing Unobtrusive JavaScript

Many of you have probably created pop-up windows by embedding JavaScript directly into your HREF tags, as shown in the following example. The biggest problem with this code is that it's embedded into your link HREF. If the user happens to have JavaScript disabled, which is rarely that case, this link won't work and there is no fallback method to enable them to view the help.

```
<a href="javascript:window.open('help.html', 'help window', 'height=800,width=600,to
  olbar=no');return false;">Help</a>
```

This HTML is an example of obtrusive JavaScript. For you Web designers, it's like when you write inline styles instead of separating the presentation layer from the content. To contrast with the example of obtrusive JavaScript, here is an example of how to use jQuery to provide an unobtrusive solution using similar code. When JavaScript is disabled, this version, instead of wrapping the code inside of a `click` function, offers users the fallback of clicking the link and being brought to the help page.

```
<!doctype html>
<html>
  <head>
    <title>Unobtrusive jQuery</title>
    <script type="text/javascript">
    $(document).ready(){
      $(".help-link").click(function() {
      var linkHref = $(this).attr('href');
      window.open(linkHref,'help window', 'height=800,width=600,toolbar=no');
      return false;
    });
  });
  </script>
  </head>
  <body>
    <a href="help.html" class="help-link">Help</a>
  </body>
</html>
```

Graceful degradation and progressive enhancement are strategies dealing with how to support newer browser features and older unsupported browsers while offering the best user experience. Progressive enhancement is the newer strategy of the two, but the main difference is the approach each of them takes. I cover these in the next couple of sections.

Graceful Degradation

With the graceful degradation approach, you get your Web site working in all modern, popular browsers and then work with older browsers to make sure they support those features. Most Web designers and developers have practiced graceful degradation by setting up specific style sheets or browser hacks for various versions of Internet Explorer (ahem, not pointing any fingers, IE6) because of layout issues with the box model.

```
<a href="javascript:window.open('help.html', 'help window', 'height=800,width=600,to
  olbar=no');">Help</a>
<noscript>
Please upgrade your browser or turn on JavaScript, as your browser is not working
  with our Website.
</noscript>
```

Progressive Enhancement

Progressive enhancement refers to a strategy of starting with a baseline of features supported by all browsers and then adding more features for the modern browsers that support them. Progressive enhancement is a great practice to adopt because it makes your sites more accessible. It's better for your users if you deliver one set of features for everyone and add special upgrades for those using more compliant browsers — that is, those compatible with features such as CSS3 and HTML 5. Currently only Safari 4 and Opera 10.6 support HTML 5 and CSS3.

The progressive enhancement approach doesn't assume that everyone has JavaScript enabled and always gives the user an alternative way of accessing the content. Consider the pop-up window used in the discussion about practicing unobtrusive JavaScript. Instead, you can use the target attribute in the anchor tag to tell the browser to open up the link in a new browser window, instead of creating a pop-up. This is supported by all popular browsers.

```
<a href="help.html" target="_blank">Help</a>
```

In this book, I focus on using jQuery with the progressive enhancement strategy to give more modern browsers a slightly better experience, while still supporting the older browsers with a baseline experience.

Unobtrusive JavaScript and jQuery

jQuery makes practicing both of these strategies (graceful degradation and progressive enhancement) easier because all of the jQuery (JavaScript) code lives outside the HTML in an external JavaScript file or in the head of the HTML file you're working with, unless you are using a hosted solution delivered by a CDN. The HTML elements contain no embedded JavaScript code, therefore a fallback action is always an option as long as the developer keeps these practices in mind when setting up their Web sites.

2

GETTING STARTED WITH JQUERY

JQUERY IS A POPULAR CHOICE among Web designers and developers because the steps required to get started developing are minimal. You just have to download a copy of the core JavaScript library file and include a `script` tag link to it on the top of your Web site. As with all JavaScript libraries, a JavaScript library `include` must be added to your Web site before you can start using its features in your Web site or application.

This chapter guides you through how to set up an optional local development environment, choose the right jQuery download, and set up the jQuery library for inclusion in your Web site. I also explain what the jQuery wrapper does.

SETTING UP YOUR DEVELOPMENT ENVIRONMENT

To get started setting up your development environment, first, choose which code editor that you want to use. There are many popular choices such as Dreamweaver, Coda, TextMate, and EditPlus to name a few. I primarily use Coda, a Mac OS X software application built for Web designers and developers to code Web sites and applications. This software is an integrated toolset that has features such as FTP, terminal (command prompt), file management, CSS and code editors, syntax highlighting, auto completion, extended find and replace functions, preview, and multi-language support. If you don't want to use a code editor, you are also are free to use regular old Notepad (Windows) or TextEdit (Mac), but you won't get all the increased features that a code editor can provide.

Before you can start writing jQuery code, you need a place to test your work: a development environment. A development environment can be either a local development setup consisting of a local Web server and Web browser or an external Web host. It basically allows you to test any work you are doing in a simulated live environment. The beauty of using an application like Coda or Dreamweaver is that you can set up your external Web host in the application, which allows you to work directly off the server and makes testing a breeze.

Some might argue that you can just work from a local folder and open each file in a Web browser, but this won't give you an accurate view of a live environment. You might end up developing a few jQuery functions like this, but when they go live, you get a different output. I believe it's better to work in an environment that's as close to live as possible from the start.

Local development environment are easy to set up and beneficial for when you aren't able to access the Internet. For Mac users, the most popular choice is MAMP (`www.mamp.info/`), which stands for Mac/Apache/MySQL/PHP, as shown in Figure 2-1. It is an all-in-one development application that you can run locally and test as if you were on a live Web server. For Windows users, the Windows version is called WampServer, which stands for Windows/Apache/mySQL/PHP Server (`www.wampserver.com/en/`). I would suggest whenever possible that you use Apache as a Web server. It's a very stable open source Web server that runs primarily on Linux.

Another alternative for Web developers using Mac OS X is to use the built-in Apache Web server on Mac OS X. To set up Apache server on a Mac, follow these steps:

1. Open System Preferences. You should see a group of icons that allow you to control settings such as Personal, Hardware, Internet and Wireless, System, and Other.

2. Click the Sharing icon to open the Sharing pane and then select the Web Sharing check box in the list of sharing services. The Sharing pane displays settings to allow you to share files, screens, printers, and so on. If the check box is already selected, skip this step.

3. Make sure the Web Sharing check box is selected, as shown in Figure 2-2. You have now started your Apache Web server. You should see a red icon turn green on the right side of the pane and text that states, `Your personal website, in the Sites folder in your home folder, is available at this address: http:// xx.xx.xx.xx/~yourname`.

4. Click the IP address to open your default Web browser. It loads your default page. The Web site files (HTML, CSS, JavaScript, Images) are located in your ~/Sites directory, similar to the way a Web server is set up. I do all of my local development using this type of setup.

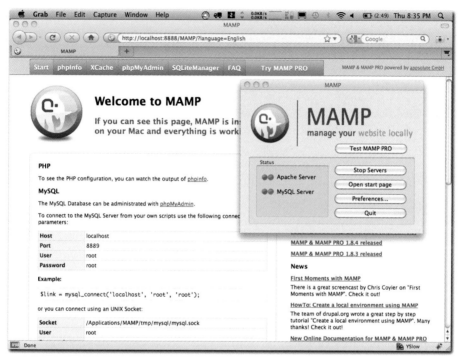

Figure 2-1: MAMP in action on my desktop

USING FIREBUG IN FIREFOX

If you aren't currently using Firefox as one of your main development browsers, I highly suggest that you download it before you proceed any further in this book. For the examples in this book, I use version 3.6.8 of Firefox and version 1.5.4 of Firebug. Joe Hewitt originally created Firebug, which is now an open-source development project, in December of 2006. Since that time, a number of updates to Firebug have been made and more than 1 million developers now use it.

Figure 2-2: The Sharing preferences dialog in Mac OS X

Firebug is an extension that provides a toolset to Web designers and developers who work with HTML, CSS, and JavaScript. Firebug is a free and open-source tool available to everyone through the Firefox extensions Web site (`addons.mozilla.org`).

21

Firebug allows you to view and edit your HTML and CSS on the fly (see Figure 2-3), and it also has a very powerful JavaScript debugger, which helps in finding errors. The console is a nice feature as you can execute JavaScript directly onto you page from within the console, and it comes in very handy!

Figure 2-3: The Firebug home page

How to Install Firebug and Enable It

To install and enable Firebug, follow these steps:

1. Open your Firefox browser and go to www.getFirebug.com.
2. Click Install Firebug for Firefox.
3. A prompt window, as shown in Figure 2-4, appears that says Install Add-Ons Only from Authors Whom You Trust. On the Install button, a number begins counting down. When it gets to 0, the Install Now button becomes enabled. Click it.
4. Next you see a progress bar that indicates that the plug-in is being installed on your browser. After the plug-in has been installed, you see a confirmation message and a button that says Restart Firefox, as seen in Figure 2-5.
5. Congratulations, you are now ready to begin using Firebug! Figure 2-6 shows the final step of the installation process.

Figure 2-4: The Firebug install prompt

Figure 2-5: The Firebug installation complete window

How to Enable Firebug

To enable Firebug, follow these steps:

1. Open up a Web page in Firefox. For demonstration purposes, I'm going to use www. mozilla.com.

2. After you have loaded the page, there are a few ways to open Firebug. The easiest way is by clicking on the Firebug icon in the bottom right of the browser. Figure 2-7 shows an example of Firebug installed and the Firebug icon on the bottom right of the browser.

   You can also start Firebug by right-clicking within the browser window and choosing Inspect Element from the drop-down menu. See Figure 2-8 for an example of the drop-down menu within the browser.

3. After you open Firebug, you see a series of tabs: Console, HTML, CSS, Script, and DOM, among others.

Figure 2-6: The Firebug installation confirmation prompt after you restart your browser

Firebug icon

Figure 2-7: A Web page and Firebug installed

Figure 2-8: How to access Inspect Element to open Firebug

How to Inspect and Edit HTML

The inspect and edit feature of Firebug is very powerful — it makes debugging HTML and JavaScript much easier, especially when you are changing the DOM on the fly. If you have a script that adds/changes HTML, you can open up the inspect window and see the HTML changes in real-time. It's always the first step I take when debugging JavaScript. I always like to first make sure that the HTML is being created properly before proceeding. See Figure 2-9 for an example of what your screen should look like after you have enabled Firebug with the HTML section open.

How to Use the Console

The Firebug console is the second step I take in debugging my JavaScript. After I have fixed any issues with the DOM, I use the console to try running my script live on the page. You see two panels in the console — the left panel is used for showing errors and the right panel is otherwise known as the command line.

1. Open up Firebug and click the Console tab.
2. If there are any errors with your JavaScript, you see them displayed on the left pane. See Figure 2-10 for an example of Firebug open with errors displayed.

Figure 2-9: The Firebug Edit HTML section

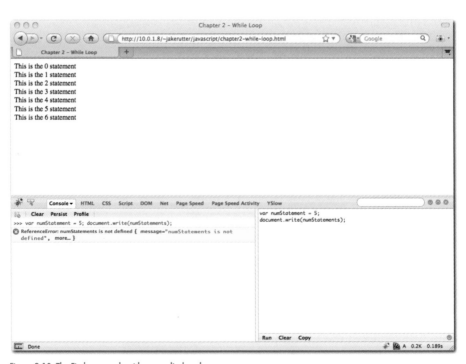

Figure 2-10: The Firebug console with errors displayed

How to Run JavaScript Live in Firefox Through the Firebug Console

The Firebug console is a great way to test jQuery or JavaScript on a page without having to add it to your HTML, run it on a Web server, and so on. The Firebug console also gives feedback in the form of error messages if your JavaScript has a problem. It's a great way to test code before committing to writing it all out in your HTML.

Advanced JavaScript Debugging with Firebug

For more advanced JavaScript applications, you can use the JavaScript debugger tool in Firebug. The JavaScript debugger is a very powerful tool that allows you to add breakpoints to different parts of the script so you can stop, start, and pause your script and take a closer look at variables and objects. I don't focus too much on the JavaScript debugger in this book because it's for more advanced JavaScript programmers.

JavaScript Debugging with Other Web Browsers

Firefox is not the only browser with Web developer tools. Apple Safari, Google Chrome, and Internet Explorer all have similar toolsets, but they are not as powerful as Firefox's Firebug. The Safari/Chrome debugger shares some common features with Firebug, including the inspect element feature and resource management tab, but they lack a powerful debugger such as the one included with Firebug. I have limited experience working with the other tools. I have used IE/Safari for spot-checking, but Firebug is always my main choice for development.

The basics of JavaScript are all concepts that Web designers and developers should be familiar with prior to entering the world of jQuery and JavaScript libraries. That being said, you can use and create basic scripts without needing a solid base in JavaScript, but knowing how JavaScript works accelerates your rate of development and understanding, which leads to high productivity.

DOWNLOADING THE JQUERY LIBRARY

Before you can start developing with jQuery, you first need to download the jQuery library from the jQuery Web site. The jQuery library is a JavaScript file that can be accessed in either of two ways:

- Download the jQuery.js and host it locally on your Web site
- Use a hosted version from a CDN (content delivery network)

I recommend downloading a copy of jQuery to your local computer for development work and testing, and specifically for when an Internet connection is unavailable. To download jQuery, follow these steps:

1. Point your Web browser to the jQuery site at `www.jquery.com`.
2. Click the Download link located in the main navigation bar at the top of the page, which takes you to a page that offers many different ways to access the jQuery Library. Figure 2-11 shows the download page.

27

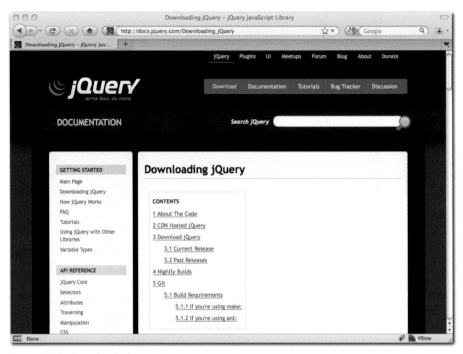

Figure 2-11: The jQuery download page

Many Web sites opt for free CDN-hosted solutions because they have proven to be reliable and fast-loading solutions that free up the bandwidth from your own site. CDN stands for content delivery network, which is a hosted solution provided by companies with large networks such as Google, Microsoft, Akamai, and so on.

Content delivery networks offer the benefit of a larger, high-speed network, which serves up the jQuery library from many locations. When a user brings up your site in their browser, their location triggers the server closest to them geographically to deliver the jQuery library, which in turn decreases the load time. The Google-hosted Ajax libraries page in Figure 2-12 has various options to include jQuery and many other libraries in your Web site or application.

When using the hosted solution, you can specify in the URL which version of jQuery to use, as shown in the following code example using Google Hosted jQuery:

```
<script src="http://ajax.googleapis.com/ajax/libs/jquery/1.4.2/jquery.min.js"></
  script>
```

Google and Microsoft are large companies with high market penetration, and many Web sites already use their hosted jQuery libraries. The more Web sites that use hosted versions, the higher the chance that you have already grabbed that file from another Web site, so it's already cached in your browser. (Browser caching occurs when you grab a file from a Web site.)

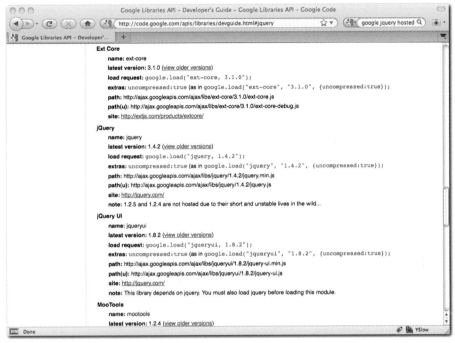

Figure 2-12: The Google-hosted Ajax libraries page

For example, say I'm a daily user of Digg (www.digg.com), an online news portal that displays news based on the popularity voted on by its users, which uses the hosted jQuery library from Google, and I decide to add the jQuery library to my Web site. When I pull up my site in the browser, it grabs a cached version of jQuery from my browser cache, unless, when requesting the library, Google sends a modified response back. In that case, the latest jQuery library would be returned instead of the file from my cache.

Table 2.1 outlines the two available versions of jQuery.

Table 2.1   jQuery Library Versions

Format	Description
Uncompressed (Estimated* 155 KB)	Main purpose is for when working in development, for debugging, and for advanced developers who would like to take a look at the code to understand how it works.
Compressed (Estimated* 55 KB)	A much smaller footprint meant for production code. It is compressed using a technique called minification, which removes unnecessary characters such as comments, line breaks, white space, and tabs to improve loading times.

* Estimated for version 1.4.2

Advanced users may want to use Git (source control software) to access the latest version of the jQuery library. I won't be going into any further detail about Git, so if you would like to learn more about it, check out www.git.com.

INCLUDING THE JQUERY LIBRARY IN YOUR WEB PAGE

After you have decided which approach you want to take — either downloading a library or using a hosted version of jQuery — you need to set it up in your Web page. The jQuery library can be included within script tags and live in between the <head></head> tags of your HTML document, or you can include the jQuery library before your closing </body> tag.

You must include any CSS (cascading style sheets) before the jQuery library and jQuery custom code because you want to ensure that all CSS is applied to the DOM (Document Object Model) before you try to change it with jQuery.

You should always include a doctype in your HTML pages. Failing to include a doctype causes all sorts of erratic behavior within your Web browser and causes your Web page to fail the validation suite check. It helps to ensure that your code works across all browsers. jQuery won't always render correctly if a doctype is not present on the page. CSS also renders incorrectly when a doctype is not present on the page.

All of the examples in this book use the HTML 5 doctype to ensure progressive enhancement and graceful degradation with older Web browsers. (See Chapter 1 if you need a reminder of what progressive enhancement and graceful degradation are.) The doctype for HTML5 is very simple to set up compared to previous doctypes, which are hard to remember.

The following code is the doctype for HTML 5:

```
<!DOCTYPE html>
```

The following example is a very basic HTML document that outlines how to include your jQuery at the top of the page. Always include all CSS files first to ensure that the page has rendered correctly before you try to manipulate the DOM:

```
<!DOCTYPE html>
<html>
  <head>
    <title>My jQuery Example</title>
    <link href="css/global.css"/>
    <script src="js/jquery.js" type="text/javascript"></script>
    <script type="text/javascript">
    //script goes here
    </script>
  </head>
  <body>
  </body>
</html>
```

Alternatively, you can also include your jQuery library at the bottom of the page. This can sometimes increase the speed at which your page loads because the JavaScript doesn't get hung up on loading at the top while the rest of the page continues to load. Also, this way, the entire DOM is guaranteed to load before the JavaScript is applied.

```html
<html>
  <head>
    <title>My jQuery Example</title>
    <link href="css/global.css"/>
    </head>
  <body>
  <h1>Hello jQuery!</h1>
  <div id="page-container">
    <p>You can place your jQuery at the end of the page too!</p>
</div>
  <script src="js/jquery.js" type="text/javascript"></script>
  <script type="text/javascript">
//script goes here
  </script>
  </body>
</html>
```

If you are using the Google-hosted version of the jQuery `include`, instead of including a relative path, insert the direct path to the library provided by Google:

```html
<html>
  <head>
  <title>My jQuery Example</title>
  <link href="css/global.css"/>
  <script src="http://ajax.googleapis.com/ajax/libs/jquery/1.4.2/jquery.min.js"
  type="text/javascript"></script>
  <script type="text/javascript">
  //script goes here
  </script>
  </head>
  <body>
  </body>
</html>
```

UNDERSTANDING THE JQUERY WRAPPER

Before you get started programming with jQuery, you need to understand what the jQuery wrapper is and how it applies to the DOM. A wrapper, in most programming languages, is something that wraps something else to extend the functionality, most often an object. To put this in perspective, the jQuery wrapper attaches itself to the DOM by using selectors and allows you to extend the DOM. jQuery doesn't actually offer any new methods; it just takes methods that already exist in native JavaScript and makes them much easier to interact with.

The power of the wrapper is being able to extend the DOM with much less code than native JavaScript. The following code is an example of the jQuery selector statement:

```
$.(selector)
```

jQuery has many event methods to choose from, but one very important one is called the `document.ready()` event handler method, which executes only after the DOM is fully loaded. In its simplest form, a method is just another way of describing a function, but in other OOP (object-oriented programming) languages, methods have increased benefits compared to functions. The power behind jQuery is in manipulating the DOM; therefore, you want to make sure the DOM is ready before you do anything with it.

The `document.ready()` event handler method allows you to put all of your JavaScript jQuery code within this event to make sure the code is executed when the DOM is ready. This event is similar to the JavaScript `onLoad` event, except the `document.ready()` event handler method only fires after the DOM has loaded.

The following code is an inline example of how to set up the `document` ready event handler method:

```
<html>
  <head>
    <title>My jQuery Example</title>
    <script src="http://ajax.googleapis.com/ajax/libs/jquery/1.4.2/jquery.min.js"
    type="text/javascript"></script>
    <script type="text/javascript"></>
    $(document).ready(function() {
    //script goes here
    });
    </script>
  </head>
  <body>
  </body>
</html>
```

You should get in the habit of setting up the `document.ready()` event handler and any other custom jQuery code in an external file. This is the method I prefer because it keeps all your code separate in its own JavaScript include. I usually call my external file with all of my jQuery code, jquery.function.js, and always make sure it's included last, after all jQuery core library file(s).

You can also use a shortened version of the `document.ready()` event handler method when you are trying to optimize the size of the jQuery functions file for increased performance, such as for a mobile application. The shortened version is set up like this:

```
<html>
  <head>
```

```
<title>My jQuery Example</title>
<script src="http://ajax.googleapis.com/ajax/libs/jquery/1.4.2/jquery.min.js"
type="text/javascript"></script>
<script type="text/javascript"></>
$(function() {
//script goes here
});
</script>
</head>
<body>
</body>
</html>
```

To explain the jQuery wrapper, I need to walk you through how to set up the `document.`
`ready()` statement. The first step involves setting up a selector that is preceded by the dollar
sign ($), which is the alias for accessing the jQuery itself. You pass the selector between the
two parentheses; in this case, I'm passing the document selector for the DOM. The alias and
the selector make up the jQuery wrapper.

```
$(document)
```

The ready event gets attached after the selector statement and is interchangeable with other
events.

```
.ready()
```

The function is the piece that holds the code, which is applied after the DOM is loaded and
ready and does not include graphics. The function is placed within the parentheses of the
ready event because you are passing the function you want to be run to the ready event:

```
.ready(function() {
  //jQuery DOM code goes here
  alert("The DOM is fully loaded and ready");
});
```

The `window.load` function is very similar to the `document.ready()` function, except
that it also waits for all of the graphics on the page to load before executing any jQuery code:

```
$(window).load {
    //jQuery Code Goes Here
    alert("The window has been loaded");
});
```

```
 $(window).load {
    //jQuery Code Goes Here
    alert("The window has been loaded");
});
```

33

RUNNING CODE OUTSIDE OF DOCUMENT READY HANDLER

Most jQuery-specific code needs to be set up within a `document.ready()` event handler method. But native JavaScript such as variables, arrays, and so on can be set up outside of the document ready event handler because they don't need to wait for the DOM to be ready and are hidden from the DOM as they are specifics within the actual script.

The following code example outlines a script that relies on the DOM to be loaded before new content can be added. There are three variables being set in this script — two of them outside of the `document.ready()` event and one being set inside for the `document.ready()` event as it needs access to the `for` loop set up inside on it.

```
<!doctype html>
<html>
  <head>
    <script src="http://ajax.googleapis.com/ajax/libs/jquery/1.4.2/jquery.min.js"></
  script>
    <script>
    var numShows = 10;
    var numTickets = 100;
    $(document).ready(function() {
      for(i=0; i < numTickets; i++)
      {
      var numTotal = i + 1;
    $('.container').append("<p>There are " + numTotal + " tickets available</p>");
      }
    });
</script>
<body>
  <div class="container">
  </div>
</body>
</html>
```

PREVENTING CONFLICTS WITH OTHER LIBRARIES

Conflicts can occur with other JavaScript libraries if you don't take the proper precautions when writing your jQuery. Most conflicts occur with the use of the $ alias, which Prototype also shares as an alias. You need to take two steps to eliminate conflicts with others libraries:

1. Add the `noConflict` function at the end of your jQuery Library. The `noConflict` function releases all dependability of the jQuery on the $ alias back to any other libraries that are also using it.

   ```
   $.noConflict();
   ```

2. Change all references of the $ alias to the jQuery alias as demonstrated in the following example. Change this:

   ```
   $(document).ready() {
       //code goes here
   ```

```
});
```

To this:

```
jQuery(document).ready() {
    //code goes here
});
```

You can also define your own alias if you don't wish to use the jQuery alias. This is done by adding a line of JavaScript to define your own alias. In the following example, I set up the new alias as $alien, instead of just $. It's that easy!

```
var $alien = jQuery;

$alien(document).ready() {
    // code goes here
});
```

USING JAVASCRIPT WITH JQUERY

Variables are a great way to store types of information, especially when writing JavaScript. I use variables frequently with jQuery and do so throughout the examples later in the book. Using variables when writing jQuery is no different than using them with JavaScript. You can set variables and call them within the jQuery wrapper because it's all basically just JavaScript.

The beauty of jQuery is that it is JavaScript, so if you have any prior knowledge of JavaScript, you can directly apply that knowledge to jQuery. You don't have to worry about learning new syntax, conventions, or methods because most of jQuery is based on JavaScript functionality, but the syntax is much easier to understand.

You may be wondering, if jQuery is JavaScript, why not just learn JavaScript? The answer is that jQuery takes everything that JavaScript does and makes it much easier to implement. The jQuery tagline — "Write less, do more" — definitely holds true. You can take 20 lines of native JavaScript and turn it into 5 lines of jQuery without having to know JavaScript. For those of you who are curious about JavaScript, learning jQuery can help you to understand the JavaScript API.

JavaScript can be hard to understand. jQuery makes it much easier for Web designers to implement features from the JavaScript API without having to understand all the complexities of JavaScript itself. jQuery has really opened up the door for so many Web designers who previously had little programming experience to add interactivity to their Web sites. It's a great time to be working with jQuery: The support and community around this library is growing at an astounding rate.

LEARNING THE JQUERY FUNDAMENTALS

Chapter 3: Using Selectors, Filters, and CSS: jQuery at Its Core

Chapter 4: Working with Events

Chapter 5: Making Your Web Site Come Alive with Effects

3

USING SELECTORS, FILTERS, AND CSS: JQUERY AT ITS CORE

SELECTORS ARE THE CORE building blocks of jQuery: Everything you do with the DOM (Document Object Model) in jQuery incorporates the use of a selector because you need to choose which elements in the DOM you are selecting and manipulating. jQuery uses common CSS and XPATH selectors that most Web designers and developers are already familiar with, as well as a few custom jQuery selectors. This makes jQuery flexible and easy to learn. Understanding how selectors work is a key component in utilizing jQuery to its fullest capability.

Filters give you more flexibility in selecting elements based on a characteristics in the DOM,

where CSS selectors can't help. Filters are often used in conjunction with selectors to give you great depth of control when selecting specific elements based on, say, their position in a group of elements, or their visibility, or a characteristic of a form input such as checked or disabled. jQuery also offers a nice range of methods for adding and removing CSS classes and also applying styling directly to a DOM element.

In this chapter, I review how to use selectors, filters, and CSS with jQuery through various real-world tutorials, which gives you a great understanding of these fundamental jQuery methods.

WORKING WITH DOM ELEMENTS USING JQUERY SELECTORS

Selectors, an essential feature of the jQuery library, are powered by the jQuery Sizzle selector engine. Sizzle can be used with other languages, but its real power is best used with all the other jQuery methods. The syntax is easy to understand for Web designers who have a solid understanding of CSS and HTML. The jQuery Sizzle selector engine is JavaScript code written to handle selectors in jQuery. The selectors are common CSS and XPATH selectors with the addition of a few custom selectors.

The jQuery selector is a string expression that classifies a single or set of DOM elements to be known as the matched set and is ready to be worked with in jQuery. The selector is always declared directly after the jQuery alias ($). After DOM elements are selected and methods have been applied, the matched set becomes a jQuery object. jQuery objects allow you to add many different types of methods including events, effects, traversal, manipulation, etc. A jQuery object is something that you may or may not encounter during your jQuery coding, but it's always there and it's important to be aware of.

The following code example shows how a selector is laid out in jQuery:

```
$(selector).method().
```

With a little practice, working with selectors in jQuery becomes second nature because many selectors are those you have worked with before using CSS. A selector is a way for you to navigate the Document Object Model (DOM), and, in its most basic form, allows you to select an element and the syntax is identical to CSS selector syntax, whether it's a ID, class, tag, or an attribute. Selectors are an essential component of any jQuery statement that you create.

When you use a selector, the statement you create automatically loops through all of the nodes in the DOM looking for the elements you have specified in your selector. The result of this loop is also known as the matched set. Web designers who are proficient with CSS and have a solid understanding of the DOM can pick up selectors quickly.

The JavaScript parts that make up a selector are

- The jQuery alias (`jQuery` or `$`).
- The DOM elements, which you are selecting, wrapped in quotes within the two parentheses.
- Anything after the selector is the jQuery method, which you are applying. The jQuery method can do anything from adding CSS to animating elements on the page. The functions, also known as methods, perform the specified action and accept arguments in the parentheses.

Table 3.1 outlines the anatomy of a jQuery selector statement:

Table 3.1   The Anatomy of a jQuery Statement

The jQuery Alias	The Selector	The jQuery Method or Action
$ or jQuery	('div')	.css('border','1px solid #333');

SELECTING PAGE ELEMENTS BY USING CSS SELECTORS

JavaScript has native functions that can select elements by ID and tag. The downside of these functions is that you have to use a different function for each of the three types of elements. Also, this creates repetition and code bloat, which can become a nightmare to manage. When you use selectors in jQuery, one selector can handle multiple types of elements. This makes writing clean and manageable code much easier.

All examples in this book show the browser output as well as the Firebug output so you can see what is being added or changed to the DOM. (See Chapter 2 for more about installing and using Firebug.) When you view the page source, you don't see the rendered source. The rendered source is the actual code that is created after the browser loads and the JavaScript has fired, which, as you are manipulating the DOM, can change quite noticeably. Firebug shows the rendered source, and can even show you the source as it changes, so it's the perfect way to test your JavaScript and jQuery.

The following list outlines the most common jQuery CSS selectors, which I explain in more depth with code and browser throughout in this chapter:

- `$('*')`
- `$('p')`
- `$('.class')`
- `$('#id')`
- `$('.parent ul li')`

In this chapter, I apply CSS to the elements using the jQuery `.css()` method. The CSS method in jQuery works by allowing you to pass any CSS properties to the CSS method that are then applied to the element matched by the selector. The CSS is added to the element, as an inline style after the DOM is loaded and ready.

In each example, you are not limited to the CSS I am applying. I'm just showing individual examples of problems you may encounter yourself and how to quickly solve them using selectors.

Selecting Elements by Using the Wildcard (*) Selector

If you would like to select all the elements in your DOM or within other elements, use the wildcard (*) selector. The wildcard is wrapped in quotes between the parentheses directly after the alias.

In the following HTML example, I select all the elements in the page with the wildcard selector and add a CSS border to each element. To add a CSS border, I use the method `.css('border','1px solid #333');`.

Figure 3-1 shows the output of the following script example with the Firebug tab open. This is where you can observe how jQuery added the borders inline to each element on the page.

```
<!doctype html>
<html>
  <head>
   <script src='http://ajax.googleapis.com/ajax/libs/jquery/1.4.2/jquery.min.js'></
  script>
   <script>
   $(document).ready(function() {
      $('*').css('border','1px solid #333');
   });
   </script>
   <body>
      <div class="container">
      <h1>Hello jQuery.</h1>
      </div>
   </body>
</html>
```

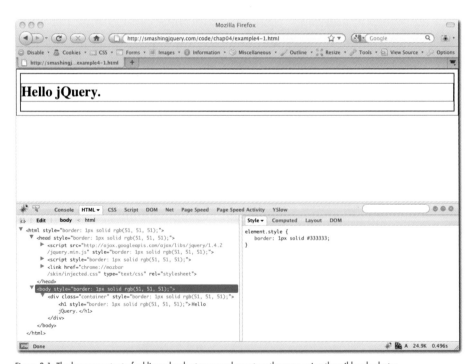

Figure 3-1: The browser output of adding a border to every element on the page using the wildcard selector

Selecting Elements by Using the HTML Tag

After you understand how the wildcard selector works, you can see that the other CSS selectors work the same way. You can select any element within the DOM using the element selector — you need to pass a tag name to the selector, which is present in the page. This selector uses the native JavaScript method `getElementsByTagName()`.

The native JavaScript function `getElementsByTagName()` retrieves all elements by their tag name. The code is set up like this:

```
document.getElementsByTagName('h1');
```

In the following HTML example, I need to set the `font-family` property of my h1 tags. I can do so by changing the CSS, but I don't want the h1 tags on other pages to be affected. Instead, I can use the tag selector together with the `css()` method to change the `font-family` property for H1 tags on this page only. I use the CSS method to apply the `font-family` property to just the H1 tag that I select.

Figure 3-2 shows the output of the following code in the browser with Firebug open. This example demonstrates how the DOM is altered by the `font-family` property being added to the h1 tag after the DOM has loaded.

```html
<!doctype html>
<html>
  <head>
  <script src='http://ajax.googleapis.com/ajax/libs/jquery/1.4.2/jquery.min.js'></
  script>
  <script>
  $(document).ready(function() {
    $('h1').css('font-family','arial,verdana');
  });
  </script>

  <body>
    <div class='container'>
    <h1>Hello jQuery.</h1>
    </div>
  </body>
</html>
```

Selecting Elements by Using the ID Selector

You can select any ID within the page using the ID (`'#'`) selector. The ID selector uses the native JavaScript method `getElementById()`. To select a class using the native JavaScript function `getElementById()`, the code is set up in the following manner:

```
document.getElementById('sidebar');
```

43

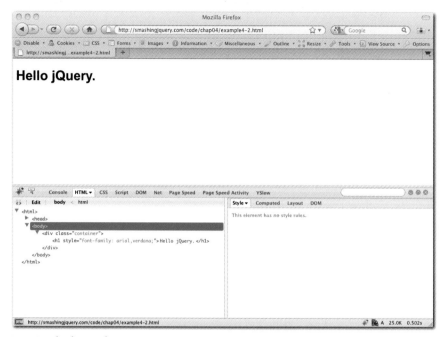

Figure 3-2: The element selector in action

The `ID` selector always includes the `#` (hash) symbol when referencing the ID in the selector. Without that symbol, the selector won't work correctly. The `ID` selector returns only the one ID that it matches. Remember that with CSS no two elements on a page should share the same ID.

In the following HTML example, I want to hide the `#sidebar div` using CSS. I use a jQuery selector to select the `#sidebar id` from the document. The ID is wrapped in quotes between the parentheses, directly after the alias. In order to hide the `div`, I use the `CSS` method and apply the following: `'display','none'`.

Figure 3-3 shows the browser output of using the `ID` selector to hide a `div` with the `ID` `"#sidebar"`:

```
<!doctype html>
<html>
  <head>
  <script src='http://ajax.googleapis.com/ajax/libs/jquery/1.4.2/jquery.min.js'></
  script>
  <script>
  $(document).ready(function() {
    $('#sidebar').css('display','none');
  });
  </script>
  <body>
  <div id='sidebar'>
  <h1>My sidebar</h1>
  <ul>
```

44

```
    <li><a href='/nav'>Navigation</a></li>
  </ul>
  </div>
  </body>
</html>
```

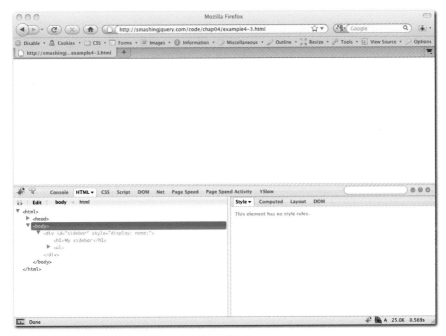

Figure 3-3: The browser output after selecting the #sidebar ID

Selecting Elements by Class

Similar to selecting by ID, you can also select elements in your page by class (.class). This selector uses the native JavaScript method getElementsByClassName(). The class selector selects all elements of the given class in the DOM. If you want to select a class using the native JavaScript method getElementsByClassName(), the code is set up as follows:

```
document.getElementsByClassName('product-image');
```

By using jQuery, I can achieve the same result as the getElementsByClassName() method, but with much less code.

In the following HTML example, I want to add a gray 1 pixel border, include 5 pixels of padding, and set a width of 150 pixels. The CSS method allows multiple CSS properties to be passed in using an object literal (a comma-separated list composed of name and value pairs that helps keep your code organized), which helps to keep this statement clean and simple.

I use a class selector to select all instances of the (.telephone) class on the page. I pass three sets of CSS properties to the CSS method, therefore I need to also enclose those properties in brackets {}. Figure 3-4 shows the output of the browser after the class selector has been called.

45

```
<!doctype html>
<html>
  <head>
  <script src="http://ajax.googleapis.com/ajax/libs/jquery/1.4.2/jquery.min.js"></
  script>
  <script>
  $(document).ready(function() {
     $('.telephone').css({'padding':'5px','border':'1px solid
#ccc','width':'150px'});
  });
  </script>
  <body>
     <div id='container'>
     <h1>Hello jQuery</h1>
     <div class='telephone'><img src="images/product.jpg"></div>
     <div class='telephone'><img src="images/product.jpg"></div>
     <div class='telephone'><img src="images/product.jpg"></div>
     <div class='telephone'><img src="images/product.jpg"></div>
     <div class='telephone'><img src="images/product.jpg"></div>
     <div class='telephone'><img src="images/product.jpg"></div>
     <div class='telephone'><img src="images/product.jpg"></div>
     <div class='telephone'><img src="images/product.jpg"></div>
     </div>
  </body>
</html>
```

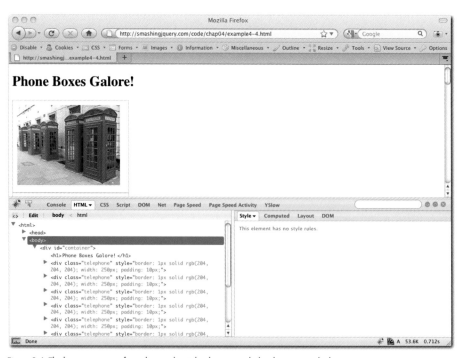

Figure 3-4: The browser output after selecting the eight elements with the class name telephone

Selecting One or Many Elements with Multiple Classes

In some cases, you may have applied multiple classes to the same element and you may want to select only elements with those classes applied. The class selector accepts multiple classes.

In the following example, I have six elements with multiple classes. I am hiding the two elements using CSS that have the "book" and "inactive" classes applied to them by using the jQuery class selector and CSS method. Figure 3-5 shows the output of the browser after the multiple elements in the selector have been called.

```
<!doctype html>
<html>
  <head>
  <script src='http://ajax.googleapis.com/ajax/libs/jquery/1.4.2/jquery.min.js'></
  script>
  <script>
  $(document).ready(function() {
    $('.book.inactive').css('display','none');
  });
  </script>

  <body>
    <div class='book inactive'>
        <p>Travel Guide to NYC</p>
    </div>
    <div class='book active'>
        <p>Travel Guide to San Francisco</p>
    </div>
    <div class='book inactive'>
        <p>Travel Guide to Seattle</p>
    </div>
    <div class='book active'>
        <p>Travel Guide to Miami</p>
    </div>
    <div class='book active'>
        <p>Travel Guide to Palo Alto</p>
    </div>

  </body>
</html>
```

Selecting Page Elements by Using Parent-Child Selectors

Parent-child selectors are a useful way to select elements within your page, when tag, CSS, and ID elements cannot be used. The parent-child CSS property is available in CSS to all popular browsers except IE6. Are you surprised? I'm not, but the beauty of using this CSS selector with jQuery is that IE6 is supported. The parent-child selector can be very useful when working with nested elements such as navigation menus.

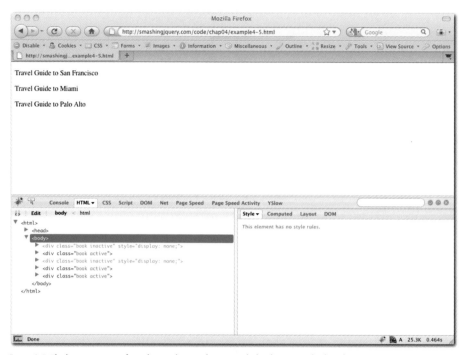

Figure 3-5: The browser output after selecting the two elements with the class names book and inactive

The parent-child selector allow you to select direct descendents of a given parent element using the > operator. Consider the following jQuery example. This statement selects all of the paragraph (p) elements found within the body as long as they are a child (that is, nested inside of the body tag):

```
$('body > p')
```

But if you had a scenario where you were trying to select a specific paragraph element inside of a specific div element, you would have to be more specific by using their class or ID names in order to select the correct descendent element.

In the following HTML example, I need to select the p tags within the elements that have the class (.inactive) and append "Sorry, this book is sold out" to the end of the p tag in the color red. I use chaining to add multiple methods to one statement. Figure 3-6 shows the output of the browser after the selector statement has been applied.

```
<!doctype html>
<html>
  <head>
   <script src='http://ajax.googleapis.com/ajax/libs/jquery/1.4.2/jquery.min.js'></
  script>
   <script>
   $(document).ready(function() {
     $('.book.inactive > p').css('display','none');
```

```
    $('.book.inactive').append('Sorry this book is sold out!').css('color','red');
});
</script>

<body>
    <div class='book inactive'>
        <p>Travel Guide to NYC</p>
    </div>
    <div class='book active'>
        <p>Travel Guide to San Francisco</p>
    </div>
    <div class='book inactive'>
        <p>Travel Guide to Seattle</p>
    </div>
    <div class='book active'>
        <p>Travel Guide to Miami</p>
    </div>
    <div class='book active'>
        <p>Travel Guide to Palo Alto</p>
    </div>

</body>
</html>
```

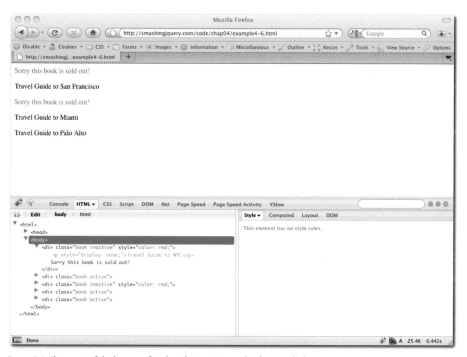

Figure 3-6: The output of the browser after the selector statement has been applied

Selecting Page Elements by Using Descendent Selectors

Parent-child selectors only work if the child is directly related to the parent, like `<li>` tags that are between two `<ul>` tags. If you run into a situation where you are trying to select an element that is two or three levels down from the parent, you need to use descendent selectors. The difference between the parent-child and descendent selector is the usage of the `>` operator — if this operator is not included, the selector matches not only child but also descendent elements.

In the following HTML example, I select the `<li>` tag that is nested within the `<ul class="sidebar-nav">` tags. After I have a matched set, I apply a CSS border to it. Figure 3-7 shows the output of the browser after the class selector has been called.

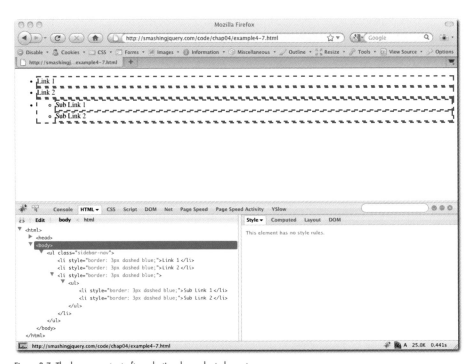

Figure 3-7: The browser output after selecting descendent elements

```
<!doctype html>
<html>
  <head>
  <script src='http://ajax.googleapis.com/ajax/libs/jquery/1.4.2/jquery.min.js'></
  script>
  <script>
  $(document).ready(function() {
    $('ul li').css('border','3px dashed blue');
  });
  </script>

  <body>
```

```
    <ul class="sidebar-nav">
    <li>Link 1</li>
    <li>Link 2</li>
    <li><ul>
        <li>Sub Link 1</li>
        <li>Sub Link 2</li>
    </li>
    </ul>
  </body>
</html>
```

Selecting Multiple Elements

You may run into a situation where you need to select multiple types of elements, which could be a combination of classes, IDs, HTML tags, as well as parent-child relationships. Using the jQuery selector, you can add multiple elements just by creating a comma-separated list.

In the following HTML example, I need to select five individual classes and two individual IDs using a comma-separated list. I then need to apply a gray background color to all of them using the CSS method, and then, with the last ID, apply the background color to the paragraph tag found within the #footer element. Figure 3-8 shows the output of the browser after the class selector has been called.

```
<!doctype html>
<html>
  <head>
  <script src='http://ajax.googleapis.com/ajax/libs/jquery/1.4.2/jquery.min.js'></
  script>
  <script>
  $(document).ready(function() {
    $('.book-one, .book-two, .book-three, .book-four, .book-five, #header,
  #footer p').css('background''','#ccc''');
  });
  </script>

  <body>
    <div id='header'><h1>Book Club</h1></div>
    <div class='book-one'>
        <p>Travel Guide to NYC</p>
    </div>
    <div class='book-two'>
        <p>Travel Guide to San Francisco</p>
    </div>
    <div class='book-three'>
        <p>Travel Guide to Seattle</p>
    </div>
    <div class='book-four'>
        <p>Travel Guide to Miami</p>
    </div>
    <div class='book-five'>
```

```
        <p>Travel Guide to Palo Alto</p>
    </div>
    <div id='footer'><p>Copyright 2010</p></div>
  </body>
</html>
```

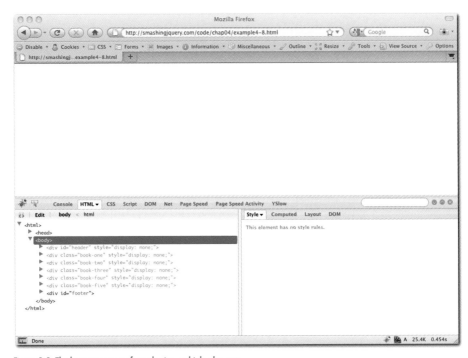

Figure 3-8: The browser output after selecting multiple elements

FILTERING DOM ELEMENTS USING JQUERY SELECTOR FILTERS

Filtering allows you to refine the elements that you are selecting. Filters are very handy when you're trying to target just one, or a few, elements within your DOM. If you have a static HTML document, it is easy to adjust the HTML. But in cases where the DOM changes with every page request or load, you need to use a dynamic front-end language such as JavaScript to add formatting on the fly.

A filter is defined by a colon that follows the actual filter: :filter.

APPLYING BASIC FILTER DEFINITIONS

As of jQuery 1.4.2, jQuery contains 20 different filters. I give real-world examples of the most common, but you can reference the following table to view the full list of filters available in jQuery.

The filters listed in Table 3.2 with a yes in the CSS3 selector column are pseudo-classes and are part of the CSS3 specification. Currently using CSS, these properties are fully supported only in newer Web browsers such as Firefox 3+, Opera 10, and Safari 3+. You can refer to www.css3.info for a full list of browsers that support new CSS3 properties. jQuery fully supports these CSS3 properties when the properties are used as filters in conjunction with selectors.

Table 3.2   Names and Functions of All of the Available Filters

Filter Name	Filter Function	CSS3 Selector
:even and :odd	Find even and odd items based on index	
:header	Finds element(s) that are H1, H2, H3, H4.... tags	
:not	Finds element(s) that are not this selector	Yes
:eq(index)	Finds an element(s) which matches this index	
:gt(index)	Finds element(s) greater than this index	
:lt(index)	Finds element(s) less than this index	
:first-child, :last-child, :only-child, :nth-child()	Finds element that is first, last, only, or you can specify which child to find with nth-child(1)	Yes
:has(p)	Finds an element(s) that has another element	
:contains('this is my text')	Finds an element(s) which that contains text	
:empty	Finds an element(s) that is empty	Yes
:parent	Finds an element(s) that is a parent	
:hidden	Finds an element(s) that is hidden	
:visible	Finds an element(s) that is visible	
:animated	Finds an element(s) that is in the process of animating	

CREATING ZEBRA-STRIPED TABLES USING THE EVEN AND ODD FILTER

Zebra striping is a common practice to make table rows easier to read by adding a lighter gray background color to each even or odd row. The :even and :odd filters in jQuery make it incredibly easy to add this type of styling to any table. This filter isn't only for zebra striping — the possibilities for how you can apply this filter are nearly endless, but zebra striping is a great example. Figure 3-9 shows the output of the browser after the page has loaded with a background color applied to all of the even rows.

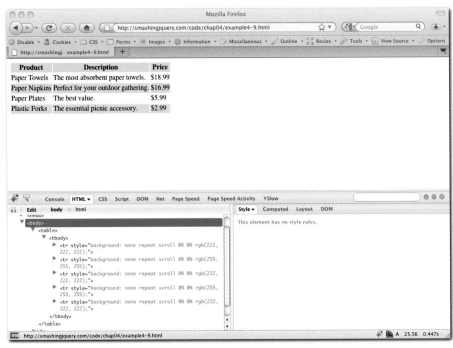

Figure 3-9: The output of the browser after the page has loaded with a background color applied to the even rows

```html
<!doctype html>
<html>
  <head>
  <script src='http://ajax.googleapis.com/ajax/libs/jquery/1.4.2/jquery.min.js'></
  script>
  <script>
  $(document).ready(function() {
    $('tr:even').css('background','#dedede');
    $('tr:odd').css('background','#ffffff');
  });
  </script>

  <body>
    <table>
      <tr>
      <th>Product</th>
      <th>Description</th>
      <th>Price</th>
      </tr>
      <tr>
      <td>Paper Towels</td>
      <td>The most absorbent paper towels.</td>
      <td>$18.99</td>
      </tr>
      <tr>
```

```
    <td>Paper Napkins</td>
    <td>Perfect for your outdoor gathering.</td>
    <td>$16.99</td>
    </tr>
    <tr>
    <td>Paper Plates</td>
    <td>The best value.</td>
    <td>$5.99</td>
    </tr>
    <tr>
    <td>Plastic Forks</td>
    <td>The essential picnic accessory.</td>
    <td>$2.99</td>
    </tr>
    </table>
  </body>
</html>
```

STYLING THE FIRST AND LAST ITEMS IN A LIST OR COLLECTION OF ELEMENTS

If you want to filter out only the first or last item from a set of elements in the DOM, you would use the :first and :last filter applied to your selector. This filter returns only one, and it's based on the index within the selector set that you choose.

In the following HTML example, I want to add a bottom border to all of the list items, except the first and last item. I can go about this two ways; one by adding a .last class to the HTML on only the last element. The other way to accomplish this is to filter the ul li selector with :first and :last filters. Figure 3-10 shows the browser output after the first and last filters have been applied to the list.

```
<doctype html>
<html>
  <head>
  <style>
  ul {width:200px;font-family:arial;}
  ul li {border-bottom:1px solid #333;}
  ul li a {text-decoration:none;}
  </style>
  <script src='http://ajax.googleapis.com/ajax/libs/jquery/1.4.2/jquery.min.js'></
script>
  <script>
  $(document).ready(function() {
    $('ul li:first').css('border','none');
    $('ul li:last').css('border','none');
  });
  </script>
  <body>
    <div id='sidebar'>
    <h1>My sidebar</h1>
    <ul>
```

```
        <li><a href='/index'>Home</a></li>
        <li><a href='/about'>About Us</a></li>
        <li><a href='/customer-service'>Customer Service</a></li>
        <li><a href='/contact'>Contact Us</a></li>
        <li><a href='/coupons'>Coupons</a></li>
      </ul>
    </div>
  </body>
</html>
```

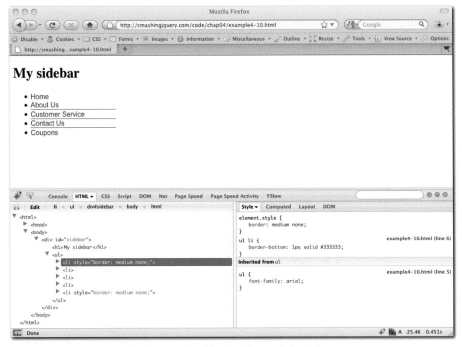

Figure 3-10: The browser output after the first and last filters have been applied to the list

FILTERING ELEMENTS THAT CONTAIN A SPECIFIC ELEMENT

You may want to add a filter that finds only elements that have a specific element inside of them. In these cases, you can use the `has()` filter. The child element contained within does not have to be a direct child of the parent container: It could instead be a descendent.

In the following HTML example, I want to add a filter that increases the font size of only `p` tags that are found within `div`'s with the class name (`.content`). Figure 3-11 shows the browser output of the `p` tag contained within the specified element.

```
<!doctype html>
<html>
  <head>
    <script src='http://ajax.googleapis.com/ajax/libs/jquery/1.4.2/jquery.min.js'></
```

```
script>
 <script>
 $(document).ready(function() {
    $('.content:has(p)').css('font-size''','''18px');
 });
 </script>

 <body>
    <div id="main">
      <div class="content">
      <p>This is my content</p>
      </div>
      <div class="alternate">
      <p>This is alternate content.</p>
      </div>
    </div>
  </body>
</html>
```

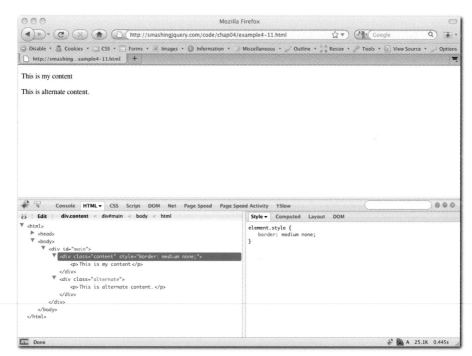

Figure 3-11: The browser output of the p tag contained within the specified element

FILTERING ELEMENTS THAT DO NOT CONTAIN ANY ELEMENTS OR TEXT

Finding empty elements in the DOM can be useful. If you have an empty element on your page, you can use the :empty filter to find it.

In the following HTML example, I want to hide the error div if it is empty. I just need to select the .error class and add the :empty filter. If the error message has content, it remains showing; otherwise, the `display:none` CSS is applied to it. Figure 3-12 shows the browser output when the selector encounters an empty element.

```html
<!doctype html>
<html>
  <head>
  <script src='http://ajax.googleapis.com/ajax/libs/jquery/1.4.2/jquery.min.js'></
  script>
  <script>
  $(document).ready(function() {
    $('.error:empty)').css('display','none');
  });
  </script>

  <body>
    <div id="main">
      <div class="error"></div>
      <div class="error">This is my error message</div>
      <div class="content">
      <p>This is my content</p>
      </div>
      <div class="alternate">
      <p>This is alternate content.</p>
      </div>
    </div>
  </body>
</html>
```

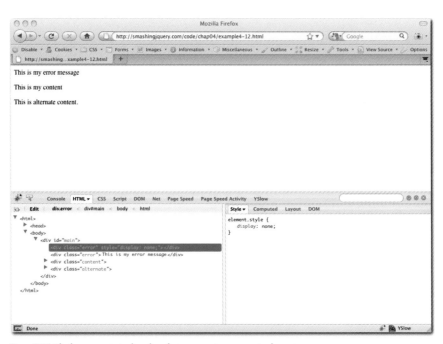

Figure 3-12: The browser output when the selector encounters an empty element

FILTERING ELEMENTS THAT CONTAIN TEXT

In some cases, you may want to filter selectors based on the text that the element contains. You can do so using the :contains filter. The text that you pass to the :contains filter can be enclosed in quotes or just plain text.

In the following HTML example, I want to hide the error div if it's empty. I just need to select the .error class and add the :empty filter. If the error message has content, it displays — otherwise, the display:none CSS is applied to it. Figure 3-13 shows the browser output after the filter finds a td cell containing the specified string 'Paper Towels'.

```html
<!doctype html>
<html>
  <head>
  <script src='http://ajax.googleapis.com/ajax/libs/jquery/1.4.2/jquery.min.js'></
 script>
  <script>
  $(document).ready(function() {
    $("tr td:contains('Paper Towels')").css('border','1px dashed #333');
  });
  </script>

  <body>
    <table>
      <tr>
        <th>Product</th>
        <th>Description</th>
        <th>Price</th>
      </tr>
      <tr>
        <td>Paper Towels</td>
        <td>The most absorbent paper towels.</td>
        <td>$18.99</td>
      </tr>
      <tr>
        <td>Paper Napkins</th>
        <td>Perfect for your outdoor gathering.</th>
        <td>$16.99</th>
      </tr>
      <tr>
        <td>Paper Plates</td>
        <td>The best value.</td>
        <td>$5.99</td>
      </tr>
      <tr>
        <td>Plastic Forks</td>
        <td>The essential picnic accessory.</td>
        <td>$2.99</td>
      </tr>
```

```
    </table>
   </body>
 </html>
```

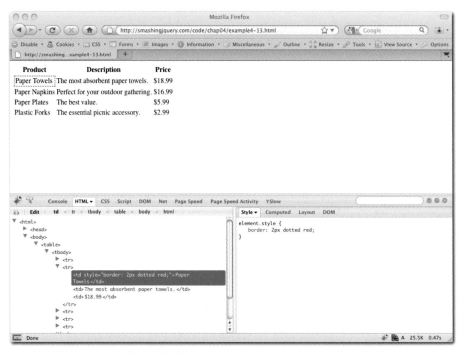

Figure 3-13: The browser output after the filter finds a td cell containing the specified string 'Paper Towels'

SELECTING ELEMENTS IN THE DOM BY THEIR ATTRIBUTES

Attributes of a tag are useful for passing extra information about the tag, or for interacting with JavaScript. A common HTML tag is the `<a>` anchor tag, which can have such attributes as `href`, `rel`, `id`, `class`, `title`, `hreflang`. Selecting by attribute works well with form fields because you can search inputs by name, type, attribute, class, ID, and so on.

You can use any of the attributes in Table 3.3 when selecting elements from the DOM. I focus on attributes in more in-depth tutorials later in the book, but for now, I'm going to go over two common examples of how to work with attributes.

Table 3.3   Attribute Names and Their Functions

Attribute Name	Attribute Function
$('[attribute*=value]')	Targets attributes that contains this value in any part of the string (wildcard)
$('[attribute|=value]')	Targets attributes with a value that starts with or is equal to a string followed by a hyphen (-)

Attribute Name	Attribute Function
$('[attribute~=value]')	Targets attributes that match this value in any part of the string, including spaces
$('[attribute$=value]')	Targets attributes that end with this value
$('[attribute=value]')	Targets attributes that match this value
$('[attribute^=value]')	Targets attributes that start with this value
$('[attribute!=value]')	Targets attributes that don't have this value
$('[attribute=value][attribute=value][attribute=value]')	Targets multiple attributes

SELECTING LINKS THAT CONTAIN A SPECIFIC WEB SITE ADDRESS

Using the wildcard with an attribute is a flexible and commonly used filter. The wildcard (*) can be used to search the DOM for any elements that contain a specific value. This selector is very fast: If you were to find all these elements manually, it could take hours. By using the wildcard attribute selector, you can achieve the same result in a matter of seconds.

In the following HTML example, I need to find all links whose HREF attributes contain the domain google.com and add a CSS class that contains a small Google icon. I filter all the HREFs that have the domain google.com in it. I then use the addClass() method to add the .google-icon class. Figure 3-14 shows the browser output after the attribute filter has found the domain google.com.

```html
<!doctype html>
<html>
  <head>
  <style>
    .google-icon {background:url(images/google_icon.jpg) no-repeat;padding:0px
  30px;}
  </style>
  <script src='http://ajax.googleapis.com/ajax/libs/jquery/1.4.2/jquery.min.js'></
  script>
  <script>
      $(document).ready(function () {
          $('ul li a[href*="google.com"]').addClass('google-icon');
      });
  </script>

  <body>
    <ul>
      <li><a href=http://www.google.com/analytics>Google Analytics</a></li>
      <li><a href="http://www.yahoo.com/sports">Yahoo Sports</a></li>
    </ul>
  </body>
</html>
```

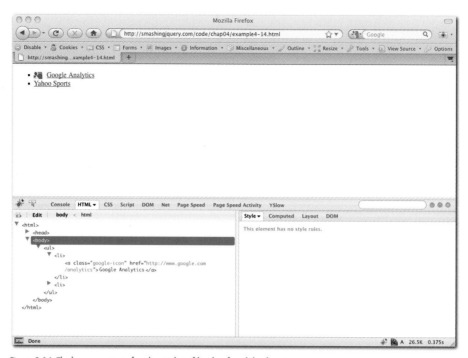

Figure 3-14: The browser output after the attribute filter has found the domain `google.com`

SELECTING ALL ELEMENTS THAT END WITH A SPECIFIC WORD

Similar to how the wildcard symbol works on attributes, you can use the dollar ($) symbol to select all elements that end with a specific string of text. In the following example, I have four `div`s with unique IDs to which I want to add a common class. Because all of my `div`s end in the word `bird`, I can use an attribute selector and select by the last word, as long as it is `bird`. Figure 3-15 shows the browser output after the attribute selector finds the word `bird`.

```html
<!doctype html>
<html>
  <head>
  <style>
  .bird {border:1px solid #ccc;width:200px;margin:5px;}
  </style>
  <script src='http://ajax.googleapis.com/ajax/libs/jquery/1.4.2/jquery.min.js'></
  script>
  <script>
      $(document).ready(function () {
          $('div[id$="bird"]').addClass('bird');
      });
  </script>
  <body>
    <div id="red-bird"></div>
    <div id="blue-bird"></div>
    <div id="green-bird"></div>
```

```
        <div id="black-bird"></div>
    </body>
</html>
```

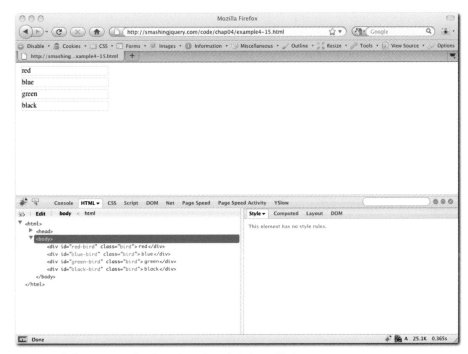

Figure 3-15: The browser output after the attribute selector finds the word bird

MANIPULATING YOUR HTML AND CSS WITH JQUERY

Learning how to use selectors to navigate the DOM is the first step to successfully understanding jQuery. But after you have selected an element, you need to do something with it, which in this case is adding, removing, cloning, replacing, or adding styling. In the future, I refer to the selected element as the matched set because I can assume that selector has returned an element.

The real fun with jQuery begins with DOM manipulation. I have touched on a few ways to add CSS properties to the DOM, but now I'm going to dive in deeper and show you how to really customize your page.

If you are familiar with the native JavaScript functions that can handle some of this editing, jQuery can do it better using syntax that's easier to understand and with less code.

Similar to manipulating HTML elements on your Web page, you can also manipulate the content.

ADDING, REMOVING, CLONING, AND REPLACING DOM ELEMENTS AND CONTENT

jQuery is extremely powerful at adding, removing, replacing, and cloning elements and content in the DOM. For example, I work at a company where, if I need to change HTML on a page, I have to get a backend developer involved, who then has to compile the code before my HTML changes show up. This process is time-consuming, especially for small changes. This is where JavaScript really comes in handy. Making updates to JavaScript files on a production server is a smaller deployment than having to upload page templates, config files, and so on.

I can use jQuery and CSS to manipulate the DOM, which is much faster than getting a backend developer involved. The following examples are common techniques for manipulating the DOM yourself with jQuery.

Adding HTML to the DOM

The `.html()` method uses the native `innerHTML` property and works by either grabbing the `html()` or passing an argument (HTML code) to the method between the parentheses.

You must understand that the `.html()` method grabs the DOM elements contained within the selector that you have targeted. Figure 3-16 shows the browser output after the DOM has loaded and the HTML method is applied.

```
<!doctype html>
<html>
  <head>
   <script src='http://ajax.googleapis.com/ajax/libs/jquery/1.4.2/jquery.min.js'></
  script>
<script>
   $(document).ready(function() {
     $('.content').html('<div class="main">Hello jQuery.</div>');
   });
   </script>

   <body>
     <div class="content">
       <p>I run 4 times a week.</p>
       <p>I lift weights 3 times a week.</p>
     </div>
   </body>
</html>
```

Adding Text to an Element in the DOM

The `text()` method works exactly like the `.html()` method, with the difference being that the `text()` method is only grabbing the text in the form of a string from the matched element. These two methods work in two ways: getting the values and setting the values by passing in arguments. You cannot pass HTML code into the text element, only strings.

```
$('.content').text('Testing 1 2 3.');
```

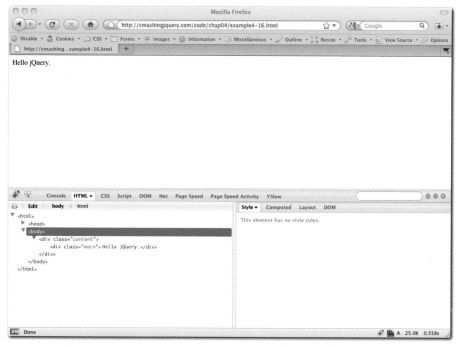

Figure 3-16: The browser output after the DOM has loaded and the HTML method is applied

Appending and Prepending HTML within an Element

If you would like to add HTML within an element, you can use the `append()` method to add it to the end or the `prepend()` method to add it to the beginning of the selected element. The HTML that you supply within the parenthesis is always inserted before or after the last child element within the element that you have selected. Figure 3-17 shows the browser output after the string is appended to the content class.

```
<!doctype html>
<html>
  <head>
  <style>
    .google-icon {background:url(images/google-icon.gif)no-repeat;}
  </style>
  <script src='http://ajax.googleapis.com/ajax/libs/jquery/1.4.2/jquery.min.js'></
  script>
  <script>
  $(document).ready(function() {
    $('.content').append('<p>I ride my bike 3 times a week.</p>');
  });
  </script>

  <body>
    <div class="content">
      <p>I run 4 times a week.</p>
```

```
        <p>I lift weights 3 times a week.</p>
    </div>
  </body>
</html>
```

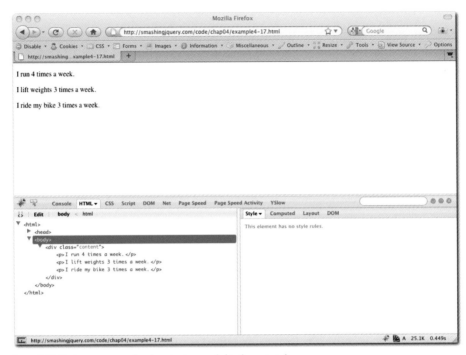

Figure 3-17: The browser output after the string is appended to the content class

Adding HTML Before and After Elements in the DOM

The `before()` and `after()` methods are very similar to the `append()` and `prepend()` methods. The main difference is where the HTML is inserted. Instead of inside the selected element, the HTML is inserted before and after the selected element. Figure 3-18 shows the output of the browser after the string is inserted after the `content` class.

```
<!doctype html>
<html>
  <head>
  <style>
    .google-icon {background:url(images/google-icon.gif)no-repeat;}
  </style>
  <script src='http://ajax.googleapis.com/ajax/libs/jquery/1.4.2/jquery.min.js'></
  script>
  <script>
  $(document).ready(function() {
    $('.content').after('<p>I ride my bike 3 times a week.</p>');
  });
```

```
    </script>

  <body>
    <div class="content">
      <p>I run 4 times a week.</p>
      <p>I lift weights 3 times a week.</p>
    </div>
  </body>
</html>
```

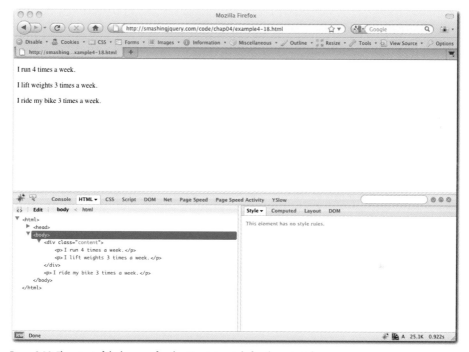

Figure 3-18: The output of the browser after the string is inserted after the content class

Removing HTML Elements from the DOM

The remove() method is useful for removing elements from the DOM. As a Web designer, I tend to hide the element with CSS, but you could alternately use the remove() method to pull it completely off the Web page.

This method is very easy to use: You just need to add the .remove() method to the selector, and after the DOM is ready, it will be removed. You can also remove specific child or descendent elements by selecting the parent and passing the child of that element to the remove() method.

The following HTML example shows the remove() method in action. Refer to Figure 3-17 to see the removal of the element from the DOM. Figure 3-19 shows the browser output after I have removed the content class from the DOM.

```html
<!doctype html>
<html>
  <head>
  <style>
    .google-icon {background:url(images/google-icon.gif)no-repeat;}
  </style>
  <script src='http://ajax.googleapis.com/ajax/libs/jquery/1.4.2/jquery.min.js'></
  script>
<script>
  $(document).ready(function() {
    $('.content').remove();
  });
  </script>

  <body>
    <div class="content">
      <p>I run 4 times a week.</p>
      <p>I lift weights 3 times a week.</p>
    </div>
  </body>
</html>
```

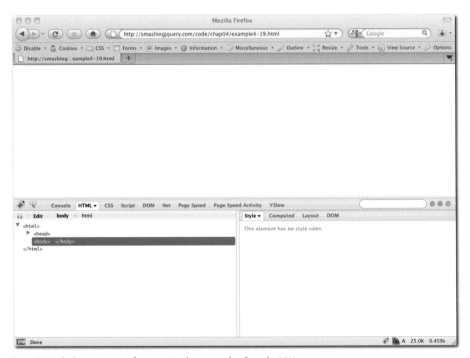

Figure 3-19: The browser output after removing the content class from the DOM

Cloning HTML Elements

You may encounter a situation where you need to copy an element in the DOM and place it somewhere else. jQuery has a method called `clone()`, which clones whichever element you select. After the element is cloned, you are free to place it where you like using other manipulation methods such as the `append()` method, as shown in the following code example:

```
$('.product').clone().append('.product');
```

WORKING WITH CSS AND JQUERY

CSS and jQuery feel like they are meant to work together. I often wonder how I survived so long without using jQuery, especially when working so extensively with CSS. Up until this point, I have been using the `.css()` method to add CSS properties to HTML elements on the page in most of my examples. The downside to using the `.css()` method is that it adds inline styles to the HTML. If you would prefer to keep the code cleaner, I would suggest adding and removing classes instead.

Table 3.4 outlines all of the CSS methods available to use when working with jQuery.

Table 3.4   Commonly Used CSS Methods and Their Abilities

Method Name	Method
.css()	Can retrieve or add CSS properties to any element
.addClass()	Can add a CSS class to any element
.hasClass()	Can test if an element has a class
.removeClass()	Can remove a CSS class from any element
.toggleClass()	Can add and remove CSS classes from any element

Adding CSS to a DOM Element

If you've been working through this chapter in order, you should be familiar by now with adding CSS to any element in the DOM because I have been using the `css()` method in all of my code examples. It is a useful method, especially if you are testing layout and would like to add borders to all of your elements.

```
$('.container').css('border','1px solid #333');
```

Adding a Class to a DOM Element

If you would like to add a class to an existing DOM element, you can use the `addClass()` method. This method works by passing the name of the class that you would like to add into the parentheses after the `addClass`. When you're adding the class name, you do not need to include the period.

```
$('.container').addClass('active');
```

If the DOM element you are adding a class to already has a class, the additional class will be added after it. If you wish to pass multiple classes to a matched set, just make sure you list each class separated by a space.

```
$('.container').addClass('active book');
```

You are not limited to adding classes by selecting classes. You can also add classes to ID and other HTML tags.

```
$('#page-wrap').addClass('alternate');
```

Removing a Class from a DOM Element

You also need to learn how to remove a class from an element. It works in the same way, but the method name changes from `addClass()` to `removeClass()`.

```
$('#page-wrap').removeClass('alternate');
```

If no class name is passed into the method, any class in that matched set is removed.

```
$('#page-wrap').removeClass();
```

You can also remove multiple classes by adding them one after another into the method, each one separated by spaces.

```
$('#page-wrap').removeClass('alternate main product');
```

Toggling a Class on a DOM Element

Toggling is the act of turning something on or off. The `toggleClass()` method is useful when you're working with dynamic Web applications where you may not always know the on/off state that an element is in.

In the following example, I toggle the class `.alternate` on the `#page-wrap div`. If the class does not exist, it is added, and vice versa.

```
$('#page-wrap').toggleClass('alternate');
```

4

WORKING WITH EVENTS

WORKING WITH EVENTS in jQuery is very similar to working with CSS in HTML. The events are separated from the elements that they are being attached to. In native JavaScript, all of the events are embedded directly into the HTML, which makes it a chore to maintain any custom events and makes it easy to screw something up. You have all of these functions in an external file, but they are added to the elements as inline JavaScript, so if something changes in one element, it has to be updated in all of the elements. With jQuery, all of the element selection and event handling is done outside of the DOM in a JavaScript file.

jQuery supports all of the native JavaScript events, but makes it much easier to integrate them into your Web sites and applications. In this chapter, I review the events that are available to you through the jQuery API, show you each event and how it works, and then walk you through a few real-world scenarios.

UNDERSTANDING EVENTS IN JQUERY

jQuery events are a fundamental piece of any Web site application or Web page. When the Internet first started, it was just static text, images, and hyperlinks. As the technology advanced, we started to see more dynamic Web pages that interacted with a database.

As the back-end technologies grew more advanced, so did the front-end, with technologies such as Adobe Flash and JavaScript, which added another dimension of interactivity. Hyperlinks have become rollovers and expanding menus, images have turned into interactive galleries with editing abilities, and static text has evolved into powerful and dynamic search engines such as the Kayak travel search engine, which offers a map-based view, as shown in Figure 4-1. jQuery allows you to use all of the native JavaScript events to capture user interactions through the keyboard and the mouse, but with less code and in an easier-to-understand syntax. That's the jQuery way!

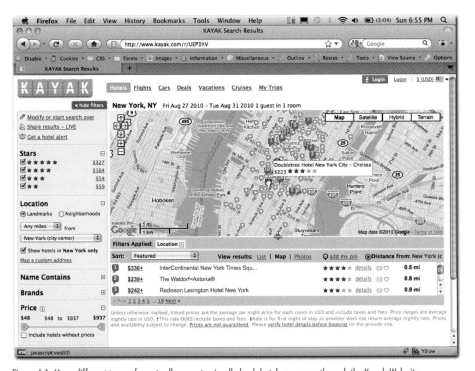

Figure 4-1: Many different types of events allow you to visually book hotels on a map through the Kayak Web site

WORKING WITH DOCUMENT AND WINDOW EVENTS

Table 4.1 introduces jQuery common document and window events, which are important events to keep in mind anytime you are writing jQuery. The table outlines each event and their function, allowing you to compare them at a glance to ensure that you are using the best-suited event for your script.

Table 4.1   jQuery Document and Window Events

Event Name	Event Function
ready()	Fires when the HTML document has loaded
load()	Fires when all assets have loaded
unload()	Fires when browser window is closed, or when a user navigates to new page via the address bar or a link
resize()	Fires when user resizes the browser window
scroll()	Fires when user initiates scroll
error()	Fires when an error is received from an HTTP request

DETECTING COMPLETE LOADING OF THE DOM WITH THE READY() EVENT

One event that is commonly used to check that the DOM (Document Object Model) has been loaded correctly is the `ready()` event. This event fires any JavaScript or jQuery code that you declare between its brackets when the DOM is ready.

The document `ready event` handler allows you to put all of your JavaScript jQuery code within this event, either inline or in an external file, to make sure the code is executed when the DOM is ready. An event handler is a function that executes your event as it occurs. It's very important that you use the document `ready event` handler to ensure the document has been correctly loaded, before you try to do any DOM manipulation. If you do not use this event, your code probably won't work in the manner that you intended.

```
$(document).ready() {
  alert("The DOM is ready");
});
```

This event is perfect for checking to be sure that the document is ready, but it doesn't include page assets such as images or video. If you would like to check for assets that have been loaded, you can use the jQuery `load()` event that is outlined in the following tutorial.

PRELOADING IMAGES WITH THE LOAD() EVENT

Preloading images is practical when you're using many images and you would like them to be available as soon as a user does something on your page. In this instance, I show an example of how to preload five images and add them to the DOM after they've been loaded. One of the worst experiences for a user is having to wait a long time for images to load on a page. This prevents that from occurring.

The images I'm using are large and not optimized for the Web; therefore, their file sizes are between 100 KB and 200 KB.

1. Using the native JavaScript array, I set up an array called `imgArray`. The array holds all of the filenames of the images that I'm adding to the page. Using an array saves me from having to create five individual statements to add the images to the page:

```
var imgArray =
["loc_portrait1.jpg",
"loc_portrait2.jpg",
"loc_portrait3.jpg",
"loc_portrait4.jpg",
"loc_portrait5.jpg"];
```

2. Add two more variables to be used with the `for` loop that will be set up in the next step. The variable `imgArrLength` stores the value that is returned for the length of the array and the variable `i` is used as the index in the `for` loop. The index in an array always starts with 0, unless it's an associative array.

```
var imgArrLength = imageArray.length;
var i = 0;
```

3. Construct a `for` loop. Using the variable `i`, set the value of it to be less than or equal to the `imgArrLength`. The `for` loop runs until it reaches the length of the array, which is 5.

```
for (i=0;i< imgArrLength ;i++) {

}
```

An index always begins with 0, so even though there are five items in the array, the index only goes to 4. The following code outlines how the index is set up using 0 through 4:

```
imgArray[0] = "loc_portrait1.jpg";
imgArray[1] = "loc_portrait2.jpg";
imgArray[2] = "loc_portrait3.jpg";
imgArray[3] = "loc_portrait4.jpg";
imgArray[4] = "loc_portrait5.jpg";
```

4. When the loop runs, it adds an image element each time until the loop is complete. Set the source of the image to `filename` and the ID of the image to be `img` plus the index (for example, `(id="img1")`) using the `attribute` method.

```
for (i=0;i <= imgArrLength;i++) {
    $('<img />').attr({'src':'images/'+imgArray[i], 'id':'img'+[i]}).
  load(function(){
    });
}
```

5. As each image finishes loading, it is appended to the `(.gallery)` container in the DOM. The images are available only as they are added to the DOM. They are added according to how long they take to load. In Figure 4-2, notice in the rendered source code that they are not in order by filename, but by file size.

```
for (i=0;i <= imgArrLength;i++) {
    $('<img />').attr({'src':'images/'+imgArray[i], 'id':'img'+[i]}).
  load(function(){
      $('.gallery').append($(this));
    });
}
```

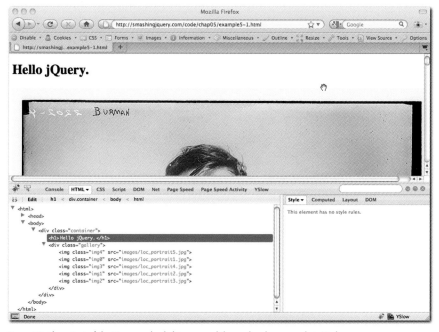

Figure 4-2: The output of the jQuery preloaded images and the rendered source code in Firebug

In the preceding code example, notice the use of the `this` keyword, which is used to reference the current object of the method or function that is being executed. You can use the `this` keyword to reference the object, or, as in the following code example, to reference the `<img>` tag. The `this` keyword is extremely useful in many situations. Figure 4-3 shows how the `this` keyword works.

```
$('.special-offer')bind('click' , function(){
    $(this).addClass('active');
});
```

Figure 4-3: How the this keyword works

6. If you pull the pieces of code together and drop it into your IDE (integrated development environment), it looks like the following:

```
<!doctype html>
<html>
  <head>
  <script src="http://ajax.googleapis.com/ajax/libs/jquery/1.4.2/jquery.min.
 js"></script>
  <script>
  var imgArray =
  ["loc_portrait1.jpg",
  "loc_portrait2.jpg",
  "loc_portrait3.jpg",
  "loc_portrait4.jpg",
  "loc_portrait5.jpg"];
  var imgArrLength = imageArray.length;
  for (i=0;i<= imageArray.length;i++) {
  $('<img />').attr('src', 'images/'+imageArray[i]).load(function(){
        $('.gallery').append($(this));
```

```
      });
    }
    </script>
    <body>
      <h1>Hello jQuery.</h1>
      <div class="gallery"></div>
    </body>
  </html>
```

SHOWING AN ALERT AS A USER LEAVES A PAGE

Have you ever wanted to show content to a user when they exit the page? Did you wish you could just give them one more opportunity to entice them with an offer that they couldn't refuse? The jQuery `unload` event can be used to do just that. This event fires when the user closes their browser window or types a new address into the browser bar. You've probably come across sites that abuse the `unload` event by hammering you with multiple windows and not letting you leave. That's the wrong way to handle those who wish to leave your site.

Instead, think about a user filling out a form on your site. He completes half of the form and then decides to bail. This is the perfect opportunity to use the `unload` event to show them an alert asking them if they want to leave. Figure 4-4 shows the alert message as the user tries to leave the page.

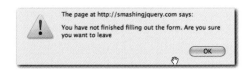

Figure 4-4: An alert message is displayed as the user tries to leave the page

The `unload` event is not handled correctly in some older browsers. Before pushing any code live, you should always thoroughly test across all the Web browsers that you support to ensure that this event works as you intend it to. The browsers that are in question are versions of Safari versions before 3 and various versions of the Firefox 3 browser — sometimes they don't fire the `unload` event when the page is closed, so a workaround might be needed for these older browsers.

The `unload` event uses the `bind` method to attach the event handler to the event.

```
$(window).bind('unload', function() {
  alert('You have not finished filling out the form. Are you sure you want to
  leave?');
});
$(window).bind('unload', function() {
  alert('You have not finished filling out the form. Are you sure you want to
  leave');
});
```

A shorthand version of the `unload` event is outlined in the following example.

```
$(window).unload(function() {
  alert('You have not finished filling out the form. Are you sure you want to
  leave?');
});
```

```
$(window).unload(function() {
  alert('You have not finished filling out the form. Are you sure you want to
  leave');
});
```

DISPLAYING A BACKUP IMAGE USING THE ERROR EVENT

I work with a handful of e-commerce sites that sell more than 200 products per site, which equals around 600 product images on each site when you take into account the different-sized images (small, thumbnail, and large) for each product. When an image link is broken on a product page, the only way I can usually find out is by browsing the site until I see the missing image. Using the jQuery `error` event, I can detect whether an image is missing and set a default image to the attribute of the matched element.

1. You need to set up an image tag first, which can be as simple as the following code. You just need to remember to give a unique ID to the image tag so that you can select it.

```
<img src="images/loc_portrait10.jpg" id="portrait" />
```

2. Next, set up a selector to set the ID equal to `portrait`.

```
$('#portrait')
```

3. Add the `error` event to the selector that you set up in the previous step. The `error` event fires only if the browser does not load the file correctly.

```
$('#portrait').error() {
});
```

4. Next, set up a handler function so that when the error event fires, something happens. In this case, set a default image to the source of the matched image element.

```
$('#portrait').error() {
  $(this).attr('src', 'images/default.jpg');
});
```

GETTING STARTED WITH EVENT DELEGATION

Event delegation and handling in jQuery refers to the execution of events by attaching event listeners to objects that wait for events to bubble up the through the elements in the DOM. Figure 4-5 shows an example of how this occurs in JavaScript. If you have ever worked with ActionScript 3.0, the concept of event bubbling should be familiar because it is handled in a similar way in jQuery and JavaScript. There are two methods that an event can trigger during the listening phase: event capturing and event bubbling.

Event capturing occurs when an event flows downwards through the descendents of the DOM. Event bubbling is what occurs when an event flows upwards through the DOM starting with the source of the event. Most events use the event bubbling flow except for focus and blur. Event capturing differs from event bubbling in the direction of how the event flows through the document, and you could argue that event bubbling is faster and more efficient. jQuery uses the event bubbling method for all of the events.

An event handler is a function that executes your code as the event occurs. A jQuery method is used to attach the event handler to an event. As of jQuery 1.4.2, the library offers three different methods for attaching events to elements: `bind()`, `live()`, and `delegate()`.

77

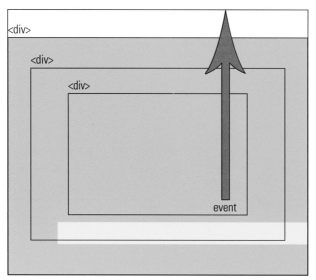

Figure 4-5: Event bubbling in action

USING BIND TO ATTACH AN EVENT HANDLER TO AN ELEMENT

The bind event handler attachment is the most basic way to capture an event and consists of passing an event type and event handler to the bind method, which is attached to an element using a selector.

```
.bind(event type, event handler)
```

In the following example, bind attaches the event handler to the click event by selecting all elements that contain the class mylink. When the event is invoked, it triggers the alertMe function:

```
$(document).ready(function(){
    $('.mylink').bind(click, alertMe);

function alertMe() {
    alert("Hello World");
}
});
```

You can also set up bind events with anonymous functions, which is often the way I set up my event handlers. The following code performs the same actions as the previous example but uses an anonymous function instead of inserting a function into the click event statement. Anonymous functions, also known as *function literals,* are best used when the code to be executed only applies in the current context. Named functions are best suited for when the code to be executed will be used in response to multiple events.

```
$(document).ready(function(){
 $('.mylink').bind(click, function(){
  alert("Hello World");
 });
});
```

The `bind` event handler works only with DOM elements that are currently in the DOM. Consider the following scenario: You have an existing element in the DOM called `box` and would like to duplicate this element and add the new element to the DOM after a link is clicked. You can set up a `click` event that is attached to a link. Each time that link is clicked, the `clone()` method is invoked on the box element and the result is appended to the container element. The following code is an example of how you can use the `click` event to change/add items that are currently in the DOM when the page has loaded:

Based on how selectors work, you might expect that the `click` event would work on this new element that you've added to the DOM. Wrong! It only works with elements that are in the DOM at the time of binding the event. The `click` event is only attached to the first element, so you can keep cloning that first element, but none of the other elements will have `click` events attached to them.

```
$(document).ready(function(){
 $('.box').bind(click, function(){
   $(this).clone().appendTo('.container');
 });
});
<div class="container">
  <div class="box"></div>
</div>
```

USING LIVE TO ATTACH AN EVENT HANDLER TO AN ELEMENT

The `live` event handler attachment is a flexible way to capture an event. It consists of passing an event type and event handler to the `live` method, which is attached to an element using a selector. The setup is very similar to the `bind` method, except that the `live` method works with current and future elements in the DOM.

```
.live(event type, event handler)
```

If we take the previous example and add the `live` event handler attachment, all of the elements, current and future, are clickable:

```
$(document).ready(function(){
 $('.box').live(click, function(){
   $(this).clone().appendTo('.container');
 });
});
<div class="container">
  <div class="box"></div>
</div>
```

The `live` method works really well with Web applications where the DOM is much more dynamic and elements are being added to and removed from the DOM constantly. This is known as DOM scripting.

The disadvantage to using the `live` event handler attachment is that you cannot chain other methods to the statement as shown in the following code example. This code won't work!

```
$(document).ready(function(){
  $('.container').first().live('click',function() {
    $(this).clone().addClass('square').appendTo('.container:first');
  });
});

<div class="container">
  <div class="box"></div>
</div>
<div class="container">
  <div class="box"></div>
</div>
<div class="container">
  <div class="box"></div>
</div>
```

USING DELEGATE TO ATTACH AN EVENT HANDLER TO AN ELEMENT

If you want to add event handlers in a similar fashion to the `live` method, but also be able to chain other methods, the `delegate` method is the most flexible and best solution. It consists of passing a selector, event type, and event handler to the `delegate` method, which is attached to an element using a selector. The selector that is passed to the `delegate` method filters the elements to target a specific element or set of elements.

```
.delegate(selector, event type, event handler)
```

When you're using the `delegate` method, which requires a slightly different setup from the `bind` and `live` methods, do the following:

1. Create the selector statement; in this case, select the container element.

   ```
   $('.container')
   ```

2. Next, attach the event with `delegate`. Within the genre element, I am filtering down to the album-cover element. With the album-cover element selected, with each click, this element is being cloned and added to the genre element.

   ```
   $(document).ready(function(){
     $('.container').delegate('.box','click',function() {
       $(this).clone().appendTo('.container');
     });
   });
   ```

The following example shows how to use the `delegate` method and chain other methods.

The difference in this example compared to the previous one is that I'm filtering the genre elements using `first()`. Only the first element will be clickable and will have the element album-cover cloned and added inside it.

```
$(document).ready(function(){
  $('.genre').first().delegate('.album-cover','click',function() {
    $(this).clone().addClass('rock').appendTo('.genre:first');
  });
});

<div class="genre">
  <div class="album-cover"></div>
</div>
<div class="genre">
  <div class="album-cover"></div>
</div>
<div class="genre">
  <div class="album-cover"></div>
</div
```

CAPTURING MOUSE EVENTS

When you are ready to add user-initiated interaction to your site, jQuery offers a wide range of mouse-initiated events that are easy to learn yet can be extended in numerous ways to propel your Web site or application to the next level.

The `bind()` method is the most common method for attaching events to functions in jQuery and I use it for the following examples.

Table 4.2 summarizes each mouse event and its function. The tutorials following the table are real-world examples of how to use these events. Most of the tutorials also incorporate concepts from the previous chapters.

Although jQuery does not have a native right-click event to offer context menus, third-party extensions that enable them are available.

Table 4.2   jQuery Mouse-Driven Events That Can Be Used with bind()

Event Name	Event Function
click	Fires when mouse button is pressed and released
dblclick	Fires when mouse button is double-clicked
mousedown	Fires when mouse button is pushed
mouseup	Fires when mouse button is released
mouseenter	Fires when mouse enters specified element
mouseleave	Fires when mouse leaves specified element

continued

Table 4.2   (continued)

Template	Function
mousemove	Fires when mouse moves on specified element
mouseout	Fires when mouse leaves specified element and parent
mouseover	Fires when mouse enters specified element and parent

ADDING AND REMOVING CONTENT TO OR FROM A PAGE WITH A MOUSE CLICK

Learning how to detect a mouse click is one of the most basic yet sought-after events in jQuery. This Internet is built on links and text, so users expect to click around your Web site. Being able to programmatically add and remove content to and from a page is useful, especially when you're creating Web applications.

If you use JavaScript to create a `click` event, you add the `onClick` action directly to the element. The `onClick` is the event handler, which then calls a function to be invoked with the click. The downside to this technique is that is muddles up your inline JavaScript actions that have to be added to each element. jQuery uses a selector statement to add the `click` event to an element or multiple elements. Introducing non-semantic code such as inline JavaScript, as in the following example, is a poor practice:

```
<a href="product.html" onClick="myFunction();">Paper Towels</a>
```

jQuery uses a selector statement to add the `click` event to an element or multiple elements using the `bind` method. The syntax for a `click` event in jQuery is more concise and isn't added inline to each individual element.

```
$(selector).bind('click', function() {
// code to be executed after element is clicked
});
```

The following tutorial explains how to add and remove one paragraph with a mouse click.

1. First, create a link that has a class of `"content-link"` and a `div` that contains the content, which is hidden upon page load.

```
<style>
.content {display:none;}
</style>
<h1>Hello jQuery.</h1>
<p>Lorem ipsum dolor sit amet, consectetur adipiscing elit. Donec gravida
  rhoncus commodo. Aenean sit amet augue iaculis sem consectetur accumsan vitae a
  arcu. Quisque quam diam, sollicitudin vel porta eget, vestibulum id justo.
  Vestibulum mattis metus sed lorem adipiscing facilisis. </p>
<a href="#" class="content-link">Show More</a>

<div id="content">
```

```
    <p>Donec diam nisi, auctor sed tristique eget, pellentesque nec nisi. Sed vel
    libero ipsum. Quisque semper, lectus in pulvinar tristique, nibh urna sceleris-
    que augue, at varius justo metus in orci. Suspendisse pretium arcu nec enim
    lacinia id cursus diam rhoncus. Praesent pulvinar volutpat luctus. Vivamus
    cursus adipiscing tellus, id fermentum turpis egestas lacinia. Aliquam tris-
    tique porttitor quam at pretium.</p>
    </div>
```

2. Using the `click` event with a selector to select the anchor tag with the class "con-tent-link". The `click` event is attached to the selector, and the content in between the curly brackets is executed after that link is clicked.

```
$('.content-link').bind('click', function() {
  // code to be executed after element is clicked
});
```

3. To get the content `div` to show after the link has been clicked, I add a selector statement, which matches the `div` with an ID of content, and add the show method to it.

The show method changes the display to block, if the matched set is hidden. If the matched set is already shown, the show method won't have an effect on anything.

```
$('#content').show();
```

4. To hide content on a page click, just switch the `show()` method to the `hide()` in the selector statement.

```
$('#content').hide();
```

5. Alternatively, if you would like to change the show effect to a toggle, so that with each mouse click it shows or hides content, use the `toggle` method. The `toggle` method can be thought of as a Boolean that toggles between the show and hide effects.

```
$('#content').toggle();
```

6. If you pull all the code together into one page, it should look similar to the following code. Figure 4-6 shows the link after it has been clicked. Firebug is open, showing that the content element's display property has been changed to "block".

```
<!doctype html>
<html>
  <head>
  <style>
  body {font-family:arial;}
  #content {display:none;}
  </style>
  <script src="http://ajax.googleapis.com/ajax/libs/jquery/1.4.2/jquery.min.js"></
  script>
    <script>
       $(document).ready(function () {
          $('.content-link').click(function () {
             $('#content').toggle();
          });
       });
    </script>
  <body>
      <h1>Hello jQuery.</h1>
```

83

```
    <p>Lorem ipsum dolor sit amet, consectetur adipiscing elit. Donec gravida
rhoncus commodo. Aenean sit amet augue iaculis sem consectetur accumsan vitae a
arcu. Quisque quam diam, sollicitudin vel porta eget, vestibulum id justo. Vestibu-
lum mattis metus sed lorem adipiscing facilisis. Vestibulum sed ipsum ut nibh
rutrum ultricies. </p>
    <a href="#" class="content-link">Show More</a>
    <div id="content">
    <p>Donec diam nisi, auctor sed tristique eget, pellentesque nec nisi. Sed vel
libero ipsum. Quisque semper, lectus in pulvinar tristique, nibh urna scelerisque
augue, at varius justo metus in orci. Suspendisse pretium arcu nec enim lacinia id
cursus diam rhoncus. Praesent pulvinar volutpat luctus. Vivamus cursus adipiscing
tellus, id fermentum turpis egestas lacinia. Aliquam tristique porttitor quam at
pretium. In ornare aliquet iaculis. Phasellus sit amet leo id urna tincidunt
fringilla. Nullam ut fringilla magna. Class aptent taciti sociosqu ad litora
torquent per conubia nostra, per inceptos himenaeos. Nunc leo arcu, sagittis eget
volutpat at, bibendum at elit. Vestibulum a nisi nec felis malesuada fringilla.
Quisque vitae mauris nec sapien porta pharetra eu vitae sapien. Cras bibendum
eleifend malesuada.</p>
    </div>
  </body>
</html>
```

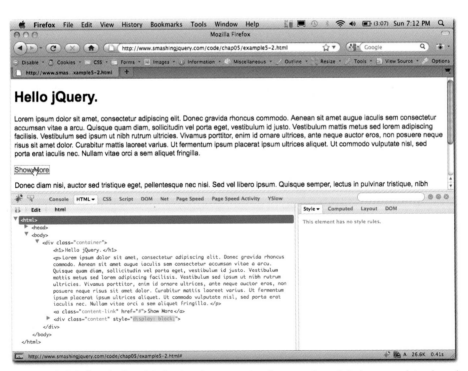

Figure 4-6: The link after it has been clicked, with Firebug open to show the content element's display property being changed via the toggle event

UNDERSTANDING HOW THE DOUBLE-CLICK EVENT WORKS

The `double-click` event is set up in the same manner as the `click` event, with the exception that it is triggered by double-clicking the mouse. I don't use the `double-click` event that often, but it can be useful for Web applications that act and/or look like desktop applications.

The jQuery `double-click` event is the same as the native JavaScript `double-click` event, which needs to be set up in a similar manner to the `onclick` event and be added directly to the element.

Desktop software often requires a double-click for an action to occur within the program. On the Internet, the double-click action can lend itself well to adding products to a shopping cart. You can also use it if your users aren't Internet-savvy and tend to always double-click. Still, the `double-click` event is not as commonly used as the `click` event.

CREATING A TOOLTIP THAT SHOWS CONTENT DURING THE HOVER EVENT

Showing tooltips or little informative bubbles on links, form elements, and other elements on your page can help your users navigate through your site while still being able to keep a consistent flow for more experienced users. Tooltips can be simple instructions on a form for users who aren't aware of what a CVV number on a credit card is, or more interactive, as in Figure 4-7, which shows an example of a hover-triggered tooltip.

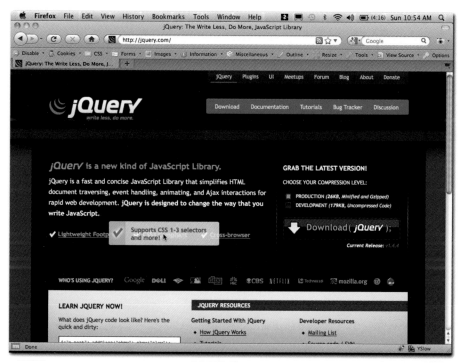

Figure 4-7: A hover-triggered tooltip on the jQuery Web site
© 2010 The jQuery Project and the jQuery UI Team

jQuery has a hover event that uses the native JavaScript `mouseover` and `mouseout` events. A tooltip is just one type of interaction that can be used with the `hover` event, but there are many other possibilities ranging from drop-down navigation menus to image previews such as those found on the Zappos Web site, shown in Figure 4-8.

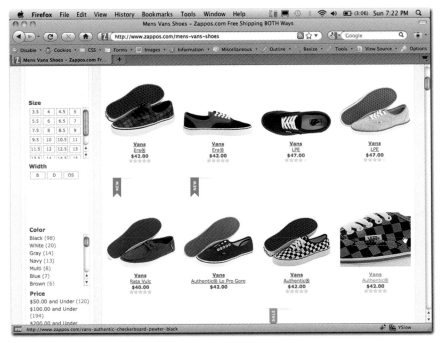

Figure 4-8: The Zappos Web site displays image previews when you roll over a product with the mouse

It's easy to add a custom tooltip that displays using the `hover` event in jQuery. This example is based around an image with a caption that I want to display directly underneath as I hover over the image, as shown in Figure 4-9. You might run into a similar situation where you don't want a caption to display all the time, but only when the user mouses over the image.

1. Start by creating the HTML for the image so that it has a title attribute set. You're using the title attribute to ensure that users without JavaScript can still see the tooltip on the image; this is a good example of progressive enhancement. (See Chapter 1 for a refresher on progressive enhancement.)

```
<h1>Hello jQuery.</h1>
<div class="cart">
  <h2>Shopping Cart</h2>
</div>
<div class="product">
<h3>Apple iPhone 4</h3>
<div class="product-image"><img src="images/iphone.jpg" title="Steve Jobs
holds up the newest iPhone 4." alt="Steve Jobs"></div>
 <p class="info">iPhone 4 is a GSM cell phone with a high-resolution display,
FaceTime video calling, HD video recording, a 5-megapixel camera, and more.</p>
 <p class="price">$299.99</p>
```

```
<div class="add-to-cart">Double-click to buy me</div>
</div>
```

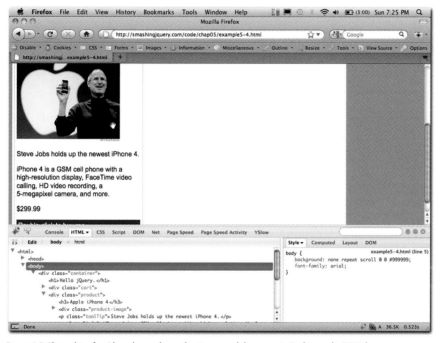

Figure 4-9: The tooltip after I have hovered over the picture, and the output in Firebug as the DOM changes

2. The next step is to add your `document.ready` event to ensure that the jQuery is applied only when the DOM is ready.

```
$(document).ready(function(){
});
```

3. Set up the `mouseenter` and `mouseleave` events to be bound to the image element found within the `product-image` element. This selector is a descendent selector because you're matching an element that is a descendent of another element. The `mouseenter` and `mouseleave` elements ensure that when the user moves their mouse over and off of the images, two different actions occur.

```
$(document).ready(function(){
$('.product-image img').bind({
  mouseenter : function () {
  },
  mouseleave: function () {
  }
});
});
```

The difference between `mouseover/mouseout` and `mouseenter/mouseleave` is the way that the event is triggered.

The `mouseover` and `mouseout` event is triggered when the mouse enters the element or child or descendent element of the element. The `mouseenter` and `mouseleave` events are triggered only when the mouse enters the element, regardless of whether it has children. The `mouseover` and `mouseout` event can trigger unintentionally and therefore cause issues within your script.

4. The `mouseenter` state is the first of the two states and fires when the mouse enters the selected element, which in this case is the image tag found within the `product-image` element. With this event, you set up a variable named `tooltip`. This variable stores the value that is extracted using the `attr` method from the `title` tag.

```
$(document).ready(function(){
$('.product-image img').bind({
  mouseenter : function () {
    var toolTip = $(this).attr("title");
    $('.info').after('<p class="toolTip">'+toolTip+'</p>');
    },
  mouseleave: function () {
        }
  });
});
```

5. The second statement inserts the value of the tooltip, which is stored in the variable `tooltip` into the DOM after the `div` with the class info. After the tooltip is inserted into the DOM, it is wrapped with a p class of `toolTip`.

```
$(document).ready(function(){
$('.product-image img').bind({
  mouseenter : function () {
    var toolTip = $(this).attr("title");
    $('.info').after('<p class="toolTip">'+toolTip+'</p>');
  },
  mouseleave: function () {
  }
  });
  });
```

6. Finally, the `mouseleave` state fires when the mouse leaves the selected element. This code hides the tooltip that you've previously added using the `hide()` method attached to the `p.tooltip` selector:

```
$(document).ready(function(){
$('.product-image img').bind({
  mouseenter : function () {
    var toolTip = $(this).attr("title");
    $('.info').after('<p class="toolTip">'+toolTip+'</p>');
  },
  mouseleave: function () {
    $('p.toolTip').hide();
  }
  });
  });
```

In the previous example, I set up the `mouseenter` and `mouseleave` events using a map of event type/handler pairs. The benefit to setting up the events in this manner is that it allows you to add more events that you would like to bind to this element within the same function.

A JavaScript object literal, also known as a map, is a collection of name and value pairs. The syntax is usually set up as opening and closing curly brackets with the name value pairs enclosed in single quotes and separated by a colon. Each name/value pair is on its own line, as shown in the following example:

```
{
'name1' : 'value1',
'name2' : 'value2',
'name3' : 'value3',
}
```

You can use `mouseenter` and `mouseleave` in another way to still obtain the same output. The `hover` event binds the `mouseenter` and `mouseleave` events together into one event, leaving you with syntax that is concise and easy to use, as you can see in the following code:

```
$(document).ready(function(){
  $('.product-image img').hover(
  function () {
    var toolTip = $(this).attr("title");
    $('.info').after('<p class="toolTip">'+toolTip+'</p>');
    },
  function () {
    $('p.toolTip').hide();
    }
  });
});
```

CREATING BASIC ADD TO CART FUNCTIONALITY WITH MOUSEDOWN AND MOUSEUP EVENTS

Drag-and-drop functionality on the Web is becoming increasingly more popular. It adds a level of deeper interactivity by allowing users to move elements around on the screen in a 3D fashion. Figure 4-10 shows the Yahoo! Sports Fantasy Baseball interface featuring a slick drag-and-drop interface.

The native JavaScript API offers the `onMousedown` and `onMouseup` events, which can be added inline to any element to capture these events. The main difference between events in JavaScript and jQuery is the addition of the on keyword that proceeds events in JavaScript. In jQuery, this extra keyword is dropped. The `onMousedown` and `onMouseup` are just known as `mousedown` and `mouseup` in jQuery.

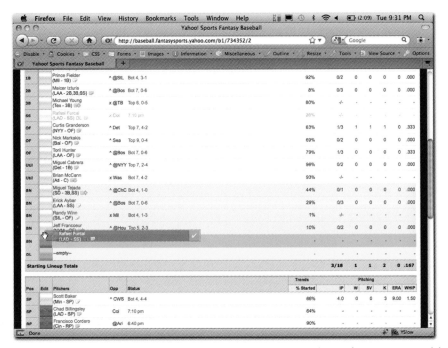

Figure 4-10: The Yahoo! Sports Fantasy Baseball interface for changing players around in your fantasy team using a slick drag-and-drop interface

In this section, I walk you through some basic concepts you can start using towards building a basic drag-and-drop system. If you are looking for robust drag-and-drop solution, jQuery UI offers a great many draggable and droppable interactions that you can easily plug into a Web application. jQuery UI is an additional library that sits on top of jQuery and offers a rich assortment of widgets, interface elements, and themes for building robust Web applications. You can visit the jQuery UI Web site at `jqueryui.com` for more information.

In Figure 4-11, I use the shopping cart sample HTML that I have used in the previous examples. The main difference is instead of using the event `dblclick()` to add the item to the shopping cart, I show you how to use the `mousedown()` and `mouseup()` events to simulate clicking and releasing an item.

1. Start by creating the necessary HTML elements on the page. I simulate a product and a shopping cart, but the script will be interacting only with the product `div` in this example.

```
<div class="cart">
  <h2>Shopping Cart</h2>
</div>
<div class="product">
<h3>Apple iPhone 4</h3>
<div class="product-image"><img src="images/iphone.jpg" title="Steve Jobs
holds up the newest iPhone 4."></div>
 <p class="info">iPhone 4 is a GSM cell phone with a high-resolution display,
FaceTime video calling, HD video recording, a 5-megapixel camera, and more.</p>
 <p class="price">$299.99</p>
```

```
<div class="add-to-cart">Double-click to buy me</div>
</div>
```

2. The next step of the process is to add your `document.ready` event to ensure that the jQuery is only applied after the DOM is ready:

```
$(document).ready(function(){
});
```

3. The next step is to add the `mousedown` and `mouseup` events. I use the `bind` method to attach the event handler to the `product` element.

```
$(document).ready(function(){
$('.product').bind({
  mousedown : function () {
  },
  mouseup: function () {
  }
});
});
```

4. The `mousedown` event fires when the mouse button is depressed on the element; when this occurs, the element is draggable and the border needs to change to a 3 px (pixel) solid red border.

```
$(document).ready(function(){
  $('.product').bind({
  mousedown : function() {
  $(this).css('border','3px solid red');
  },
  mouseup: function() {
  }
  });
});
```

5. The `mouseup` event fires when the mouse button is released. A few changes take place in the following code after this occurs. First, the border is set back to the 3 px solid `#cccccc` (light gray) that it started with. Then the `cart` element is selected. Text that says `Apple iPhone 4 is now in the cart` is appended, and the H2 element changes to `Shopping Cart contains 1 item!`. The final statement hides the `product` element.

```
$(document).ready(function(){
  $('.product').bind({
  mousedown : function() {
  $(this).css('border','3px solid red');
  },
  mouseup: function() {
  $(this).css('border','3px solid #ccc');
  $('.cart').append('Apple iPhone 4 is now in the cart<br>');
  $('.cart h2').text('Shopping Cart contains 1 item!');
  $(this).hide();
  }
```

```
    });
    });
```

The important concept is that we can detect when the mouse button is down and when the mouse button is up and offer two completely different functions. Figure 4-11 shows the drag-and-drop basic functionality with Firebug open to outline the changes to the DOM.

All of the mouse-initiated events can also be written in shorthand format, which offers a more concise way for developers to build jQuery functionality into their Web sites and applications.

This is the `click` event written in longhand format using the `bind` method:

```
$('.container').bind('click', function(){});
```

The same `click` event as in the preceding example using `bind`, but written in shorthand:

```
$('.container').click(function(){});
```

The downside to using the shorthand format is that you are then unable to bind multiple events to one event handler:

```
$('.container').bind('click dblclick', function())};
```

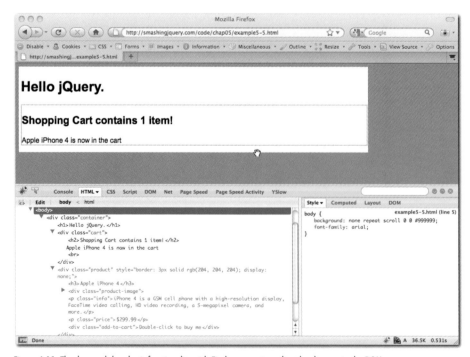

Figure 4-11: The drag-and-drop basic functionality with Firebug open to outline the changes to the DOM

CREATING A ROLLOVER EFFECT ON A BUTTON WITH IMAGES

Setting up a rollover effect is pretty painless with jQuery. I remember when I first started working with HTML and CSS about 10 years ago, setting up a rollover effect with an image. I was using a WYSIWYG editor at the time called Macromedia HomeSite, which created all of this crazy JavaScript code — probably about 25 lines of who knows what — to do a simple rollover. In the following tutorial, I show you how you can do that same with just four lines of code!

1. First you need to add a class to your image so that you can easily target it with a jQuery selector.

```
<img src="images/rollover_off_btn.gif" class="button" alt=""/>
```

2. Next, set up a hover event.

```
$('.button').hover(
  function() {
  },
  function() {
});
```

3. Use the two event handlers inside the hover event function to change the source on the image path. The first event handler is for the mouseenter state, and the second is for the mouseleave state. Using the attribute method, you pass over the src attribute followed by the path of your images:

```
$('.button').hover(
  function() {$(this).attr('src','images/rollover_on_btn.gif');},
  function() {$(this).attr('src','images/rollover_off_btn.gif');
});
```

Here is the complete code for the tutorial for setting up a rollover image:

```
<!doctype html>
<html>
  <head>
  <script src="http://ajax.googleapis.com/ajax/libs/jquery/1.4.2/jquery.min.
  js"></script>
  <script>
  $(document).ready(function(){
    $('.button').hover(
      function() {
        $(this).attr('src','images/rollover_on_btn.gif');
      },
      function() {
        $(this).attr('src','images/rollover_off_btn.gif');
    });
  });

</script>
<body>
    <img src="images/rollover_off_btn.gif" class="button" alt="Button"/>
  </body>
</html>
```

CAPTURING FORM EVENTS

Similar to how mouse-initiated events use the `bind` event handler attachment, you can also use the `bind` method to attach event handlers to form events. Forms are especially common across Web sites and applications. You can find them on every application you use, used for anything from a basic search to a full-blown three-step registration form. In some cases, longer forms that ask the user for lots of information can be both daunting to fill out and can create hard-to-clean-up data. jQuery events can lend a hand in triggering actions, such as form validation when a user leaves a field or alerting the user that a certain field needs attention. Form events can enhance the user experience in many ways.

jQuery offers a handful of form events, which are common events also found in native JavaScript, to help enhance the experience your users encounter when filling out a form. Table 4.3 summarizes each form event and its function.

Table 4.3   Names and Functions of the jQuery Form Events

Form Event Name	Form Event Function
change()	Triggers when you make a change inside of a field
focus()	Triggers when you tab into or select a text field
focusin()	Triggers when you tab into or select a text field contained within an element
focusout()	Triggers when a text field or text area loses focus to another element contained outside the element
blur()	Triggers when a text field or text area loses focus to another element
select()	Triggers when text within an element is selected
submit()	Triggers when the form is submitted, either by clicking a Submit button or pressing Enter on keyboard
reset()	Triggers when the form is reset using the input type="reset"

ADDING A BORDER TO A FORM FIELD WHEN THE USER ADDS FOCUS

The focus event is often used to guide your users through fields in a form. The `focus` event fires when there is focus on an element, usually a form field. After the user starts typing, you can set a function to execute using the callback from the focus event.

In the following example, I show you how to set up a focus event that adds a CSS border to a form field when a user clicks into it. This is helpful to users when they are presented with a Web page with many form fields. It helps to notify the user which field they are currently filling out.

1. The first step involves setting up the HTML. Set up an input field and give it an ID of `firstname"`.

   ```
   <input type="text" name="firstname" id="first-name"/>
   ```

2. Create a selector statement that matches the `"container"` element and binds the `focus` event to the event handler.

```
$('.first-name').bind('focus', function()};
```

3. Add the border property within the CSS method to the event handler function.

```
$('.first-name').bind('focus', function(){
  $(this).css('border','1px solid red');
})};
```

The input field "first-name" now has the focus event bound to it, when the user clicks inside or tabs into this field, the border will change to a 1px solid red. It's as easy as that.

SHOWING A MESSAGE AFTER A USER LEAVES AN INPUT FIELD

The `blur` event is opposite of the focus event and is triggered when a user's mouse or cursor leaves the current selected input field or element and another input field or element is selected. User-interface changes such as a border around an input field changing to red or validation occurring on an e-mail address field are real-world examples of what can occur as a result of the `blur` event. I focus on more ways to create interactive form elements in Chapter 8.

CAPTURING KEYBOARD EVENTS

Keyboard events are similar to mouse events, but instead they capture events that originate from the keyboard such as the pressing of a key or text changing inside of a form field. Often keyboard events are used with in-browser games and inline form validation. On some sites that require a username, username validation script often validates the data as you type and is probably triggered by capturing events that originate from the keyboard. Table 4.4 introduces the list of keyboard events and what each function does.

Table 4.4   Names and Functions of the jQuery Keyboard Events

Keyboard Event Name	Keyboard Event Function
keydown()	Triggers when a key is first depressed
keypress()	Triggers when a key is pressed once or many times
keyup()	Triggers when a key goes up after being pressed

Validation is a key part of any Web form. The data that you receive from users is only as good as the methods you put in place to make sure that the data is clean and usable. The change event is one of many from Table 4.4 that allows you to check a text field as soon as the text or number has been changed inside of it. Contrary to what many amateur developers may think, JavaScript-only validation methods are not secure and need back-up server side validation, depending upon what data is being validated.

A frequently used implementation, as seen in Figure 4-12, is the Twitter status input field that allows you to type up to a maximum of 140 characters. Each time a letter is entered into the input field, it is subtracted from the total amount of allowed characters. Text on the page shows how many remaining characters are left.

The change event is set up with the `bind` method in the same way as other events.

```
$('.container').bind('change', function())};
```

In this tutorial, I show you how you can make a remaining character script similar to the one used on Twitter. The final result of this tutorial is shown in Figure 4-13.

1. The first step involves setting up the HTML. Set up an input field and give it an ID of `status`. This input is used with the `change` event to detect the characters being added.

   ```
   <textarea cols="50" rows="5" id="status"></textarea>
   ```

2. Add an empty `div` called `counter`. This is where the remaining character number shows up as you type into the input field.

   ```
   <div class="counter"></div>
   ```

3. Set up a variable called `maxNum`, which is the maximum amount of characters allowed, and set it to `100`.

   ```
   var maxNum = 100;
   ```

Characters remaining in a 140 char. limit

Figure 4-12: The max limit function on the Twitter status field

© 2010 Twitter. www.twitter.com

4. Create a selector statement that matches the `status` element and binds the `keypress` event to the event handler. The `keypress` event fires each time a key on the keyboard is pressed, which is the perfect event for testing input on form fields while focus is inside the `status` element.

```
$('#status').bind({
  keypress : function() {
  });
});
```

5. After the `keyup` fires, I need to capture the value of the `status` input field. I have set up a variable called `inputText` that stores this value. I have set up another variable called `numChar` that stores the length of the `inputText` variable. I then create a variable called `harRemain` that holds the result of subtracting `numChar` from `maxNum`.

```
$('#status').bind({
  keypress : function() {
          var inputText = $(this).val();
          var numChar = inputText.length;
          var charRemain = numChar - maxNum;
  });
});
```

6. After setting up all the variables, I need to add a conditional statement using a comparison operator to check if the value of `numChar` is less than or equal to `maxNum`. If the expression returns `true`, I select the `counter` element and change the text within to the variable `charRemain` (number of remaining characters).

```
$('#status').bind({
  keypress : function() {
    var inputText = $(this).val();
    var numChar = inputText.length;
    var charRemain = numChar - maxNum;
    if (numChar <= maxNum) {
      $('.counter').text(charRemain);
    }
  });
});
```

7. Finally, you have to add an `else if` statement that checks to see if the `maxNum` is greater than `numChar`. If this expression returns `true`, prevent the user from typing any more letters into the text field using `event.preventDefault()`. `event.preventDefault()` is equivalent to the native JavaScript statement return `false`, which prevents the default event from occurring.

```
$('#status').bind({
  keypress : function() {
          var inputText = $(this).val();
          var numChar = inputText.length;
          var charRemain = numChar -- maxNum;
          if (numChar <= maxNum) {
                  $('.counter').text(charRemain);
          }
    else if (numChar > maxNum){
      event.preventDefault();
    }
  }});

});
```

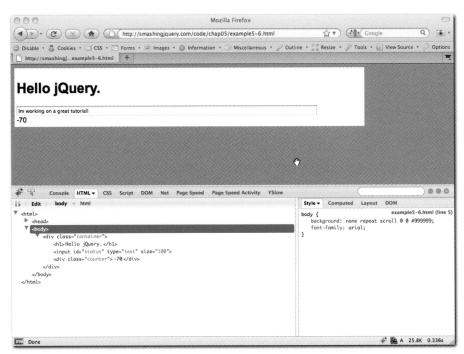

Figure 4-13: The script in action as text is entered into the field and the counter counts down

MAKING YOUR WEB SITE COME ALIVE WITH EFFECTS

IN RECENT YEARS, JavaScript effects have really come of age in an industry where Adobe Flash used to rule the online effects universe. Web sites with image slideshows, animated menus, or video-like animations that used to be done exclusively in Flash are now often done in JavaScript to facilitate cross-browser and mobile compatibility. This increase in JavaScript effects usage has become a major reason for Web designers and developers to utilize the effects API in jQuery.

jQuery utilizes native JavaScript effects that you might already be familiar with to provide robust offerings that can be easily integrated into any Web site. Because they are written in jQuery, the effects are incredibly easy to set up, which makes them a popular choice among Web designers and developers.

In this chapter, I review the effects that are available to you through the jQuery API, show you each effect and how it works, and then walk you through a few real-world scenarios.

DISCOVERING WHAT JQUERY EFFECTS CAN DO

As Web designers and front-end developers, it's our job to make the user interface for a Web site usable. Often that involves moving elements on and off the screen in order to fit more content on one page. Users want and expect instant gratification: They don't want to wait around for clunky Web sites that have many, many pages and take forever to load.

Facebook, the most popular social network, with more than 500 million users, has a very interactive and fun interface driven by JavaScript. If you log in to your Facebook page, you can chat with friends and check your friend feed without having to request a new page. This user experience is created using JavaScript effects such as show/hide and animations. Web sites like Facebook are setting the bar high for what users are expecting from an online experience.

Geolocation-based applications are starting to gain more popularity. Many of these Web sites incorporate front-end JavaScript Google Maps-type technologies. Figure 5-1 shows the Gowalla Web site, a geo-location–based social community.

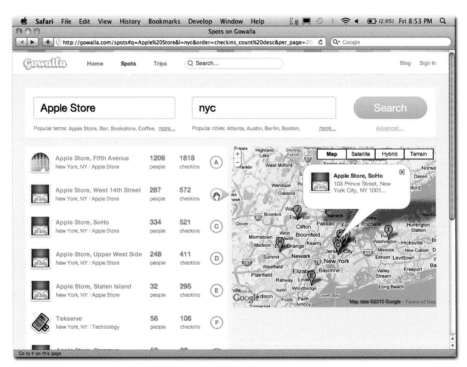

Figure 5-1: The Gowalla Web site, a geo-location–based social community

© 2010 Gowalla Incorporated

jQuery provides basic effects, such as showing, hiding, sliding, and fading. Table 5.1 outlines the basic effects that are all set up in a similar fashion and have the same optional parameters that can be passed into the methods.

Table 5.1   Basic jQuery Effects

Effect Name	Effect Function
show()	Shows an element
hide()	Hides an element
toggle()	Toggles between show and hide using click event
slideDown()	Slides element down
slideUp()	Slides element up
slideToggle()	Toggles between sliding down and sliding up
fadeIn()	Fades element in to opaque
fadeOut()	Fades element out to transparent
fadeTo()	Fades element to specified opacity

SHOWING AND HIDING ELEMENTS USING SHOW AND HIDE

Showing and hiding elements using jQuery is a basic effect. I showed examples of this effect being used in previous chapters, but usually these effects can be seen used in conjunction with the click event. It is commonly used across the Internet. In Figure 5-2, Google Gmail uses the show/hide effect to show the new Call Phone feature overlay.

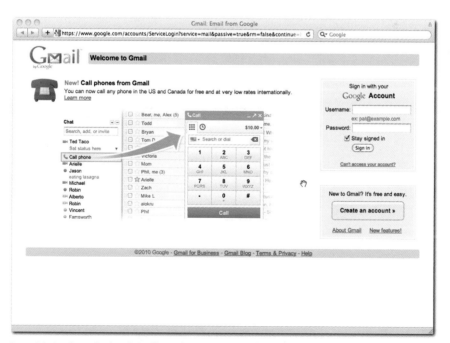

Figure 5-2: Gmail uses the show/hide effect to show new Call Phone feature overlay

Reproduced from 2010 © Google

The `show` or `hide` effect is attached to a selector and two optional parameters can be passed into it. The `duration` parameter determines how long the animation runs and can be set using the keywords `fast` or `slow`, as well as milliseconds (600, 200, 700, and so on). The `callback` parameter allows you to link up a function, which executes when the `show` effect is complete.

```
$(selector).show(duration, callback)
```

The following example shows a link with a `click` event attached. When the link is clicked, an element with the class `recipe` is shown. This is the `show` effect in its most basic form.

```
<style>
.recipe {display:none;}
</style>
$('.recipe-name').bind('click', function() {
  $('.recipe').show();
});


<a href="#" class="recipe-name">Key Lime Pie</a>
<div class="recipe">Key lime pie is an American dessert made of key lime juice, egg
  yolks, and sweetened condensed milk in a pie crust.</div>
```

jQuery enables the div to be shown by adding a `display:block` inline style to the selected element. Figure 5-3 shows how the previous code example is rendered in the browser.

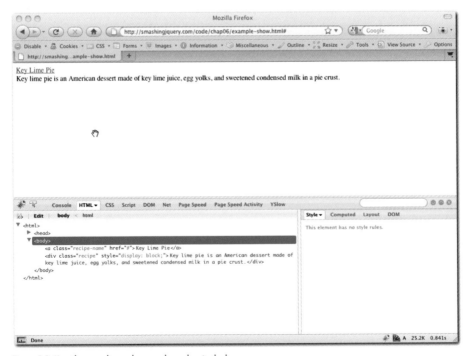

Figure 5-3: How the preceding code example renders in the browser

The `hide` event works exactly like the `show` event, except that it hides the selected element. The inline style is changed to `display:none`.

```
$('.recipe-name').bind('click', function() {
  $('.recipe').hide();
});
```

```
<a href="#" class="recipe-name">Key Lime Pie</a>
<div class="recipe">Key lime pie is an American dessert made of key lime juice, egg
  yolks, and sweetened condensed milk in a pie crust.</div>
```

If you would like more control over the speed of the `show` effect, just pass either the specific keyword (`fast/slow`) or number of milliseconds to the `show` method.

```
$('.recipe').show('slow');
```

You can also pass a `callback` function to the `show` method, which fires after the effect has finished rendering.

SETTING A MESSAGE TO APPEAR ONLY ONCE ON SITE USING THE SHOW METHOD AND COOKIES

Suppose you are in a situation where you may want to display a special offer or special message to your users, but you only want to show them the message once. I've often seen messages like this on Basecamp, a Web-based project management tool, when a login message is displayed telling me about some new feature. You can use the `show` method coupled with a return function that drops a cookie on your user's computer to prevent them from seeing this message again on the same computer, under that user account.

To get started, create the message and "bake" the cookie:

1. Create the HTML for the message that you wish to show and include a link to allow the user to hide it. Include a link on the page to show the message after it has been hidden:

   ```
   <a href="#" class="special-offer">View this special offer!</a>

   <div id="message">
     Special Offer for Members! 50% off your first purchase.<br/>
     <a href="#" class="hide">Hide this message</a>
   </div>
   ```

2. Set up a `click` event for the special offer link to show the message and set the `hideMessage` `callback` function which we create shortly. Within the `click` event, add a selector statement for the message element with the `show` effect added to it. You do not need the pass the `duration` parameter into the `show` method. But you need to add the `callback` function that you want to execute after the `show` method has finished. In this case, it's `hideMessage`.

   ```
   $('.special-offer').bind('click', function(){
     $('#message').show(hideMessage);
   });
   ```

3. Set up another `click` event for the hide link to hide the message and set the `hide Message` callback function.

```
$('.hide').bind('click', function(){
    $('#message').hide(hideMessage);
});
```

4. Next, set up the `hideMessage()` function that drops a cookie on the user's computer after they have viewed the message.

```
function hideMessage() {
}
```

5. Create a cookie called `hideCookie` and set it to expire 30 days after today. The date is set up using the JavaScript `date` object. This is a good example of mixing native JavaScript functions with jQuery. Figure 5-4 shows a screenshot of the cookie with its values set in Firefox.

```
function hideMessage() {
    var expirDate=new Date();
    expirDate.setDate(expirDate.getDate()+30);
    document.cookie = "name=hideCookie;expires="+expirDate.toUTCString();
}
```

At this point, you should be able to show and hide the message and set the cookie. But what about the users who have already seen the message? If they come back to the site tomorrow, you want to make sure they don't see it again. You can do that by creating another function that runs using the `load` event to hide the message if the cookie is found, as shown in Figure 5-5:

1. Add a variable that is assigned to the cookie. Using the JavaScript cookie object, you can retrieve a cookie by using `document.cookie`.

```
var messageCookie = document.cookie;
```

2. Create a conditional statement that tests whether the `messageCookie` has a value and then hides the special offer link; otherwise, do nothing.

```
if (messageCookie) {
    // if message cookie is present, then hide special offer link
    $('.special-offer').hide();
}
else {
    // do nothing
}
```

TOGGLING BETWEEN SHOW AND HIDE

You may encounter a situation where you need to toggle between the `show` effect and the `hide` effect. jQuery has a nice solution to that called `toggle()`. The `toggle()` method binds an event handler to the `click` event and lets you toggle between `show` and `hide`, based on what the current visibility of the element. The important part of the following example is to set the recipe element to `hidden` using CSS; the toggle works based off of that property.

```
<style>
.recipe {display:none;}
</style>
$('.recipe-name').toggle(
 function() {
  $('.recipe').show();
 },
 function() {
  $('.recipe').hide();
 }
);
<a href="#" class="recipe-name">Key Lime Pie</a>
<div class="recipe">Key lime pie is an American dessert made of key lime juice, egg
 yolks, and sweetened condensed milk in a pie crust.</div>
```

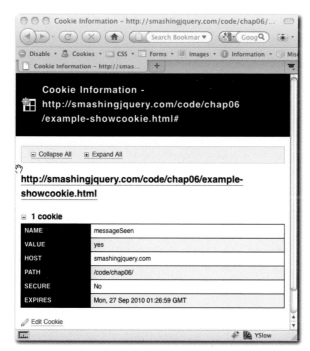

Figure 5-4: The cookie with its values set in Firefox

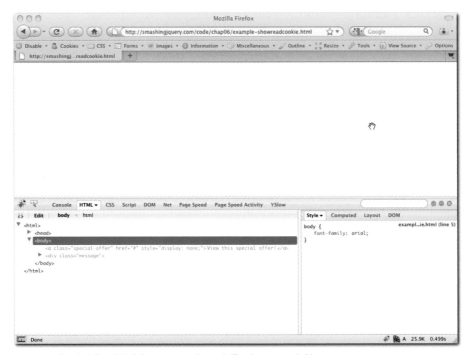

Figure 5-5: After the link is clicked, the message and special offer elements are hidden

SLIDING ELEMENTS UP AND DOWN

The sliding effect can be seen in many places across the Web, most often with image galleries where images slide in and out of view. In addition, with the recent flux of real-time conversation brought on by Facebook and Twitter, sliding in and out of recent activity on a page is more common too. Check out Figure 5-6 for a look at how Twitter (www.twitter.com) has integrated a sliding-in effect for its home page when new tweets are posted. As each new tweet is posted, the tweet slides down from the top, pushing the tweets currently on the page down, one by one, until the tweet makes its way off the page and out of visibility.

The slideDown and slideUp methods are set up in exactly the same manner as are the show and hide methods. By adding the method to the selector, you can pass in two optional parameters (duration and callback). The names of the methods often can be confusing to jQuery newbies. These slideDown method makes elements visible and the slideUp method makes elements hidden.

```
$('.message').slideDown();
```

Figure 5-6: Twitter has integrated a sliding effect for its home page when new tweets are posted

© 2010 Twitter. www.twitter.com

DISPLAYING ALTERNATIVE SEARCH OPTIONS WITH THE SLIDETOGGLE METHOD

Searching is an integral part of the Web and quite possibly why Google is the most successful company around today. Every user expects to be able to search and easily find what they are looking for on your site. Building a better user interface that gives your users the ability to find everything your site offers right at their fingertips is an important improvement. Mozilla has a large community of developers who create add-ons for the Firefox browser. Figure 5-7 is an example of their search bar with advanced options. If you click the advanced options, the advanced option search bar slides down, which is a nice touch because it keeps you on the same page but allows you to expand your search. This feature can be easily added with jQuery using the `slideToggle` method.

The `slideToggle` method is very similar to the `toggle` method for showing and hiding elements, except that it isn't already attached to a `click` event. If the element is already shown and `slideToggle` is invoked, it is set to `slideUp`. The opposite happens if the element is hidden.

```
$('.message').slideToggle();
```

Figure 5-7: A Firefox plug-in Web site that has an advanced search slide-down effect implemented

In the following tutorial, I show you how to set up an advanced search menu that slides into place using the `slideToggle()` method, similar to the Web site example shown in Figure 5-7.

1. Create the HTML for the search input and advanced search options:

```
<style>
body {font-family:arial;}
.advanced {display:none;
padding:3px;
border:1px solid #ccc;
width:300px;
}
</style>
<div id="search">
  <h1>Johnny's Superstore</h1>
  <input type="text" width="60" />
  <input type="submit" value="search"/><br>
  <a href="#" class="advanced-search">Advanced Search</a>
    <div class="advanced">
      <input type="radio" name="category"/> Clothing<br/>
      <input type="radio" name="category"/> Electronics<br/>
      <input type="checkbox" name="sale"/> Clearance Only<br/>
    </div>
</div>
```

2. Set up a selector statement for the `advanced-search` element and bind a `click` event handler to it. Within the event handler, set up a selector for the `advanced` element and add the `slideToggle` method to it.

```
$('.advanced-search').bind('click',function(){
    $('.advanced').slideToggle();
    });
```

Each time the advanced-search input button is clicked, the advanced search options element slides either up or down, depending upon which state the element is in when the page loads. In this case, the advanced-search element is hidden using a CSS style on page load. Figure 5-8 shows the output in the Firefox and Firebug; similar to `hide/show`, the element is shown by jQuery adding an inline style of `display:block` to the element.

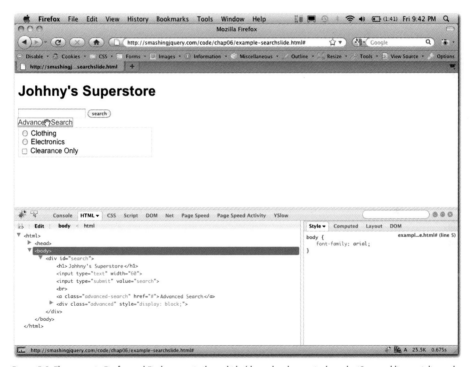

Figure 5-8: The output in Firefox and Firebug — similar to hide/show, the element is shown by jQuery adding an inline style of display:block to the element

FADING ELEMENTS

The fade-in and fade-out effects can add another dimension of interactivity to the elements on a Web site. Most often, the fade effect is used with image galleries or image slideshows where one image fades out as another image fades in. Up until a few years ago, it seemed the only way to achieve such an effect was by using Flash to create an animated image slideshow or by using advanced JavaScript that required many lines of code.

jQuery has made it possible to use native JavaScript effects without having to interact directly with the hard-to-understand JavaScript API. With the effects introduced by jQuery, the same animated slideshow can now be implemented in JavaScript. Using JavaScript-based slideshows instead of Flash gives you a SEO (search engine optimization) advantage because not all search engines are able to index the content found within Flash files.

A key CSS property that is used in conjunction with the fading of elements on a Web page is the opacity property, as shown in Figure 5-9. The opacity property takes a value from 0 to 100 or 0.0 to 1.0 and is used in the fadeIn and fadeOut methods.

Figure 5-9: An example of how an image fades using the opacity property

The fadeIn effect is set up in a similar way to the show effect. You have two optional parameters that can be passed in: duration and callback. The duration parameter determines how long the animation runs in fast or slow, as well as milliseconds (600, 200, 700, and so on). The callback parameter allows you to link up a function that executes when the show effect is complete.

```
$(selector).fadeIn(duration, callback)
```

The fadeOut is identical to fadeIn except that instead of fading an element in, it fades it out. The fadeTo effect allows you to distinguish an opacity level that you would like the selected element to fade to.

```
$(selector).fadeIn(duration, opacity, callback)
```

BUILDING A BASIC IMAGE GALLERY WITH A FADE TRANSITION

To showcase how to use fading with your Web site, in this section I run through how to set up a simple image gallery. This gallery has five images with a list of numbers that can be clicked to change the images. When the image changes, the current image fades out and the newly selected image fades in. I break this script down into multiple steps so you can see the progression of how to build incrementally to make your scripts more dynamic:

1. Start off with some basic HTML. I add all of the necessary HTML for the slideshow through jQuery, which makes the script ultra-portable and easy to set up.

```
<div class="container">
  <h1>jQuery Images Galore.</h1>
</div>
```

2. Next, set up a style sheet to ensure the image gallery will be laid out correctly on the page.

```css
body {
font-family:arial;
}

ul#nav {
list-style-type:none;
margin:10px 0 10px;
padding:0;}

ul#nav li {
float:left;
width:30px;}

ul#nav li a {text-decoration:none;
background:#05609A;
color:#fff;
padding:5px;}

ul#nav li a.active {
background:#B4F114;
}

.slide-image {width:400px;
height:300px;
border:2px solid #05609A;
overflow:hidden;
}

.slide-image img {
display:none;
}
```

3. Create an array to hold all of the images and assign it to the variable `slideArray`. This array determines how many navigation links to create, depending upon how many images are in this array. More or fewer can be inserted at any time and the script automatically adjusts.

```javascript
var slideArray = [
"ansel_adams1.jpg",
"ansel_adams2.jpg",
"ansel_adams3.jpg",
"ansel_adams4.jpg",
"ansel_adams5.jpg"
];
```

Also, create a variable called `imgDir` to hold the value of the path, relative or absolute, of your images folder for the slideshow. This variable is included when you set up the images in the slideshow later in the tutorial.

```javascript
var imgDir = 'images/ansel_adams';
```

4. Append the element `slide-image` into the DOM inside of the `container` element. This inserted element holds all of the images as they are added into the DOM.

```javascript
$('.container').append('<div class="slide-image"></div>');
```

111

5. After the `slide-image` element is set up, you need to add an image to show up in the element after the page has loaded.

```
$('.slide-image').html('<img src="images/'+slideArray[0]+'"/>');
```

6. Insert the unordered list element `nav` into the DOM after the `slide-image` element. This contains all of the links for the images in the slideshow.

```
$('.slide-image').after('<ul id="nav"></ul>');
```

7. Use the `length` property to determine how many items are in the `slideArray` array, and assign that value to the variable `lengthArray`.

```
var slideLength = slideArray.length;
```

8. Set up a `for` loop that will iterate through all of the items in the `slideArray` using the `slideLength` variable to limit the amount of times the loop runs to 5.

```
for(i=0; i < slideLength; i++){

}
```

9. Because there are 5 items in the array, the length returns as 5. I add a variable called `slideText` and assign it a value of `1 + i` (index). This ensures that the anchor text starts with 1 and ends with 5, instead of starting with 0 and ending with 4.

```
for(i=0; i <= slideLength; i++){
   var slideText = i + 1;
}
```

10. Next, using the `nav` element, which I added to the DOM in step 5, I append an `li` element for each index in the array. Within each `li` element, I include an `anchor` tag with a `rel` attribute set to the value of `slideText` and I also insert `slideText` as the anchor text. I use this `rel` attribute to select which image is inserted. Figure 5-10 shows the loop being evaluated in the browser with the result being HTML, which can be seen through Firebug.

```
for(i=0; i < slideLength; i++){
   var slideText = i + 1;
$('#nav').append('<li><a href="#" rel="'+slideText+'">'+slideText+'</a></li>');
}
```

11. After creating the navigation list, I need to set up a `click` event for each link element. Set up a basic `click` event using the `bind` method to attach the `nav` selector statement to the handler function.

```
$('#nav li a').bind('click', function(){
});
```

12. Add a variable called `numSlide` to hold the value of the attribute `rel`. This value is set only when a slide number anchor tag is clicked; that is, when the event is fired, not bound.

```
$('#nav li a').bind('click', function(){
   var numSlide = $(this).attr('rel');
});
```

13. Select the `slide-image` element and insert an image tag with the `imgDir` and `numSlide` variables included. This adds the correct image and server path as the link is clicked to the page.

```
$('#nav li a').bind('click', function(){
   var numSlide = $(this).attr('rel');
   $('.slide-image').html('<img src="'+imgDir + numSlide+'.jpg"/>');
});
```

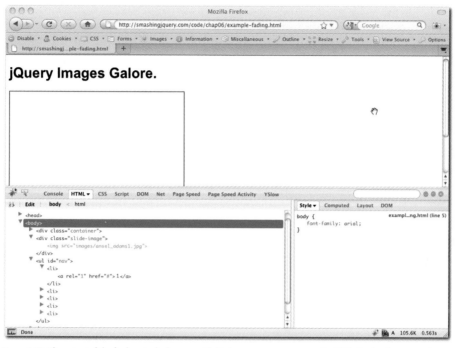

Figure 5-10: The output of the for loop in the browser, with Firebug open so you can see the HTML that has been created

14. It's always an added bonus to know where you are in the navigation after you click a link. I add two more statements to the `click` event. The first one removes all instances of the active class from the anchor tags in the navigation list that previously had the class. The second statement adds an active class to only this anchor tag that was clicked.

```
$('#nav li a').bind('click', function(){
var numSlide = $(this).attr('rel');
$('.slide-image').html('<img src="'+imgDir + numSlide+'.jpg"/>');
$('#nav li a').removeClass('active');
$(this).addClass('active');
});
```

Now that you have learned how to create a basic slideshow, I show you how to add the fading effects to make it really come to life. It only takes one line to fade in an image.

15. Select the image tag that is a descendent of the `slide-image` element and add the `fadeIn()` effect.

```
$('#nav li a').bind('click', function(){
  var numSlide = $(this).attr('rel');
  $('.slide-image').html('<img src="'+imgDir + numSlide+'.jpg"/>');
  $('.slide-image img').fadeIn();
  $('#nav li a').removeClass('active');
  $(this).addClass('active');
});
```

16. To ensure that the first slide is loaded when the page loads, set up a selector statement to select the first anchor tag in the navigation and simulate a click on it:

```
$('#nav li a').eq(0).click();
```

ADDING DELAY TO CREATE A TIMED ANIMATION

Because animations are usually a series of events occurring within a given timeframe, being able to delay elements to create a timed animation is a basic requirement. jQuery offers a way to add delay to an animation with the `delay` method.

The `delay` method was added recently to version 1.4 of the jQuery library to allow you to add a delay to the methods that follow it, which are attached by chaining. The `delay` method is only to be used with effects in the jQuery library. If you are looking for a more flexible timer function, give the native JavaScript `setTimeout` function a shot.

If you are looking to display a message to your users and have it disappear after a certain amount of time, the `delay` effect is the perfect solution. In this example, I want to display a message when the user hovers their mouse pointer over a link. If the user's mouse leaves the link, after 10 seconds, I want the message to fade out.

1. Set up HTML for the tooltip element that contains the message and the show-tip link that the user mouses over to see the message.

```
<a href="#" class="show-tip">Learn more about Peaches</a>
    <div class="tool-tip">
    Although its botanical name Prunus persica suggests the peach is native to
Persia, peaches actually originated in China where they have been cultivated
since the early days of Chinese culture. Peaches were mentioned in Chinese
writings as far back as the 10th century BC and were a favoured fruit of kings
and emperors. Recently, the history of cultivation of peaches in China has been
extensively reviewed citing numerous original manuscripts dating back to 1100
B.C.
    </div>
```

2. Next, set up a `hover` event. The `hover` event toggles between the `mouseenter` and `mouseleave` events. In the first statement, the `mouseover`, select the tooltip message and fade it in over a duration of 900 milliseconds.

```
$('.show-tip').hover(
  function(){
  $('.tool-tip').fadeIn(900);
  },
  function() {
  });
```

3. In the second statement, the `mouseleave`, select the tooltip message, but this time, delay it for 10,000 milliseconds (10 seconds) and then fade it out over a duration of 900 milliseconds.

```
$('.show-tip').hover(
  function(){
    $('.tool-tip').fadeIn(900);
```

```
    },
      function() {
        $('.tool-tip').delay(10000).fadeOut(900);
      });
```

CHAINING MULTIPLE EFFECTS TOGETHER

By now, you should be pretty familiar with the concept of chaining in jQuery. Chaining allows you to add multiple methods to the same statement. This helps to keep your amount of code smaller and increases the performance of your scripts.

In the following example, I use chaining to illustrate how you can add multiple methods to a `selector` statement. The tooltip is first set to hidden, and then the element is faded in at a speed of 900 milliseconds. A one-second delay occurs, and then it fades out at a rate of 900 milliseconds.

```
$('.tooltip').hide().fadeIn(9000).delay(1000).fadeOut(9000);
```

If you were to write that same statement without chaining, it would require three separate statements on three individual lines:

```
$('.tool-tip').fadeIn(900);
$('.tool-tip').delay(10000);
$('.tool-tip').fadeOut(900);
```

The preceding sequence of jQuery statements results in the same output as the chained example, but chaining saves space and keeps your code cleaner. Consider a scenario where you need to select three different `li` elements using their respective `ID` names and style each of them differently:

```
<ul id="news">
    <li id="politics">Politics</li>
    <li id="sports">Sports</li>
    <li id="finance">Finance</li>
    <li id="world">World</li>
    <li id="local">Local</li>
</ul>
```

You can do this in one of two ways. The first is by creating three statements that each select the element and apply CSS to it:

```
$('#politics').css('border','1px solid red');
$('#finance').css('display','none');
$('#local').css('border','1px solid green');
```

The second way of achieving this is by chaining all of the elements and methods into one statement by utilizing the `end()` method. The `end()` method puts a stop on the current methods and allows you to start chaining new methods again after it, without any overlap of the methods before the `end()` method. Figure 5-11 shows the result of chaining multiple methods together from the previous code example.

```
$('#news').find('#politics').css('border','1px solid red').end().find('#finance').
  hide().end().find('#local').css('border','1px solid blue');
```

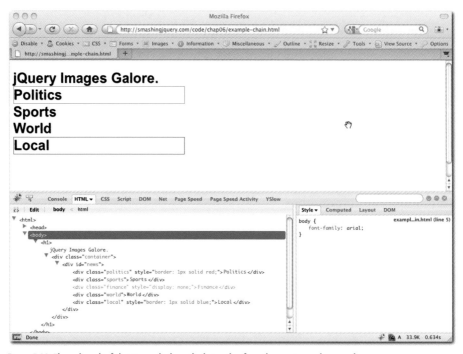

Figure 5-11: The end result of chaining multiple methods together from the previous code example

CREATING A NEWS FEED TICKER WITH MULTIPLE EFFECTS

With the increased appeal of being able to reach a broader audience by delivering news content through RSS (Really Simple Syndication) feeds, news tickers, and widgets have become much more common. News tickers can be anything from a box of 10 news articles that gets refreshed whenever the page is reloaded, to more advanced news tickers that show real-time updates such as the Google Real Time Search Engine, as seen in Figure 5-12.

Here I show you how to create a basic news feed ticker that pulls in static content using multiple effects to fade-in and slide the items into view. This news ticker can be expanded to include live RSS feeds with a few tweaks, but this should be enough to get you started:

1. The first step is to create a basic HTML structure. The goal is to make this news ticker as dynamic as possible, so it can be dropped onto any page without having to modify the page itself. In this case, I have created a page with an `H1` element, which I use in my `selector` statement to drop in the news ticker directly after.

```
<body>
  <h1>jQuery Latest News</h1>
</body>
```

2. I have set up ten headlines in an array called `newsArray`. This is static content that is looped around in the news ticker.

```
var newsArray = [
"Delhomme, Wallace sharp early for Browns",
"Bucs expect to have injured QB Freeman for opener",
"Report: Haynesworth likely has rhabdomyolysis",
"QB Orton effectively leading Broncos in preseason",
"Vernon Gholston not offended by set-up fight",
"Cubs' Piniella to retire after Sunday",
"Bradley interested in Aston Villa job",
"Federer beats Fish for Cincinnati title",
"Garcia 3-hits Giants, Cardinals roll 9-0",
"Cano, CC power Yankees over M's 10-0"
];
```

3. I set up two variables: `newsLength` is set to the length of the `newsArray`. And `newsInterval` holds the numeric value in milliseconds for how often to grab a new headline and insert it into the news ticker.

```
var newsLength = newsArray.length;
var newsInterval = 2000;
```

4. Select the `H1` element and insert the unordered list element `news-feed` after it.

```
$('h1').after('<ul id="news-feed"></ul>');
```

117

Figure 5-12: The Google Real Time Search Engine, which slides in new content from Twitter as it is posted

5. Create a `for` loop to loop through all of the headlines in `newsArray`. For each headline, add a list item to the `news-feed` unordered list with the headline name in between the two `li` tags:

```
for(i=0; i < newsLength; i++){
$('#news-feed').append('<li>'+newsArray[i]+'</li>');
}
```

6. Next, I set up a function called `slideHeadline()` that contains all of the effects to make the news ticker work. The first statement inside of the function selects the last item in the `news-feed` unordered list, clones it, and adds inserts it back into the list, but at the top using the `prepend` method.

```
function slideHeadline() {
$('#news-feed li:last').clone().prependTo('#news-feed').hide();
}
```

7. The second statement added to the function selects the first item (the cloned element that was just created in the news feed) and adds the `slideDown` effect to it.

```
function slideHeadline() {
$('#news-feed li:last').clone().prependTo('#news-feed').css('display','none');
$('#news-feed li:first').slideDown();
}
```

8. Not only do I want to slide down the first item at a speed of 500 milliseconds, but I also want to fade the item, at a rate of 1,000 milliseconds, as it slides into place. I do that by chaining the `fadeIn` method into the same statement that contains the `slideDown` method.

```
function slideHeadline() {
$('#news-feed li:last').clone().prependTo('#news-feed').css('display','none');
$('#news-feed li:first').fadeIn(1000).slideDown(500);
}
```

9. One last statement is added to the `slideArticle` function that removes the last item in the list. These three statements all occur one after the other, which simulates a nice fade and sliding effect, as illustrated in Figure 5-13.

```
function slideHeadline() {
$('#news-feed li:last').clone().prependTo('#news-feed').css('display','none');
$('#news-feed li:first').fadeIn(1000).slideDown(500);
$('#news-feed li:last').remove();
}
```

10. This last piece of JavaScript is probably the most important. I need set up the `set Interval` native JavaScript function to execute the `slideArticle` function at the `newsInterval` rate (2,000). This function continuously loops the news ticker. Without this function, the news ticker doesn't run.

```
setInterval(slideHeadline, newsInterval);
```

The `setInterval` function is a native JavaScript timer function that allows a specific function to run after a given interval of time has passed. There is a similar JavaScript timer function called `setTimeout`, but the main difference between these two functions is `setInterval` continues looping until you tell it to stop, whereas `setTimeout` only runs once. Two functions will stop these timers from running: `clearTimeout()` and `clear Interval()`. The jQuery library uses `setTimeout` and `setInterval` to power the jQuery Effects APIs.

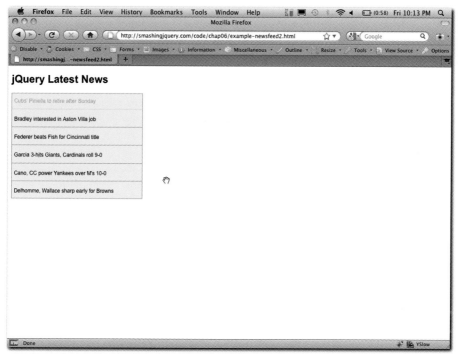

Figure 5-13: An illustration of the top element fading and then sliding into view while the bottom element is removed from view

CREATING ADVANCED ANIMATIONS

jQuery offers a method called `animate` that you can use to create customized animations. Instead of chaining `fade`, `slide`, and `show` together, which can be quite limited in scope, the `animate` method allows you to use any CSS property that is controlled by a numeric value. The CSS properties that can be used with `animate` are listed in Table 5.2.

Table 5.2   Common CSS Properties That Can Be Used with the Animate Method

CSS Property	Sample Value
opacity	0.5
top	10 px
height	100 px
width	200 px
margin	10 px
padding	15 px

BUILDING AN IMAGE GALLERY WITH TEXT CAPTIONS USING ADVANCED ANIMATIONS

I worked with Flash and ActionScript until about two years ago, when I decided to change course and start working more with JavaScript and jQuery. I made the switch because I can have more control over the DOM using JavaScript and because of the lack of Flash and ActionScript support on mobile devices such as iPhone. Flash is good for advanced animation, but image galleries have come a long way in JavaScript. The major benefit I found to learning ActionScript is how similar the languages are to each other in how they handle events and effects.

Understanding the basic concepts behind any programming language gives you a huge advantage when trying to learn another language: Most of the concepts stay the same; only the language syntax changes. Both ActionScript 3 and JavaScript are based on ECMAScript, so they have many similarities. On more than one occasion, I have encountered a déjà vu moment when working with JavaScript because the syntax and conventions closely resemble those in ActionScript.

Back in 2006, I built my first Flash 8 XML-driven animated slideshow. It was a pretty slick little application. If you passed a formatted XML file into the Flash file, it would iterate through the XML, add the slides, and animate them, allowing you to click on each slide and have it take you to a link, as shown in Figure 5-14. I was very proud of this script — so proud, in fact, that I released it on my blog (`onerutter.com`) and it has been downloaded more than 13,000 times. The size of the Flash file was about 5 KB and there were 136 lines of code, which was quite compact and impressive at the time. It wasn't until I started working with jQuery that I began to realize how much code is too much!

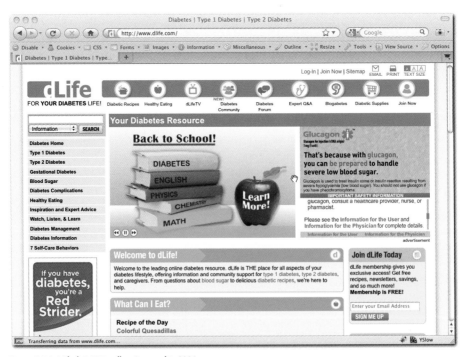

Figure 5-14: A Flash 8 XML gallery I created in 2006

The following animated image gallery tutorial allows you to create one similar to the one I built in 2006 with Flash, with the exception that it's not XML-driven and is only about 85 lines of code. You can extend the image gallery by adding support for XML feeds if you like, but I'll leave that up to you. Figure 5-15 illustrates how the image slideshow will work.

Figure 5-15: How the image slideshow will work

1. The only HTML required on the page is an element called `container`. All of the necessary HTML is DOM-scripted into this element by the script.

```
<div class="container"></div>
```

2. Next you need to set up a style sheet to style the image gallery. If you decide to use different-sized images, you need to change the `.container` property to reflect the new image size. The `.text-strip` class has been set up to show the text on top of the images as each image is changed.

```
body {font-family:arial;}

ul#nav {
list-style-type:none;
margin:10px 0 10px;
padding:0;}

ul#nav li {
float:left;
width:30px;}

ul#nav li a {text-decoration:none;
```

121

```css
background:#05609A;
color:#fff;
padding:5px;}

ul#nav li a.active {
background:#B4F114;}

.container {position:relative;
height:250px;
width:400px;
border:1px solid #333;
overflow:hidden;}

.slide-container {
position: absolute;
top: 0;
left: 0;}

.slides {
float:right;}

.slide-text {
display:none;
font-size:18px;}

img {border:0;}

.textStrip {top:0px;
display:block;
position:absolute;
left:-400px;
padding:5px;
background:#333333;
opacity:.9;
color:#ffffff;
width:100%;
}
```

3. The first step is to create three arrays. The first array, called `slideArray`, is used to hold the image files, which you would like to appear as slides in the slideshow. The second array, called `textArray`, holds the captions that appear on each slide. The third array, called `urlArray`, is used to hold the URLs that you would like to apply to each slide. These arrays can hold as many or as few items as you want to display in the slideshow.

```javascript
var slideArray = ["photo1.jpg","photo2.jpg","photo3.jpg","photo4.jpg"];
var textArray = ["Rusty Cable.","Watch Dogs.","Plant Sink.","Urban Cowboy"];
var urlArray = ["http://www.google.com", "http://www.onerutter.com", "http://
  www.flickr.com", "http://www.facebook.com"];
```

4. Append an element called `slide-container` to your container element on the page. `slide-container`, as the name suggests, holds all of the slides.

```javascript
$('.container').append('<div class="slide-container" />');
```

5. After the `slide-container` element, insert an unordered list called `nav`. This element contains the navigation links to control the slides in your slideshow and has a class named `clearfix` added to it, which sets up a clear CSS property after the navigation list.

```
$('.container').after('<ul id="nav" class="clearfix"></ul>');
```

6. Create a `for` loop limited by the value of `slideArray.length`. The `slideArray` has four values in it, so the highest index will be 3. Set up a variable within the `for` loop called `slideNum` with a value of `i + 1`. This is set up because the first value of `i` will be 0, and the first image in the array has a 1 in the filename, so it won't get matched correctly up unless we create this variable.

```
for(i=0; i < slideArray.length; i++){
var slideNum = i + 1;
}
```

7. The first statement that is added to the `for` loop appends a list item with the value of `slideNum`.

```
for(i=0; i < slideArray.length; i++){
var slideText = i + 1;
$('#nav').append('<li><a href="#" rel="'+slideNum+'">'+slideNum+'</a></li>');
}
```

8. Next, add a variable called `slideInfo`, which holds the HTML that needs to be added to the page in order to display each slide. The HTML spans multiple lines, so if there is any extra spacing after each line, the JavaScript won't work. To remedy this, create multiple lines and concatenate them using the `+=` operator. It keeps the code cleaner and easier to read.

   The first line adds an element called `slide-image`, and use the `SlideNum` variable to insert a unique number for each. The second line adds an element called `slide-text`, which is wrapped around the caption text that is pulled from the `textArray`. The third line adds the image stored in the `slideArray` using the index from the loop.

```
for(i=0; i < slideArray.length; i++){
var slideNum = i + 1;
$('#nav').append('<li><a href="#" rel="'+slideNum+'">'+slideNum+'</a></li>');
var slideInfo = '<div class="slide-image'+slideNum+' slides">';
slideInfo += '<div class="slide-text">'+textArray[i]+'</div>';
slideInfo += '<img src="images/'+slideArray[i]+'"/></div>';
}
```

9. After the HTML has been set up, append it to the `slide-container` element.

```
for(i=0; i < slideArray.length; i++){
var slideText = i + 1;
$('#nav').append('<li><a href="#" rel="'+slideText+'">'+slideText+'</a></li>');
var slideInfo = '<div class="slide-image'+slideText+' slides">';
slideInfo += '<div class="slide-text activeInfo'+[i]+'">'+textArray[i]+'</div>';
slideInfo += '<img src="images/photo'+slideText+'.jpg"/></div>';
$('.slide-container').append(slideInfo);
}
```

10. Next, add three more variables: `slideTotal` holds the total number of slides derived from `slideArray.length` (four items), `slideWidth` is the width of each slide, and `slideContainer` is the width multiplied by the `slideTotal`. The `slideContainer` is equal to 1600.

```
var slideTotal = slideArray.length;
```

123

```
slideWidth = 400;
var slideContainer = slideWidth * slideTotal;
```

11. Using the CSS method, set the width of the `slides-container` element to the new value stored in the variable `slidesContainer` that was created in the preceding step.

```
$(".slide-container").css({'width' : slideContainer});
```

12. Create a `click` event by selecting the `anchor` tag, which is a descendent of the list item (`li`) tag in the #`nav` unordered list.

```
$('#nav li a').bind('click', function(){
});
```

13. Active item highlighting means that when a link is clicked, it stays active to let you know which slide you are currently on. To enable active item highlighting, you need to add two statements. The first statement removes the active class from all elements. The second statement adds the active class to the element that was clicked using the `this` keyword.

```
$('#nav li a').bind('click', function(){
$('#nav li a').removeClass('active');
  $(this).addClass('active');
});
```

14. The next statement added to the `click` event handler resets the position of the `slide-text` element for the next slide, using the CSS method, if the `slide-text` has not finished animating.

```
$('#nav li a').bind('click', function(){
$('#nav li a').removeClass('active');
$(this).addClass('active');
$(".slide-text").css({
  'top':'-100px',
  'right':'0px'
  });
});
```

15. The preceding statement resets the position of the `slide-text`, but the next two statements stop the animation and clear the queue. This prevents any further effects from taking place by using the `stop()` and `clearQueue()` methods to ensure all remaining effects are cleared from the queue. The addition of effects into the animation queue, without clearing the queue can cause unintended results.

```
$('#nav li a').bind('click', function(){
$('#nav li a').removeClass('active');
$(this).addClass('active');
$(".slide-text").css({
  'top':'-100px',
  'right':'0px'
  });
$(".slide-text").stop();
$(".slide-text").clearQueue();
});
```

16. Create three more variables. The first one is called `active`, which stores the value of the current active nav list item's `rel` tag attribute and subtracts 1. The second variable, `slideNum`, stores the same value as the previous value, but without subtracting 1. The third variable is called `slidePos` and is equal to the value of `active` multiplied by `slideWidth`.

```
$('#nav li a').bind('click', function(){
  $('#nav li a').removeClass('active');
  $(this).addClass('active');
  $(".slide-text").css({
    'top':'-100px',
    'right':'0px'
  });
  $(".slide-text").clearQueue();
  $(".slide-text").stop();

  var active = $('#nav li a.active').attr("rel") - 1;
  var slidePos = active * slideWidth;
  var slideNum = $('#nav li a.active').attr("rel");
});
```

17. Using the variables that were set up in the preceding step, if the value of active equals 2 and the value of slideWidth equals 400, slidePos will equal 800. This is a key variable and is used to move the slides left by attaching the animate method to the slide-container element in the following example. The animate method is also passed duration, 1000, and a callback function.

```
$('#nav li a').bind('click', function(){
$('#nav li a').removeClass('active');
$(this).addClass('active');
$(".slide-text").css({
  'top':'-100px',
  'right':'0px'
});
$(".slide-text").clearQueue();
$(".slide-text").stop();

var active = $('#nav li a.active').attr("rel") - 1;
var slidePos = active * slideWidth;
var slideNum = $('#nav li a.active').attr("rel");

$(".slide-container").animate({
  left: -slidePos,
  },1000, function(){
});
});
```

18. You set up the animation for the slide text within the callback function for the first animate statement. Create a selector on the unique slide-text class and uses the CSS method to set up the necessary styles that allow the slide-text to display over the current image.

```
$('#nav li a').bind('click', function(){
  $('#nav li a').removeClass('active');
  $(this).addClass('active');

  $(".slide-text").css({
  'top':'-100px',
  'right':'0px',
```

```
});

$(".slide-text").stop();
$(".slide-text").clearQueue();

var active = $('#nav li a.active').attr("rel") - 1;
var slidePos = active * slideWidth;
var slideNum = $('#nav li a.active').attr("rel");

$(".slides-container").animate({
left: -slidePos,
},1000, function(){
  $('.slide-text').addClass('textStrip'});
});
```

19. In the final callback, add one more `animate` method to move the `slide-text` element onto the current slide for 1 second, and then slide the text up off the slide. Figure 5-16 shows the final result of this script in the browser.

```
$('#nav li a').bind('click', function(){
  $('#nav li a').removeClass('active');
  $(this).addClass('active');

  $(".slide-text").css({
  'top':'-100px',
  'right':'0px'
  });

  $(".slide-text").stop();
  $(".slide-text").clearQueue();

  var active = $('#nav li a.active').attr("rel") - 1;
  var slidePos = active * slideWidth;
  var slideNum = $('#nav li a.active').attr("rel");

  $(".slide-container").animate({
  left: -slidePos
  },1000, function(){
    $('.slide-image'+slideNum+' .slide-text').addClass('textStrip').animate({
        top:0,
        left:slidePos,
        right:0
      }, 1000, function(){
        $('.slide-text').delay(5000).animate({
        top:-100
        }, 1000);
        });
    });
});
```

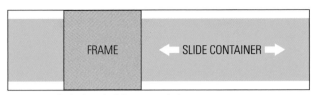

Figure 5-16: The final result of this script in the browser

ADDITIONAL EASING EFFECTS USING THE JQUERY EASING PLUG-IN

The jQuery Easing plug-in provided by GSGD (`http://gsgd.co.uk/sandbox/jquery/easing/`) allows you to add 30 different types of easing effects to your Web site. The `animate` method already has two easing effects — `swing` and `liner`, but they're very limited — to be able to create more realistic easing effects such as bounce and elastic effects, it's best to use a plug-in. Easing controls an animation by accelerating or decelerating the rate at which it falls into place, commonly seen as an animation snapping into place. Easing gives animation a more realistic effect.

```
.animate(duration, easing, callback);
```

jQuery is extendable with plug-ins — as you know, you can write your own jQuery functions — but you can also write your own jQuery plug-ins if you would like to reuse the code for a certain task or release it to the jQuery open-source community for other users. I go into more detail about jQuery plug-ins in Chapter 11.

Some sample effects included with the Easing plug-in are

- `easeOutBounce`
- `easeInBounce`
- `easeInElastic`
- `easeInCubic`

The easeOutBounce and easeInBounce effects use a combination of easing with a bounce effect to simulate an object bouncing into the screen. The easeInElastic effect shows the element snapping into place like an elastic band. The easeInCubic is similar to the plain old ease-in effect, but it's much slower. The Easing plug-in Web site offers examples of each of the thirty effects included with the plug-in.

After you have downloaded the easing plug-in and included it in your page directly after the jQuery library file, you are ready to begin using it. To demonstrate, I add an easing effect into the previous tutorial.

Take the following code snippet from the previous example. If you set the easing parameter to `easeOutBounce`, the animation uses the `easeOutBounce` effect from the custom easing plug-in. It's that easy!

```
$(".slide-container").animate({
  left: -slidePos,
},'easeOutBounce',1000, function(){
  $('.slide-image'+slideNum+' .slide-text').css(
    {'display':'block',
    'position':'absolute',
    'top':'0px',
    'left':'-400px',
    'padding':'5px',
    'background':'#333333',
    'opacity':'.9',
    'color':'#ffffff',
    'width':'100%'
    }).animate({
    top:0,
    left:slidePos,
    right:0,
    },'easeOutBounce',1000, function(){
      $('.slide-text').delay(5000).animate({
      top:-100,
      }, 1000);
  });
});
```

III

APPLYING JQUERY TO YOUR WEB SITE

Chapter 6: Improving Navigation: Menus, Tabs, and Accordions

Chapter 7: Creating Interactive and Exciting Tables

Chapter 8: Creating Advanced Forms with jQuery

6

IMPROVING NAVIGATION: MENUS, TABS, AND ACCORDIONS

NAVIGATION ON THE WEB allows you to maneuver through a Web site, find a product, read daily news articles, or log in to your bank account to check your balance. Using navigation on the Internet has become second nature to many users; you can use jQuery to improve this experience using events and effects you learned in previous chapters.

Improving navigation and how users interact with content on your Web site can improve the customer experience, which can lead to more visitors. In this chapter, I introduce you to a few real-world navigation difficulties and how you can overcome them using jQuery, HTML, and CSS.

SETTING ALL LINKS ON A PAGE TO OPEN IN A NEW WINDOW

One of the more attractive features of jQuery is being able to select many elements at once and change some part of the selected elements. You may run into a situation on a page where you need to quickly change all of the hyperlinks to open in a new window, but you don't have access to the source code. The code is being generated dynamically in a PHP, JSP (Java Server Pages), or ASP (Active Server Pages) file somewhere and you can't access it.

Instead, you can write a little jQuery, which saves you a lot of work editing various files and so on compared to making changes to the source code. The beauty of using jQuery is that it's extremely easy to comment out or delete the code when you no longer need it.

Here I show you how to set up all the hyperlinks on a page to open in a new window. You can apply many other options to hyperlinks on your Web page, such as

- Assigning a new class to all hyperlinks
- Setting the `title` tag on all hyperlinks to be the same as the anchor text
- Adding a `rel` tag to all hyperlinks
- Removing `href` from all hyperlinks so that they are disabled

In the following tutorial, I guide you through how to set up a jQuery script that loops through all of the links in a given list, adds a `title` tag, and sets them up to open in a new window, as shown in Figure 6-1.

1. The HTML structure in this example is an unordered list with an `ID` set to links. The `ID` is used to select the list of links.

```
<ul id="links">
        <li><a href="http://www.yahoo.com">Yahoo</a></li>
        <li><a href="http://www.google.com">Google</a></li>
        <li><a href="http://www.bing.com">Bing</a></li>
    </ul>
```

2. Create a selector statement to select all anchor tags that are a descendent of the `#links li` elements. Use the `attr()` method to apply the `target` parameter and `_blank` value to all the links that are a child of the `#links` unordered list.

The `attr()` method allows you to get or set the value of an attribute.

```
$('#links li a').attr('target', '_blank');
```

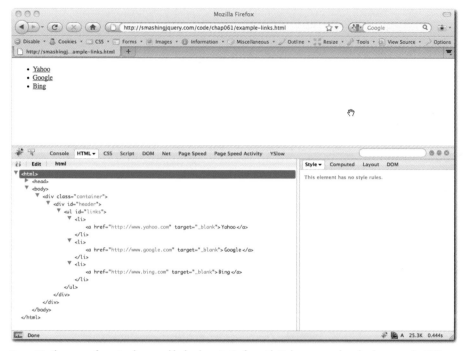

Figure 6-1: The output of running the target blank selector in Firefox, with Firebug open to show the changes to the DOM

SETTING AN ACTIVE ITEM IN YOUR NAVIGATION MENU

Users must always know where they are within a Web site and where they are visually on the navigation menu. This basic user interface requirement can be overlooked and often is. Figure 6-2 shows an example of how the menu items stay active on Mashable (www. mashable.com) when you navigate to a specific section. I have seen few solutions in jQuery or JavaScript for this issue — most solutions often involve backend programming using PHP, JSP, or ASP.

The following tutorial guides you through how to set up active menu items on your Web site's navigation menu using jQuery. The jQuery script is set up to determine the selected element in the menu based on the address in the URL.

1. Create a variable named path and set its value to location.pathname, which is part of the location object in native JavaScript. It returns everything after the domain name.

   ```
   var path = location.pathname;
   ```

   Assume that we are currently on this page: www.smashingjquery.com/mycode/myexample.html.

   The location.pathname is equal to /mycode/myexample.html.

Menu items stay visible.

Figure 6-2: The menu items stay active on Mashable when you navigate to a specific section

Reproduced by permission of Mashable.com

2. Create another variable name `pathArray` and use the native `split()` method from native JavaScript to split the path string using the `'/'` into an array.

```
var pathArray = path.split('/');
```

The result of `pathArray` is `['mycode', 'myexample.html']`. This result is reached by the splitting the value of path (`/mycode/myexample.html`) into two separate strings.

3. Create a final variable and set the value to the length of `pathArray`.

```
var pArrLength = pathArray.length;
```

4. Set up a `for` loop to iterate through the values in the array. Using the attribute selector, set up a selector statement to match all anchor tags that contain a value from `pathArray` and add the class `selected`. The attribute selector that is specified here uses the `wildcard` select, which matches the value in any part of the `href`:

```
for(i=0; i < pArrLength; i++) {
  $("a[href*='"+pathArray[i]+"']").addClass("selected");
}
```

The active menu item script is limited and works in situations only where there is a navigation menu with no drop-down. When a drop-down menu is added and you would like to highlight a menu item that is a parent of the page you are on, you need to alter the script to not only highlight the top-level pages, but also the children of these top level pages. For example, if you had a top-level item called About Us and under this drop-down list were items such as Our Story, Careers, and Contact Us, which are considered children of the top-level item, you would need to use `parent()` and `children()` selectors and build an array of possible URL matches to set this up.

CREATING A BASIC DROP-DOWN MENU

The drop-down menu is one of the most popular ways to approach navigation on a Web site. Many Web sites have categories or sections with many pages in those sections. Creating a navigation system that showcases every page on your site all at once would be challenging, and it would be extremely daunting for the user experiencing this scenario.

The benefit of drop-down menus are that you can list all of your pages in the menu, show the top-level entry points, and hide the rest. Then it's up to the user to decide if they want to see more by hovering over the top-level category, which shows the rest of the categories available.

Drop-down menus can be set up horizontally, with the submenu appearing below the main menu, or they can be set up vertically, as shown in Figure 6-3.

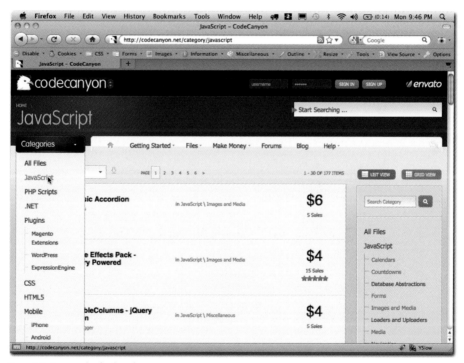

Figure 6-3: An example of a drop-down menu

Reproduced by permission of envato.com

Here, I show you how to build a basic drop-down menu, as shown in Figure 6-4, and then add some fancy effects, as shown in Figure 6-5:

1. The drop-down menu is built using nested unordered lists, which give you the flexibility of being able to add more levels and more links easily without breaking the design. In the following code, I create five links across the top and two drop-down menus appearing below Our Work and Services. You can add as many or as few drop-down menus as you like. Just make sure they are added before the closing list item tag of the top level where you would like the menu to appear.

```
<div id="header">
  <ul id="navigation">
    <li><a href="#">Home</a></li>
    <li><a href="#">Our Work</a>
      <ul class="subnav">
        <li><a href="#">Example 1</a></li>
        <li><a href="#">Example 2</a></li>
        <li><a href="#">Example 3</a></li>
      </ul>
    </li>
    <li><a href="#">Services</a>
      <ul class="subnav">
        <li><a href="#">Service 1</a></li>
        <li><a href="#">Service 2</a></li>
        <li><a href="#">Service 3</a></li>
      </ul>
    </li>
    <li><a href="#">About Us</a></li>
    <li><a href="#">Contact</a></li>
  </ul>
</div>
```

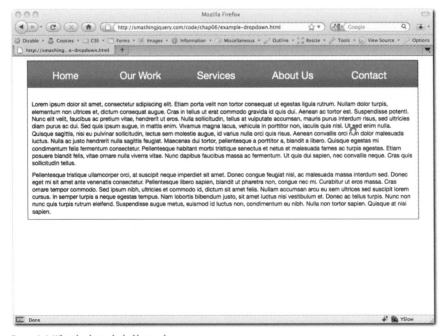

Figure 6-4: What the design looks like in a browser

2. Next, set up a style sheet to make sure the menu is laid out correctly on the page. I always include a CSS reset at the beginning of the style sheet; recently, I've been using a portion of the YUI (Yahoo! User Interface) reset and it works quite well.

A CSS reset style sheet resets all of the styles to a baseline value of 0 to put all the browsers on a level playing field, which can make it easier to make your Web site cross-browser compatible. After setting up a reset style sheet, you need to set up new values based on the 0 baseline. The case against using a reset style sheet is that it can take a lot of extra CSS and time to add in all the necessary styles just to get things looking right because all of the browser defaults have been reset.

I have included the reset in the following CSS for you to use.

```
body, div, dl, dt, dd, ul, ol, li, h1, h2, h3, h4, h5, h6, pre, form, fieldset,
  input, textarea, p, blockquote, th, td{margin:0; padding:0}
h1, h2, h3, h4, h5, h6{font-size:100%; font-weight:normal}
```

3. The remaining CSS controls how the menu and drop-down menus are laid out on the page. You can either build all the CSS before starting the jQuery or create the foundation for how it will look and work as you go:

```
.container{
width:950px;
margin:10px auto;
font:14px "Helvetica Neue",Arial,Helvetica,Geneva,sans-serif;
border:1px solid #333;
}
p{margin:10px;}

ul#navigation{
list-style-type:none;
background:#CE0100;
height:63px;
font-size:24px;
}

ul#navigation li{
float:left;
width:175px;
text-align:center;
position:relative;
height:63px;
padding:20px 5px 10px 5px;
}

ul#navigation li a{
color:#fff;
text-decoration:none;
display:block;
}

ul#navigation li a.active{
border:1px solid blue;
}
```

```
ul#navigation li ul.subnav{
background:#E7F1D2;
width:175px;
clear:both;
display:none;
position:absolute;
top:63px;
-moz-border-radius-bottomleft:8px;
-moz-border-radius-bottomright:8px;
-webkit-border-bottom-left-radius:8px;
-webkit-border-bottom-right-radius:8px;
border-radius: 8px;
border-left:2px solid #998;
border-right:2px solid #998;
border-bottom:2px solid #998;
}

ul#navigation li ul.subnav li{
clear:both;
height:40px;
padding:0;
text-align:center;
margin:0px;
}

ul#navigation li ul.subnav li a{
background:none;
font-size:18px;
color:#333;
text-decoration:none;
padding:10px 0;
border:none;
}

ul#navigation li ul.subnav li a:hover{
background:#DBF1AD;
font-size:18px;
color:#333;
border:none;
}
```

4. Next, set up a `hover` event and select the list item by using the descendent selector `#navigation li`. The `hover` event combines the `mouseenter` and `mouseleave` events. The first event handler is the `mouseenter` event, where you need to find the nested unordered list element called `subnav` using the `find()` method and attach the `slideDown` effect to the statement. The second event handler is the `mouseleave` event, which does the opposite of what `mouseenter` does. Use the `find` method to

search for an element called `.subnav` and attach the `slideUp` effect to the statement. For those list items that do not contain a .subnav element, nothing happens when they are hovered over because a `.subnav` will not be found using the `find` method.

```
$(document).ready(function(){
  $('#navigation li').hover(function() {
    $(this).find('.subnav').slideDown('slow');
```

The `find()` method allows you to filter through the descendents of the element you have selected and hopefully to create a match. After the match has been found, the element is your new matched set.

```
  }, function() {
    $(this).find('.subnav').slideUp('fast');
  });
});
```

You may be wondering why you can't just set up the statement to select the `.subnav` element directly and apply the effect to it like the following code example:

```
$('.subnav').slideDown('slow');
```

If you set up the selector statement without the `this` specifier, it matches all of the elements with a class of `subnav` and applies the `slideDown` effect to them. This is incorrect. By first selecting the `#navigation li` elements and attaching a `hover` event, you can reference the element that is hovered on using the `this` keyword to ensure that the `slideDown` effect is applied only to the `.subnav` element that belongs to the list item being hovered over.

5. In the final step, the drop-down menu must stay visible while the mouse is on a top-level link or any child element below the top level. Figure 6-5 shows an example of how the `mouseenter` event bubbles down from the parent element to the children. Use the `find` method to locate the anchor tag and add or remove the active class depending upon whether the `mouseenter` or `mouseleave` event fires.

```
$(document).ready(function(){
  $('ul#navigation li').hover(function() {
    $(this).find('.subnav').slideDown('slow');
    $(this).find('a').addClass('active');

  }, function() {
    $(this).find('.subnav').slideUp('fast');
    $(this).find('a').removeClass("active");
  });
});
```

After you have a working drop-down menu, the jQuery code that adds the interactivity to the menu is very simple. You spend most of your time either working with a designer to style the menu or designing it yourself. Figure 6-6 shows the drop-down menu being used in Firefox with Firebug open so you can view the changes to the DOM.

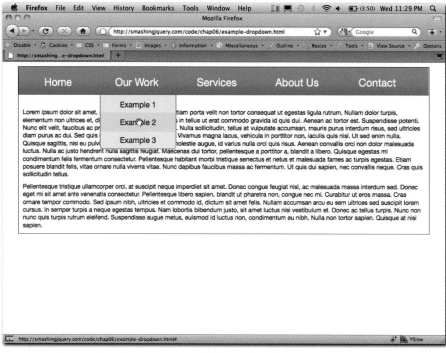

Figure 6-5: An illustration of how the mouseenter event bubbles down from the parent element to the children

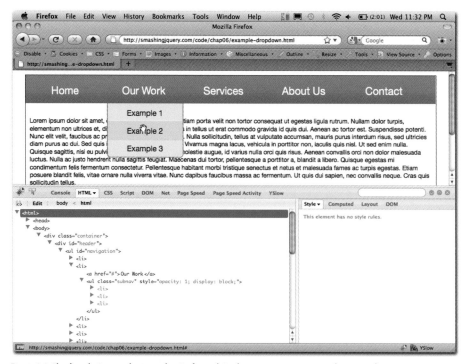

Figure 6-6: The drop-down menu being used in Firefox with Firebug open so you can view changes to the DOM

ADDING ADVANCED EFFECTS TO THE BASIC DROP-DOWN MENU USING ANIMATE

In this section, I show you how to add an opacity change that occurs as the menu slides down, which is an advanced animation effect that uses the `animate` method to the basic drop-down that I showed you how to create in the previous tutorial. All of the code from the previous example is the same, except for two lines in the jQuery. The `animate` method gives you more control over how you want the drop-down to appear on the screen by allowing you to pass in up to four arguments: CSS `properties`, `duration`, `easing`, and `callback`. In this particular example, I want to toggle the height and change the opacity and set the duration to 500 milliseconds. You can also use the keyword `fast` for 200 milliseconds and `slow` for 600. The result is shown in Figure 6-7.

In both statements, switch the `slide` effect with the `animate` method. Pass along the opacity and height CSS properties to the `animate` method to alter the display of the DOM elements on the hovering of the user's mouse pointer:

```
$(document).ready(function(){
  $('ul#navigation li').hover(function() {
    $(this).find('.subnav').animate({opacity: 1.0,height: 'toggle'}, 500);
    $(this).closest('a').addClass('active');
}, function() {
    $(this).find('.subnav').animate({opacity: 0,height: 'toggle'}, 500);
    $(this).find('a').removeClass("active");
        });
  });
```

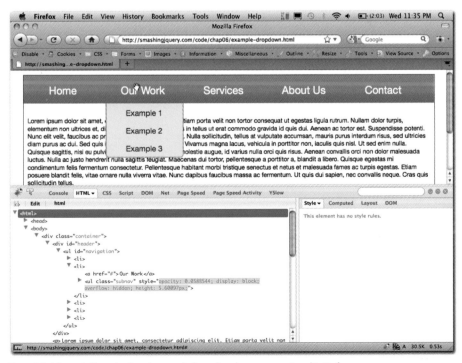

Figure 6-7: Advanced effects that have been applied to a drop-down menu as viewed in Firefox

CREATING AN ACCORDION MENU

The accordion menu is a fashionable choice among Web designers and user interface designers for Web sites that need to show a lot of content in a small space. The accordion hides all of the content except one section. When the mouse hovers over or clicks on a specified item, the content associated with that item expands to show or contracts to hide. Accordions can be used for navigation elements, but recently they have also been used for content-related purposes such as showing large amounts of content in small spaces. Magento, the open-source e-commerce platform, has implemented an accordion-style checkout process, as shown in Figure 6-8.

Click to show hidden content

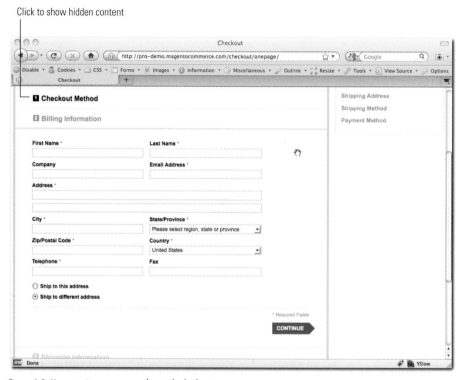

Figure 6-8: Magento sites use an accordion-style checkout process

In this section, I guide you through a tutorial that shows you how to set up a vertical accordion, which can be used for a site navigation sidebar. The accordion always has one content section open while the rest are closed. The header elements display an icon to help show the user which content section is open or closed.

1. The first task is to define the HTML structure of the accordion menu. The goal is to create a clean code structure, which is easy to set up and maintain with jQuery. The HTML structure requires two elements: an accordion header element and an accordion content element. The header element is given a class of accordion-header and wrapped around H3 tags, which display the header text. The header is the element that is clicked on to show or hide the content underneath it. The content element is set up as an unordered list and

given a class of `accordion-content`. It contains the elements which are shown or hidden as each header is clicked.

```
<div id="accordion">
  <div class="accordion-header">
    <h3>Books</h3>
    <span></span>
              </div>

  <ul class="accordion-content">
    <li><a href='#'>Business</a></li>
    <li><a href='#'>Education</a></li>
    <li><a href='#'>Tech</a></li>
    <li><a href='#'>Romance</a></li>
  </ul>

  <div class="accordion-header">
    <h3>Electronics</h3>
    <span></span>
  </div>

  <ul class="accordion-content">
    <li><a href='#'>Audio</a></li>
    <li><a href='#'>Video</a></li>
    <li><a href='#'>Automobile</a></li>
    <li><a href='#'>Appliances</a></li>
  </ul>

  <div class="accordion-header">
    <h3>Sporting Goods</h3>
    <span></span>
  </div>

  <ul class="accordion-content">
    <li><a href='#'>Baseball</a></li>
    <li><a href='#'>Basketball</a></li>
    <li><a href='#'>Football</a></li>
    <li><a href='#'>Tennis</a></li>
  </ul>
</div>
```

2. Next, set up a style sheet to make sure the accordion is laid out correctly on the page. Similar to other tutorials, a CSS `reset` is added:

```
body, div, dl, dt, dd, ul, ol, li, h1, h2, h3, h4, h5, h6, pre, form, fieldset,
  input, textarea, p, blockquote, th, td{margin:0; padding:0}
h1, h2, h3, h4, h5, h6{font-size:100%; font-weight:normal}
```

3. The remaining CSS controls the look and feel of the accordion menu. You will be setting up different styles for the menu and content elements; the menu item includes an icon that displays which menu item has been selected.

The menu icon is set up using a sprite. A sprite is a way of creating one large image that can be applied to different elements on a Web site using background positioning. The major benefit to using sprites is that they can severely cut down the number of requests your Web site makes to the Web server for images, which increases the performance and decreases the load times. You see a benefit if you are using more than, say, 20 images. Also, sprites combat against image-loading flicker, which occurs when you create a rollover with two separate images and the onhover image hasn't loaded yet.

```css
#accordion{
width:225px;
margin:10px 0 10px 10px;
}

#accordion .accordion-header{
background:#3971AC;
color:#fff;
border-bottom:1px solid #fff;
position:relative;
}

#accordion .accordion-header h3{
margin:0;
cursor:pointer;
text-indent:10px;
padding:5px 0;
}

#accordion .header-active{
background:#48ABC3;
}

#accordion .accordion-header span{
background:url(../images/accordion_sprite.gif) no-repeat;
display:block;
position:absolute;
width:11px;
height:12px;
top:5px;
left:200px;
}

#accordion .accordion-header span.icon-active{
background:url(../images/accordion_sprite.gif) no-repeat;
background-position:0 -12px;
display:block;
position:absolute;
width:11px;
height:12px;
top:5px;
left:200px;
}

#accordion ul.accordion-content{
margin:0px 0 0px 0;
```

```
padding:5px 5px 10px 5px;
list-style-type:none;
background:#A8D7E2;
}


#accordion ul.accordion-content li{
padding:1px 0px;
display:block;
margin:0;
padding:2px 5px;
}


#accordion ul.accordion-content li a{
color:#D16C3A;
}
```

4. After the page loads, ensure that only the first menu element and content element are displayed. The following jQuery statement hides all of the instances of accordion-content (content element) that are not the first element by using a combination of the not() method and :first filter.

```
$('.accordion-content').not(':first').hide();
```

The .not() method filters any elements or selectors that are matched using the selector that precedes it. This can be in the form of a filter, as seen in this example, or you can pass it a specific element, such as seen in the example in the next step:

5. After you've hidden all of the instances of accordion-content that are not the first element, create another statement to apply the show effect to only the first accordion-content element:

```
$('.accordion-content:first').show();
```

6. To create an active or selected menu item, I added a class to the CSS file called header-active. Apply this class to the first accordion-header element using the following statement:

```
$('.accordion-header:first').addClass('header-active');
```

I have also added icons to the accordion menu and use the empty span tags to place the icons on the header. I have set up a class called icon-active that shows a down arrow graphic notifying the user of which content section is open. When the icon-active class is not applied, a right arrow graphic is displayed using the span tag. Use the :first filter to select the first accordion-header element, and then chain a find method to search for the span tag and add the class icon-active.

```
$('.accordion-header:first').find('span').addClass('icon-active');
```

7. Now begins the fun stuff: making the accordion react to a user input. Attach a click event to the accordion-header menu element.

```
$('.accordion-header').click(function () {
});
```

8. The first statement that gets added to the click event handler function is to make sure any item already clicked retracts and any active classes are removed. You can do this by selecting any visible instance of accordion-content and applying the slideUp effect to it. Then use the prev method to go back up the DOM tree one element, which in this case is the accordion-header, and remove the class header-active from it.

```
$('.accordion-header').click(function () {
  $('.accordion-content:visible').slideUp('slow').prev().
  removeClass('header-active');
});
```

The `prev()` method allows you to search the DOM for the previous sibling and you can take it a step further by passing a selector string (`'.active'`) into the method as an argument.

9. Add a statement to guarantee that any visible `icon-active` element is hidden by removing the class `icon-active`.

```
$('.accordion-header').click(function () {
  $('.accordion-content:visible').slideUp('slow').prev().
  removeClass('header-active');
    $('.icon-active:visible').removeClass('icon-active');
      });
```

Note: An important thing to remember is that the `addClass()`, `removeClass()`, and `hasClass()` methods do not require the period to be included when passing class names into them. This is often overlooked and can create errors in your jQuery scripts; however, the `is()`, `filter()`, and `not()` methods do require that the period be included before the class name.

10. Add a statement that selects the header that was clicked using the `this` keyword and add the class `header-active`. Then choose the next element using the `next()` method and slide it down slowly.

```
$('.accordion-header').click(function () {
  $('.accordion-content:visible').slideUp('slow').prev().
  removeClass('header-active');
    $('.icon-active:visible').removeClass('icon-active');
    $(this).addClass('header-active').next().slideDown('slow');
});
```

The `next()` method is the opposite of the `prev()` method. Instead of the previous sibling, this method returns the next sibling.

11. The final statement that is added inside of the `click` event handler function uses the `"this"` keyword in conjunction with the `find` method to add the class `icon-active` to the `span` tag found within the `accordion-header` element.

```
$('.accordion-header').click(function () {
  $('.accordion-content:visible').slideUp('slow').prev().
  removeClass('header-active');
    $('.icon-active:visible').removeClass('icon-active');
    $(this).addClass('header-active').next().slideDown('slow');
    $(this).find('span').addClass('icon-active');
});
```

If you work with a Web site or application that adds menu and content elements dynamically to the accordion, just make sure to switch the `click` event attachment method from `bind` to `live`. Otherwise, the `click` event won't register new elements that are added to the DOM after the page has loaded.

After pulling all of the HTML, CSS, and jQuery together and loading your page in a browser, you should see the accordion in full swing, as shown in Figure 6-9.

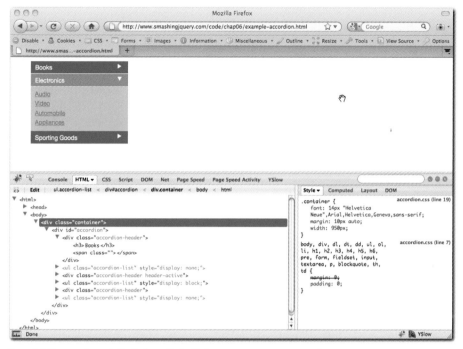

Figure 6-9: The accordion script in Firefox, with the Firebug pane open so you can see the guts

147

The accordion script helps you to display a large amount of content in a small space, but it has limitations, including

- As you add more menu items to the accordion, you need to scroll farther down the page to select or view the content embedded within those items. If you use an accordion in a real-world application, this limitation can greatly limit the user interface, which can decrease usability or even sales and conversions, if it's an e-commerce site.

- The accordion does not remember the content section that you are in if you refresh the page, although this type of functionality could be set up using cookies and jQuery. There is also a better, cookie-less technique that involves using anchors and query string handling, which you can find out more about on Rebecca Murphey's blog (http://blog.rebeccamurphey.com/2007/12/04/anchor-based-url-navigation-with-jquery/).

- The accordion section location can't be saved via a bookmark. If you get to a page and bookmark the page expecting the accordion to stay open in that particular section, it won't. The solution would be to set up anchors as mentioned in the preceding paragraph.

- If your Web site audience is not Internet-savvy, they may not be familiar with accordions and therefore won't understand how they work.

CREATING TABBED CONTENT

Tab navigation is popular with Web designers and developers as an easy and intuitive way for users to navigate through a Web site or application. The tab structure is reminiscent of the days of storing files in filing cabinets using tabbed hanging folders to identify what files were included. The tab structure has been transferred to the Web as a great way of organizing your data into logical "filing cabinets" or Web pages. Figure 6-10 shows an example of how Basecamp, a project management tool, uses tabs to organize and display content within the tools sections.

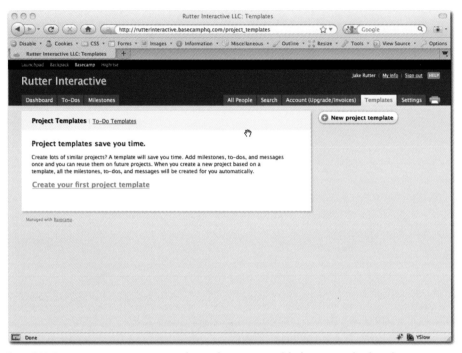

Figure 6-10: Basecamp, a project management tool, uses tabs to organize and display content within the tools sections

Tab-style navigation is not only seen on the Web, but also on computer desktops. Web browsers such as Mozilla Firefox and Google Chrome use tabs to display multiple Web pages within one window, and recently Internet Explorer 7 has also adopted this type of user interface as well. The chat programs Adium for Mac and Trillian for PC have adopted tab-style navigation for organizing multiple chat sessions into one window.

Some Web sites have taken tab-style navigation to the next level by coupling it with dynamic content switching. Instead of using tabs to navigate to different areas within their Web sites, dynamic content switching occurs when the tabs are used to show different content within the same page, similar to how an accordion menu is used to display large amounts of data in smaller spaces, but in a more user-friendly way. Some Web sites have even gone the extra mile of showing content that is loaded via Ajax when a tab is clicked, which is dynamic content in the pure sense because it's not actually on the page and can change every time. In Figure 6-11, the Coda Web site (www.panic.com/coda) uses tabs to show dynamic content on the page. The content is shown using animation effects, which is pretty nifty. As the user clicks each tab, content slides on and off the screen from left to right, or vice versa.

Figure 6-11: The Coda Web site uses tabs to show dynamic content on the page

© 2007 PANIC INC. Panic, the Panic Logo, and Transmit are registered trademarks of Panic Inc. www.panic.com

In the following tutorial, I walk you through how to set up a dynamic content switcher using tabs. The content and tabs are set up in a way that allows for more content to be added dynamically without breaking the jQuery:

1. Define the HTML structure of the tabs. The tabs require two elements: navigation and a content element. The tabs are set up using an unordered list called `#tabs`. Each list item has an anchor tag wrapped around the text, which should be displayed in the tab. In this example, I have added five navigation tabs.

```
<ul id="tabs" class="clearfix">
  <li><a href="">Home</a></li>
  <li><a href="">Shop</a></li>
  <li><a href="">Community</a></li>
  <li><a href="">Customer Service</a></li>
  <li><a href="">About</a></li>
</ul>
```

2. Set up the tab content. Each piece of content is wrapped in an element called `.content`. You can add as many or as few tabs of content as you like — just make sure that the number of elements matches up to the number of tabs. All of the tabs need to be wrapped with an element called `.content-container`. In this example, I've added five content elements:

```
<div id="content-container">
<div class="content">
<p>Lorem ipsum dolor sit amet, consectetur adipiscing elit. Integer euismod nunc
  id mauris placerat iaculis. Integer viverra velit eros, sed semper ante. Ut at
  turpis in tellus tincidunt dignissim non vitae felis. Donec nec sem ut est
```

```
    tincidunt ullamcorper.
</div>


<div class="content">
<p>Lorem ipsum dolor sit amet, consectetur adipiscing elit. Integer euismod nunc
    id mauris placerat iaculis. Integer viverra velit eros, sed semper ante. Ut at
    turpis in tellus tincidunt dignissim non vitae felis. Donec nec sem ut est
    tincidunt ullamcorper.
</div>


<div class="content">
<p>Lorem ipsum dolor sit amet, consectetur adipiscing elit. Integer euismod nunc
    id mauris placerat iaculis. Integer viverra velit eros, sed semper ante. Ut at
    turpis in tellus tincidunt dignissim non vitae felis. Donec nec sem ut est
    tincidunt ullamcorper.
</div>


<div class="content">
<p>Lorem ipsum dolor sit amet, consectetur adipiscing elit. Integer euismod nunc
    id mauris placerat iaculis. Integer viverra velit eros, sed semper ante. Ut at
    turpis in tellus tincidunt dignissim non vitae felis. Donec nec sem ut est
    tincidunt ullamcorper.
</div>


<div class="content">
<p>Lorem ipsum dolor sit amet, consectetur adipiscing elit. Integer euismod nunc
    id mauris placerat iaculis. Integer viverra velit eros, sed semper ante. Ut at
    turpis in tellus tincidunt dignissim non vitae felis. Donec nec sem ut est
    tincidunt ullamcorper.
</div>


<div class="content">
<p>Lorem ipsum dolor sit amet, consectetur adipiscing elit. Integer euismod nunc
    id mauris placerat iaculis. Integer viverra velit eros, sed semper ante. Ut at
    turpis in tellus tincidunt dignissim non vitae felis. Donec nec sem ut est
    tincidunt ullamcorper.
</div>
</div>
```

3. Next, set up a style sheet to make sure the accordion is laid out correctly on the page. Similar to other tutorials, a CSS reset is added:

```
body, div, dl, dt, dd, ul, ol, li, h1, h2, h3, h4, h5, h6, pre, form, fieldset,
    input, textarea, p, blockquote, th, td{margin:0; padding:0}
h1, h2, h3, h4, h5, h6{font-size:100%; font-weight:normal}
.clearfix:after{content:".";display:block;height:0; clear:both;
    visibility:hidden}
```

4. The remaining CSS controls the look and feel of the tab and content elements on the page. One important bit of CSS to remember is that all .content elements are hidden by default.

```
body{background:#8CCAD9}

ul#tabs{
```

```
    list-style-type:none;
    position:relative;
    }

    ul#tabs li{
    float:left;
    width:155px;
    text-align:center;
    position:relative;
    margin:0 3px;
    position:relative;
    }

    ul#tabs li a.tab-active{
    color:green;
    background:#fff;
    position:relative;
    top:1px;
    }

    ul#tabs li a{
    border-top:1px solid #9B4C24;
    border-left:1px solid #9B4C24;
    border-right:1px solid #9B4C24;
    background:#2E7D91; ;
    padding:10px 5px 10px 0px;
    display:block;
    text-decoration:none;
    font:bold 14px "Helvetica Neue",Arial,Helvetica,Geneva,sans-serif;
    color:#fff;
    position:relative;
    }

    #content-container{
    border:1px solid #333;
    background:#fff;}
```

`.content{display:none;}`

All of the following jQuery should be wrapped within the `document.ready()` function to ensure that the DOM is ready before any of the jQuery can be executed.

5. After the page loads, you want to ensure that only the first tab element is shown. Create a statement that selects the `.tab` element using the `:first` and attach the `show()` effect.

`$('.content:first').show()`

6. After setting the first content element to show, select the first navigation element (`#tabs li a`) and add the class `.tab-active`. This ensures that the first tab is selected after the page has loaded:

`$('#tabs li a:first').addClass('tab-active');`

7. Attach a `hover` event to the navigation element (`#tabs li a`). The `hover` event includes the `mouseenter` and `mouseleave` events. This `hover` event is added for effect only and is completely optional.

```
$("#tabs li a").hover(
  function () {
  // mouseenter event
  },
  function () {
  // mouseleave event
  }
);
```

8. You only need to add a statement to the `mouseenter` or `hover` event handler function, which uses the `animate` method because the animation only occurs as the mouse hovers the tab. When the user hovers her mouse over the tab after 300 milliseconds, the tab moves 20 pixels from the left in a span of 50 milliseconds, which is the duration, and then it snaps back into place. You can tweak the `animate` method by adding different CSS properties if you would like a different effect.

The `animate()` method works only with CSS properties that have numeric properties such as `margin`, `padding`, `left`, `top`, and `opacity`.

```
$("#tabs li a").hover(
  function () {
  // mouseenter event
    $(this).animate({left:20}, 300, function (){
      $(this).animate({left:0}, 50);
    });
  },
  function () {
  // mouseleave event
  }
);
```

9. Attach a `click` event to the `navigation` element (`#tabs li a`). The `click` event controls the showing and hiding of content on the page. Add a return `false` statement to the `click` event to prevent the default event, which is the browser trying to navigate to the link (#) that was clicked, from occurring.

```
$('ul#tabs li a').bind('click',function () {
  return false;
});
```

10. The first statement that is added to the `click` event handler is to get the index value of the tab that was clicked. Set up a variable called `linkIndex`. Create a `selector` statement using the `navigation` element (`#tabs li a`), attach the index method and pass in `this` as the parameter and assign it to the variable `linkIndex`.

```
$('ul#tabs li a').bind('click',function () {
  var linkIndex = $('#tabs li a').index(this);
  return false;
});
```

Using an index instead of static class or ID names allows the script to be able to handle changes in the HTML such as adding or removing tabs, without having to rewrite the script as if you had hard-coded elements into the script. This script is much more valuable when it can be applied to any number of tabs and is therefore easily scalable.

The `index()` method returns the index position of an object when a selector or element is passed into the method as a parameter and evaluated.

11. Add a statement to the `click` event handler that selects the navigation element (`#tabs li a`) and removes the `tab-active` class. This statement is to ensure that only one navigation element is selected at a time.

```
$('ul#tabs li a').bind('click',function () {
    var linkIndex = $('ul#tabs li a').index(this);
    $('#tabs li a').removeClass('tab-active');
    return false;
});
```

12. Add a statement to the `click` event handler that selects the content element that is visible and applies the `hide` effect to it.

```
$('ul#tabs li a').bind('click',function () {
    var linkIndex = $('ul#tabs li a').index(this);
    $('ul#tabs li a').removeClass('tab-active');
    $(".tab:visible").hide();
    return false;
});
```

13. Add a statement to the `click` event handler that filters the content elements based on the current index and only shows the content whose index matches that of the content element. This statement controls the showing and hiding of the content elements based on their index values. Even though there is no relationship in the DOM between the list items and content elements, when a list item is clicked, it is matched up based solely on the order of the index values in both sets of elements. It's a great way to keep the code autonomous.

```
$('ul#tabs li a').bind('click',function () {
    var linkIndex = $('ul#tabs li a').index(this);
    $('ul#tabs li a').removeClass('tab-active');
    $(".tab:visible").hide();
    $(".tab:eq("+linkIndex+")").show();
    return false;
});
```

The `eq(index)` method returns the set of element(s) at the given index.

14. The final statement added to the `click` event handler adds a `tab-active` class to each element that is clicked to show the user which tab they are currently on.

```
$('ul#tabs li a').bind('click',function () {
    var linkIndex = $('ul#tabs li a').index(this);
    $('ul#tabs li a').removeClass('tab-active');
    $(".tab:visible").hide();
    $(".tab:eq("+linkIndex+")").show();
    $(this).addClass('tab-active');
    return false;
});
```

If you work with a Web site or application that adds tab and content elements dynamically to the tabbed content script, just make sure to switch the `click` event attachment method from bind to live. Otherwise, the `click` event won't register new elements that are added to the DOM after the page has loaded.

After pulling all of the HTML, CSS, and jQuery together and loading it up in a browser, you should see the accordion in full swing, as in Figure 6-12.

Figure 6-12: The tab content script in Firefox with the Firebug tab open

7

CREATING INTERACTIVE AND EXCITING TABLES

IN THE LATE NINETIES, during the explosive growth of the Internet and the World Wide Web, tables were often used for page design and layouts, which is not what they were originally intended for. The problem with using tables for design and layout stems from their lack of support for semantic principles, where content is separated from design, and the usage of *nested tables*, which add unnecessary page bloat to your code and lead to an accessibility and maintainability nightmare. Nested tables occur when you create a page layout with table upon table nested into each other to match up to a complex design. Most Web designers and developers are now able

to work purely with HTML and CSS to create semantic designs that no longer use tables for layout and therefore separate the content from the presentation layers.

HTML tables were used improperly because alternative layout options did not exist until the advent of CSS — even then, browsers didn't support CSS correctly for quite a few years. Tables have a really bad reputation, but if they're used correctly for tabular data, they can be quite useful for showing data in a clean, structured format. In the following chapter, I share some ways to enhance your tabular data using jQuery.

STYLING THE DATA IN TABLES WITH CSS

Figure 7-1 shows an example of using tables to show data on the eWedding Web site (www.ewedding.com/packages.php).

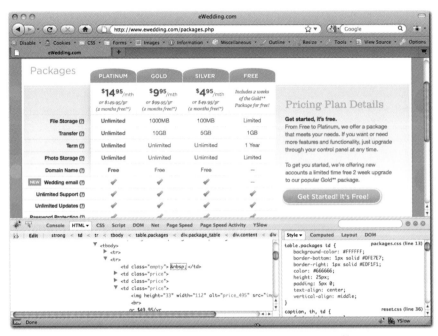

Figure 7-1: An example of using tables to show data — in this case, comparisons — on eWedding

Reproduced with permission of ewedding.cp

You can add CSS styling to your tables in such a way as to help to make them more usable and easier to digest for your users. I use the following HTML table in the tutorials:

```
<table border="1" cellpadding="4">
  <thead>
 <tr>
    <th>Category</th>
    <th>Product</th>
    <th>Price</th>
    <th>Status</th>
  </tr>
</thead>
  <tbody>
 <tr>
    <td>Clothing</td>
    <td>North Face Jacket</td>
    <td>$189.99</td>
    <td>In-stock</td>
  </tr>
  <tr>
    <td>Shoes</td>
```

```
      <td>Nike</td>
      <td>$59.99</td>
      <td>In-stock</td>
    </tr>
    <tr>
      <td>Electronics</td>
      <td>LED TV</td>
      <td>$589.99</td>
      <td>Out of stock</td>
    </tr>
    <tr>
      <td>Sporting Goods</td>
      <td>Ping Golf Clubs</td>
      <td>$159.99</td>
      <td>In-stock</td>
    </tr>
    <tr>
      <td>Clothing</td>
      <td>Sweater</td>
      <td>$19.99</td>
      <td>In-stock</td>
    </tr>
  </tbody>
</table>
```

ADDING ALTERNATING ROW COLORS USING FILTERS

Zebra striping is a common practice used by Web designers to make table rows easier to read by adding a background color to each even or odd row, as in Figure 7-2, an example of zebra striping from the Web site for Performable (www.performable.com). Zebra striping can be done using backend programming languages such as PHP or ASP.net, but the downside is that a developer must be involved. The :even and :odd filters in jQuery make it incredibly easy to add this styling to any table.

Set up a document ready function and, within it, add two statements to select the odd and even rows using filters. The first statement selects all of the even rows and applies the CSS property background:#dedede (light gray). The second statement is just to ensure that all of the odd rows have a background of white. Figure 7-3 shows the example as output in the browser after the page has loaded.

```
$(document).ready(function() {
    $('tbody tr:even').css('background','#dedede');
    $('tbody tr:odd').css('background','#ffffff');
  });
```

ADDING A SIMPLE HOVER EFFECT TO ROWS

You can increase the interactivity of your tables by adding a hover effect to all the rows in your table. As in the following example, it could be as simple as adding a different color background to the table row as the user moves their mouse over each row. Figure 7-4 shows the final result of the code in Firefox.

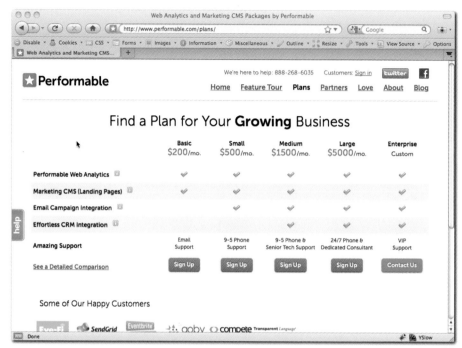

Figure 7-2: Zebra striping used on a table at the Performable.com Web site

Reproduced with permission of performable.com

1. Set up a document ready handler and attach a hover event to the tr element. The beauty of the selector is that it will automatically apply to all of the rows in the table and attach a hover event, with just a few lines of code.

```
$(document).ready(function(){
    $('tr').hover(function() {
    }, function() {
    });
});
```

2. Add two statements into the hover functions, one for mouseenter and one for mouseleave. On mouseenter, the background color changes to pink and on mouseleave, the background color changes back to white using the this keyword to point to the current tr element that the event has been triggered on.

```
$(document).ready(function(){
    $('tr').hover(function() {
        $(this).css('background','pink');
    }, function() {
        $(this).css('background','white');
    });
});
```

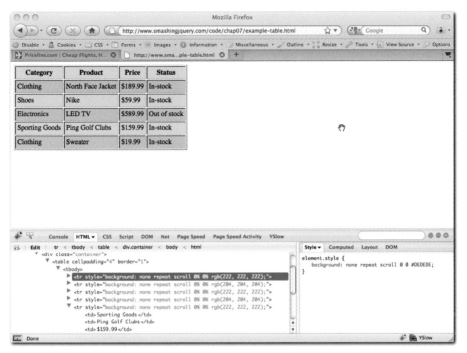

Figure 7-3: The output of the browser after the page has loaded — all of the even rows have a background color applied to them

ADDING AN ADVANCED HOVER EFFECT TO ROWS

If you want to get more complex, you can add a hover effect that displays editing options to the user, as seen in Figure 7-5. This type of user interface solution is often used to show editing capabilities alongside inline editing.

Set up a document ready handler with a hover event attached to the table row (tr) element. Create two selector statements; one each for the mouseenter and mouseleave events. For the first statement (mouseenter), use the this keyword and attach the after method to insert the HTML anchor tag into the DOM (document object model). The first statement appends the Edit Me link into all of the children of the row that is being hovered over. The second statement removes the editme element after the mouse has been moved off.

```
$(document).ready(function(){
    $('tr').hover(function() {
      $(this).children().append('<div class="editme"><a href="">Edit Me</a></div>');

    }, function() {
      $('.editme').remove();
    });
});
```

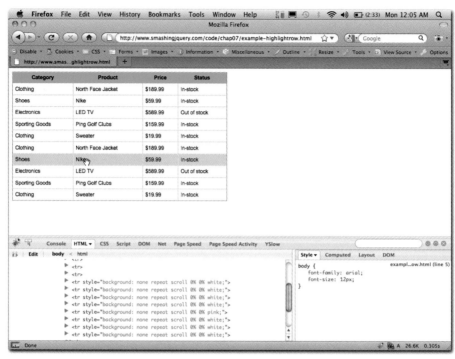

Figure 7-4: The output in Firefox and Firebug as the user moves their mouse over a row

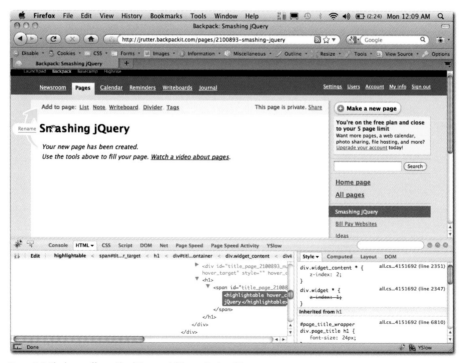

Figure 7-5: The hover effect with editing capabilities on BackpackIt.com

MANIPULATING THE DATA IN TABLES

Now that you have seen how to add simple styling and effects to tables, I'm going to show you how to manipulate the data that is in the tables. When I say manipulate, I mean add, remove, and filter the data contained, which results in changes to the DOM. All of the selectors, events, and effects that I have discussed up until now can be applied to tabular data. The possibilities of what you can do are endless. In this section, I explain the following solutions:

- Adding a row after the first/last rows of the table
- Adding a row after a row based on index
- Adding a row after rows with specific content
- Removing a row using a filter selector
- Removing a row based on index
- Removing a row based on its content

I use the following HTML table in all of the tutorials within this section. Take note of the structure. Figure 7-6 shows an example of this table in Firefox.

```
<table border="1" cellpadding="4" id="products">
    <thead>
  <tr>
      <th>Category</th>
      <th>Product</th>
      <th>Price</th>
      <th>Status</th>
  </tr>
  </thead>
    <tbody>
  <tr>
      <td>Clothing</td>
      <td>North Face Jacket</td>
      <td>$189.99</td>
      <td>In-stock</td>
  </tr>
  <tr>
      <td>Shoes</td>
      <td>Nike</td>
      <td>$59.99</td>
      <td>In-stock</td>
  </tr>
  <tr>
      <td>Electronics</td>
      <td>LED TV</td>
      <td>$589.99</td>
      <td>Out of stock</td>
  </tr>
  <tr>
      <td>Sporting Goods</td>
      <td>Ping Golf Clubs</td>
```

```
    <td>$159.99</td>
    <td>In-stock</td>
  </tr>
  <tr>
    <td>Clothing</td>
    <td>Sweater</td>
    <td>$19.99</td>
    <td>In-stock</td>
  </tr>
 </tbody>
</table>
```

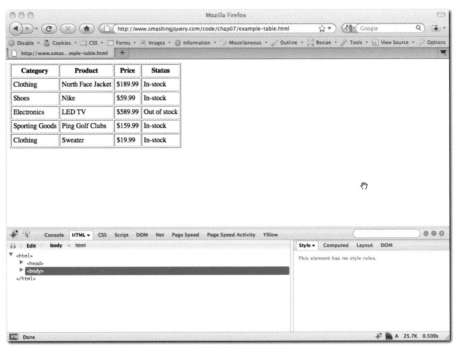

Figure 7-6: The table created in the preceding code as it appears in Firefox

ADDING A MESSAGE AFTER THE FIRST/LAST ROWS OF THE TABLE

Adding content dynamically to a page can be done server-side, which requires a request to the server and, depending on the size of the database that needs to be searched, can take quite a bit of time and processing power. An easier way to dynamically insert content is using jQuery to either add static content stored in a jQuery function or to load content in via Ajax without disrupting other activities on the page.

You can specifically target areas within the table if you have a search results page and you would like to insert a special message after the first search result. This is similar to the way Google always keeps paid results at the top of every search results page, and all other organic listings follow afterwards.

jQuery allows you to do this by using a combination of the `:first` filter and the `after()` method. The Priceline Web site (`www.priceline.com`) uses a similar method in their hotel search results page. Figure 7-7 shows an example of how Priceline inserts a special offer after every two hotel listings.

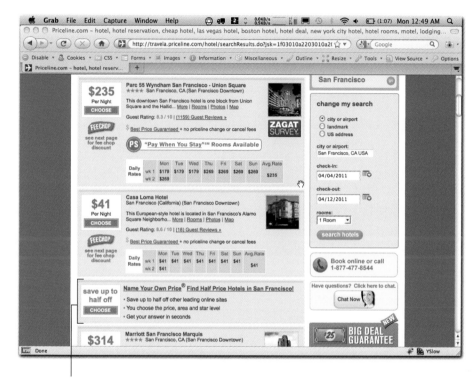

The special offer follows every two listings.

Figure 7-7: Priceline inserts a special offer after every two hotel listings on the search results page

Using the HTML table from the preceding example, I show you how easy it is to add a special message dynamically before the first row in the table:

1. Create a class named `special` and apply different CSS properties to it so that it stands out after it is added to the table.

```
.special
  {background:#6AAF18;text-align:center;font-size:22px;color:#fff;font-
  weight:bold;}
```

2. Set up a `document ready` handler and, within it, add a statement that selects the first `tr` in the table and inserts the special offer row directly after it.

```
$(document).ready(function() {
  $('#products tr:first').after('<tr><td colspan="4" class="special">Special
  Offer TODAY</td></tr>');
});
```

Alternatively, you can use the `:last` filter to show content only after the last row in the table. Figure 7-8 shows the special message script in action using Firefox.

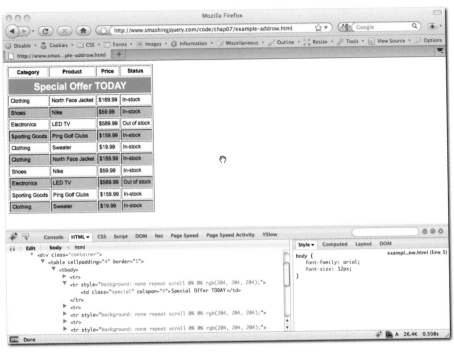

Figure 7-8: The special message script in action using Firefox

REMOVING A ROW USING A FILTER SELECTOR

I work in an environment where removing content, whether it be temporarily or permanently, can be quite a challenge. We have a schedule of weekly deployments and code that needs to be compiled and tested, which prevents quick changes to most pages on the sites. If we need to do a quick fix such as removing a product, image, text, or any type of element from the DOM, we can use the `remove()` method, which makes the backend developers happy because they don't have to get involved. Sometimes, content makes it onto a site when it shouldn't, after work hours during times of limited support. Being able to quickly go in and remove the content using jQuery really saves the day and allows the developers to fix the issue the next day from the core.

The `remove()` method removes whatever matched set it is attached to from the DOM.

Set up a `document ready` handler and add a `selector` statement with `remove()` method attached at the end. The matched set, in this case, the last `table-row`, is removed from the DOM. Figure 7-9 shows the result of the last row of the table being removed.

```
$(document).ready(function(){
    $('tr:last').remove();
});
```

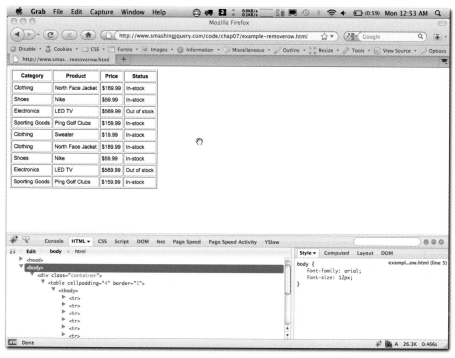

Figure 7-9: The last table-row is removed

Here are some ideas for extending the functionality of the special message tutorial:

- Add a timer to show a special message after 10 seconds has gone by and make it disappear 30 seconds later.
- Use the `animate` method to add advanced animation effects to a special message.
- Use cookies to only show the special message to first-time visitors.

ADDING A ROW AFTER A ROW BASED ON ITS INDEX VALUE

Just as you add a row based on its position in the table as first or last, you can also insert a row based on the index value of the row proceeding or following it. Set up a selector that selects all elements that have an index of 5 using the `:eq()` filter and insert the `Special Offer TODAY` HTML content directly after the matched element.

:eq() is a filter selector that allows you to filter by index.

```
$("tr:eq(5)").after('<tr><td colspan="4">Special Offer TODAY</td></tr>');
```

REMOVING A ROW BASED ON ITS INDEX VALUE

Similar to adding a row based on index, you can also remove a row by its index value. Set up a selector that selects any `tr` elements that have an index of `1` and removes them from the DOM using the `remove()` method. In this case, it would only be equal to one row:

```
$("tr:eq(1)").remove();
```

ADDING A MESSAGE AFTER ROWS WITH SPECIFIC CONTENT

If you would like to insert rows into a table before or after a text string contained in the table rows, you can do so by using the `:contains` filter. Similar to the Priceline example in Figure 7-7, you can use this filter in conjunction with tables to show special messages to your users.

Consider this scenario: You would like to match all rows (`Clothing`) and add a special message after each row that contains this string. The message contains HTML that mentions a special offer. It's a clever way to call out specific elements and highlight them within the DOM. It's important to note that the `contains` filter is case-sensitive. If it came across any strings in a lowercase, if you had specified uppercase, they would be skipped over.

Create a `selector` statement using the `tr` elements on the page. Using the `:contains` filter, you can match all table rows that contain the string `Clothing`. After each matched set, insert a `Special Offer` table row. Figure 7-10 shows how an example of adding special content using the `:contains` filter is rendered in a browser.

`:contains` is a filter that allows you to filter the DOM elements based on their content.

```
$('tr:contains("Clothing")').after('<tr><td colspan="4" class="special">Special
   Offer TODAY</td></tr>');
```

REMOVING A ROW BASED ON ITS CONTENT

Just as you can add a row based on specific content, you can also remove elements based on the content contained within them. Set up a selector statement that selects all `tr` elements that have contain the string `Clothing` and removes them from the DOM.

```
$("tr").remove(":contains('Clothing')");
```

SETTING UP TABLE PAGINATION WITH JQUERY

Pagination involves breaking up content into manageable page-sized pieces. On the Web, pagination is everywhere; Figure 7-11 shows pagination on the Google search results page. Pagination helps to limit the number of results shown at one time to make it easier for users to navigate and digest the content delivered to them.

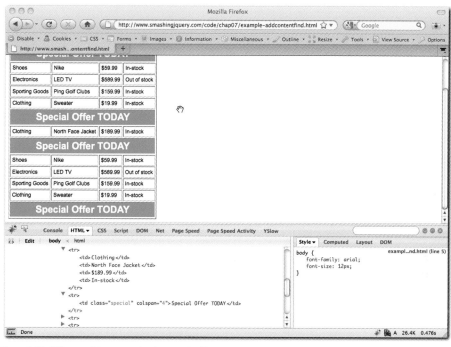

Figure 7-10: Adding special content using the :contains filter

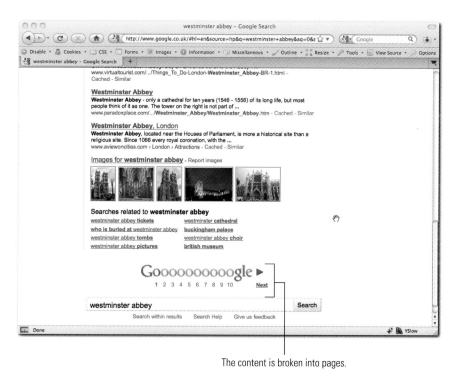

The content is broken into pages.

Figure 7-11: Pagination on the Google search results page

Reproduced from 2010 © Google

Pagination is frequently set up using server-side programming languages like PHP, ASP.NET, and Java. The major benefit to using a server-side solution is the Web page doesn't need to load all of the records at once; they are loaded only when the user requests them. You can use jQuery to set up pagination, but I recommend doing it to paginate only results that aren't heavy-loading (where there are more than 100 results), which could weigh the page loading time down considerably.

If your skills are advanced enough, you can build jQuery that loads only 10 results and, each time a page is clicked, that content is loaded via Ajax and inserted into the current page.

In the following pagination example, I explain how you can paginate a collection of table rows with just a few lines of jQuery. The script automatically paginates the records that you pass into the selectors and also creates a navigation menu underneath that shows all of the pages available. When you click on a page, the page number stays active to let the user know which page they are on.

1. Before you can add pagination, you need some data to paginate. In this example, I use a table, but you could use anything from an unordered list to a group of divs. In the following HTML, 12 table rows are set up:

```
<table border="0" cellpadding="0" cellspacing="0" id="data">
  <tr>
    <td>1</td>
    <td>Clothing</td>
    <td>North Face Jacket</td>
    <td>$189.99</td>
    <td>In-stock</td>
  </tr>
  <tr>
    <td>2</td>
    <td>Shoes</td>
    <td>Nike</td>
    <td>$59.99</td>
    <td>In-stock</td>
  </tr>
  <tr>
    <td>3</td>
    <td>Electronics</td>
    <td>LED TV</td>
    <td>$589.99</td>
    <td>Out of stock</td>
  </tr>
  <tr>
    <td>4</td>
    <td>Sporting Goods</td>
    <td>Ping Golf Clubs</td>
    <td>$159.99</td>
    <td>In-stock</td>
  </tr>
  <tr>
    <td>5</td>
```

```
    <td>Clothing</td>
    <td>Sweater</td>
    <td>$19.99</td>
    <td>In-stock</td>
  </tr>
  <tr>
    <td>6</td>
    <td>Clothing</td>
    <td>North Face Jacket</td>
    <td>$189.99</td>
    <td>In-stock</td>
  </tr>
  <tr>
    <td>7</td>
    <td>Shoes</td>
    <td>Nike</td>
    <td>$59.99</td>
    <td>In-stock</td>
  </tr>
  <tr>
  <td>8</td>
    <td>Electronics</td>
    <td>LED TV</td>
    <td>$589.99</td>
    <td>Out of stock</td>
  </tr>
  <tr>
    <td>9</td>
    <td>Sporting Goods</td>
    <td>Ping Golf Clubs</td>
    <td>$159.99</td>
    <td>In-stock</td>
  </tr>
  <tr>
    <td>10</td>
    <td>Shoes</td>
    <td>Nike</td>
    <td>$59.99</td>
    <td>In-stock</td>
  </tr>
  <tr>
    <td>11</td>
    <td>Electronics</td>
    <td>LED TV</td>
    <td>$589.99</td>
    <td>Out of stock</td>
  </tr>
  <tr>
    <td>12</td>
    <td>Sporting Goods</td>
    <td>Ping Golf Clubs</td>
    <td>$159.99</td>
```

```
        <td>In-stock</td>
    </tr>
</table>
```

2. Using the table ID #data, create a selector statement that inserts a div with an ID #nav after the #data element on the page, which will show up underneath the table. The #nav element is used to hold the page number links.

```
$('#data').after('<div id="nav"></div>');
```

3. Set up a variable called rowsShown, which holds the value for how many rows you want to show on each page.

```
var rowsShown = 4;
```

4. Set up a variable called rowsTotal, which gets the number of the rows in the element that you will be paginating. The #data element is selected and the length property is added to the end, which in this case should return 12.

```
var rowsTotal = $('#data tr').length;
```

5. Set up a variable called numPages, which will be equal to the value of rowsTotal divided by rowsShown. Notice that the equation is wrapped by the Math.round native JavaScript method. Math.round rounds the product of the equation to the nearest number.

```
var numPages = Math.round(rowsTotal/rowsShown);
```

In any of the tutorials, when you create a variable, if you would like to quickly see that the variable is returning a number, insert an alert statement with the variable inside of the parenthesis, like this: alert(rowsTotal). This doesn't just relate to jQuery, but is a native JavaScript function that is central to all JS debugging.

6. Set up a for loop to iterate through the number of pages and create page number links that are used to navigate through the pages. Add a variable called pageNum; the value is set to the i + 1, i being the iteration variable in the loop. This ensures that the page number starts at 1 instead of 0. Next, add a selector statement to the for loop that selects the #nav element and adds an anchor link with the rel tag set to the index. The page number is set to the pageNum value.

```
for(i = 0;i<numPages;i++) {
    var pageNum = i + 1;
    $('#nav').append('<a href="#" rel="'+i+'">'+pageNum+'</a> ');
}
```

7. Add a statement to hide of all of visible rows in the #data table.

```
$('#data tr').hide();
```

8. Add a statement that selects the first row and shows it.

```
$('#data tr:first').show();
```

9. Add a statement that selects all of the rows in the #data table and use the slice jQuery method to limit only first four rows to be shown. The slice method allows you to pass two parameters (start and end) to slice out a section of an array.

```
$('#data tr').slice(0, rowsShown).show();
```

10. Add a statement that selects the first page number and adds a class, active, to it. This ensures that the first page anchor link is selected when the page loads.

```
$('#nav a:first').addClass('active');
```

11. Attach a `click` event to all of the page number links in the `#nav` element. This `click` event is used to control the pagination; this event contains the guts of the script.

```
$('#nav a').bind('click', function(){
});
```

12. The first statement that is added to the `click` event removes the `active` class from whichever link is currently active.

```
$('#nav a').bind('click', function(){
  $('#nav a').removeClass('active');
});
```

13. The next statement adds only the `active` class to the page number link that has been clicked.

```
$('#nav a').bind('click', function(){
  $('#nav a').removeClass('active');
  $(this).addClass('active');
});
```

14. Add a variable called `currPage`, which stores the value of the `rel` tag that was set up in the `for` loop.

```
$('#nav a').bind('click', function(){
  $('#nav a').removeClass('active');
  $(this).addClass('active');
  var currPage = $(this).attr('rel');
});
```

15. Add a variable named `startItem`, which stores the product of `currPage` multiplied by `rowsShown`.

```
$('#nav a').bind('click', function(){
  $('#nav a').removeClass('active');
  $(this).addClass('active');
  var currPage = $(this).attr('rel');
  var startItem = currPage * rowsShown;
});
```

16. Add a variable named `endItem` that stores the product of `startItem` plus `rowsShown`.

```
$('#nav a').bind('click', function(){
  $('#nav a').removeClass('active');
  $(this).addClass('active');
  var currPage = $(this).attr('rel');
  var startItem = currPage * rowsShown;
  var endItem = startItem + rowsShown;
});
```

17. The final statement that is added to the `click` event controls which records are shown when a particular page anchor tag is clicked. Using a selector, grab all the table rows within the `#data` table. The results of this tutorial are shown in Figure 7-12.

```
$('#nav a').bind('click', function(){
  $('#nav a').removeClass('active');
  $(this).addClass('active');
  var currPage = $(this).attr('rel');
  var startItem = currPage * rowsShown;
  var endItem = startItem + rowsShown;
  $('#data tr').css('opacity','0.0').hide().slice(startItem, endItem).
  css('display','table-row').animate({opacity:1}, 300);
});
```

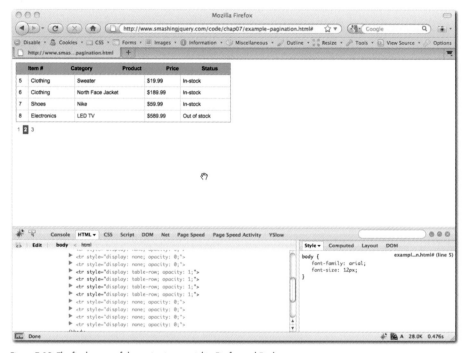

Figure 7-12: The final output of the pagination tutorial in Firefox and Firebug

CREATING ADVANCED TABLES USING JQUERY PLUG-INS

jQuery has an extensive community of developers who create jQuery plug-ins. In Chapter 10, I explain how to create your own plug-ins and also review some popular plug-ins that I suggest you use in your own projects. The only downside to having so many options to choose from is that sometimes the quality of code and support for a plug-in is lacking. You can usually tell a good plug-in from a bad one by the documentation that accompanies it.

You can build your own jQuery code to do table sorting and filtering, but quite a few powerful plug-ins can also do this. Using a plug-in can rapidly speed the implementation of a solution, and because most plug-ins are open source, it gives you a good base to get started upon. I review how to work with two plug-ins in particular: tablesorter and Visualize.

SORTING ROWS USING THE TABLESORTER PLUG-IN

The tablesorter plug-in allows you to apply sorting to any table. The tablesorter plug-in has been around for a few years and is well supported with excellent documentation. It works on all the popular browsers. Table 7.1 outlines some basic configuration options that can be passed into the `tablesorter` method to give you more control and flexibility. This tutorial references version 2.0.5 of the tablesorter plug-in.

For example, if you have a table that contains more than one hundred records and you would like to sort all of them by clicking on one header item, you can easily set this up using the tablesorter plug-in.

The benefit to sorting the tabular data using jQuery instead of a server-side method is that jQuery is faster in reorganizing the records. If you use a server-side solution, the Web site has to reload each request whenever a reorder is submitted, which slows down the results.

Table 7.1 tablesorter Configuration Options

Option	Description	Default
cssAsc	Allows you to specify a class for ascending order	"headerSortUp"
cssDesc	Allows you to specify a class for descending order	"headerSortDown"
cssHeader	Allows you to specify a class for the header in the unsorted state	"header"
sortForce	Allows you to force the sorting	null
sortList	Allows you to specify how the data is sorted by passing in values to columnIndex and sortDirection	null
sortMultiSortKey	Allows you to specify the key used for multi-column sorting	shiftKey

For more information about tablesorter, visit: http://tablesorter.com/

In the following example, I show you just how easy it is to use the tablesorter plug-in to add sorting options off of existing data in a table:

1. Before you can apply the tablesorter plug-in to your table, you need to make sure the table is set up correctly. If it's not, the plug-in won't work. You need to wrap all of the table header cells with a `thead` tag and all of the table cells with a `tbody` tag, as in the following HTML example:

```
<table border="0" cellpadding="0" cellspacing="0" id="data">
  <thead>
    <tr>
    <th>Item #</th>
    <th>Category</th>
    <th>Product</th>
    <th>Price</th>
    <th>Status</th>
    </tr>
  </thead>
  <tbody>
```

```
  <tr>
    <td>1</td>
    <td>Clothing</td>
    <td>North Face Jacket</td>
    <td>$189.99</td>
    <td>In-stock</td>
  </tr>
  <tr>
    <td>2</td>
    <td>Shoes</td>
    <td>Nike</td>
    <td>$59.99</td>
    <td>In-stock</td>
  </tr>
  <tr>
    <td>3</td>
    <td>Electronics</td>
    <td>LED TV</td>
    <td>$589.99</td>
    <td>Out of stock</td>
  </tr>
  <tr>
    <td>4</td>
    <td>Sporting Goods</td>
    <td>Ping Golf Clubs</td>
    <td>$159.99</td>
    <td>In-stock</td>
  </tr>
  <tr>
    <td>5</td>
    <td>Clothing</td>
    <td>Sweater</td>
    <td>$19.99</td>
    <td>In-stock</td>
  </tr>
  <tr>
    <td>6</td>
    <td>Clothing</td>
    <td>North Face Jacket</td>
    <td>$189.99</td>
    <td>In-stock</td>
  </tr>
  <tr>
    <td>7</td>
    <td>Shoes</td>
    <td>Nike</td>
    <td>$59.99</td>
    <td>In-stock</td>
  </tr>
  <tr>
    <td>8</td>
    <td>Electronics</td>
```

```
        <td>LED TV</td>
        <td>$589.99</td>
        <td>Out of stock</td>
    </tr>
    </tbody>
</table>
```

2. When using a plug-in with jQuery, you always need to include it at the top of your page. You should load plug-ins before any code that references them. Any code that doesn't reference the plug-in can happily be loaded before the plug-in, but always after the jQuery library.

```
<script src="js/tablesorter.min.js"></script>
```

3. Set up a `document ready` function and, within it, add a statement that selects the `#data` table and applies the `tablesorter()` method to it. If you apply the `table-sorter` method without any options, the default options referenced in the Table 7.1 are automatically applied and the table sorting should reflect Figure 7-13.

```
$(document).ready(function(){
    $("#data").tablesorter();
});
```

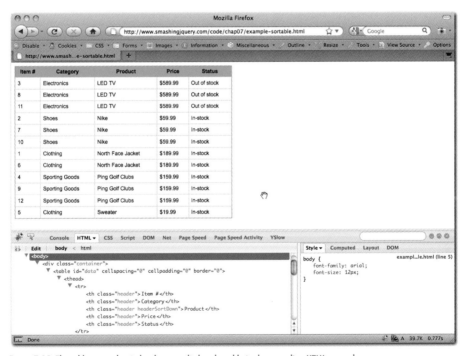

Figure 7-13: The tablesorter plug-in has been applied to the table in the preceding HTML example

CHANGING DEFAULT SORT ORDER

You can change the default sort order by using the `sortList` parameter to pass in an array:

```
[columnIndex, sortOrder]
```

Using the `tablesorter` statement you have set up from the previous example, pass in the `sortList` parameter. The first number in the array is the column index and the second number is the `sortOrder` (0 equals ascending and 1 equals descending).

```
$("#data").tablesorter({sortList:[[1,0]]});
```

If you wish to configure tablesorter further, you can pass in any of the options from Table 7.1. The tablesorter plug-in is a quick and easy way to add sorting to any table. If you use this plug-in, you will spend less time writing JavaScript and can effectively spend more time designing a table that is easy to use and visually appealing. By passing different CSS classes into the `tablesorter` function, you can customize the look and feel. This option is necessary if you have multiple tables on a page and would like to style them all slightly differently.

CREATING SEXY CHARTS WITH TABULAR DATA USING VISUALIZE

Interactive graphs are most often creating using Adobe Flash for dynamic graphs, such as those seen in Google Analytics in Figure 7-14. Recently, a number of developers have created jQuery plug-ins that can create comparable charts but without the dependency of Flash. The Visualize plug-in, created by Filament Group, is one of the better solutions for creating charts. The Visualize plug-in allows you to create graph, line, bar, and pie charts using tabular data. It has a number of options that can be passed into the function to set up and alter a chart on any page using data pulled from HTML tables. Table 7.2 lists the Visualize configuration options.

Figure 7-14: Google Analytics using Flash for charts and graphs

Table 7.2   Visualize Configuration Options

Option	Description	Default Behavior
type	Allows you to choose the type of chart	Bar chart
width	Allows you to set the width of the chart	Width of table
height	Allows you to set the height of the chart	Height of table
appendTitle	Allows you to add title to chart	True, title will be applied
title	Allows you to set the title for the chart	Title from caption tag will be applied
appendKey	Allows you to add color key to the chart	True, title key will be applied
colors	Allows you to determine colors	Default colors will be applied
textColors	Allows you to change color of text	N/A
parseDirection	Direction to parse the data	X-axis by default
pieMargin	Allows you to change space around pie chart	Default value: 20
pieLabelPos	Allows you to set position of labels on pie chart	Default position: Inside
lineWeight	Allows you to set stroke weight in line and area charts	Default value: 4
barGroupMargin	Allows you to add spacing around each group of bar graphs	Default value: 10
barMargin	Allows you to add spacing around bar graphs	Default value: 1

Other notable jQuery charting plug-ins include Highcharts, Flot, jqplot, and jQuery Sparklines.

CREATING A BAR CHART

In the following example, I show you just how easy it is to use the Visualize plug-in to create a bar chart based off existing data in a table. The results are shown in Figure 7-15.

1. Before you can apply the chart plug-in to your table, you need to make sure the table is set up correctly. If the table is not set up correctly, the plug-in won't work. You need to wrap all of the table header cells with a thead tag and all of the table cells with a tbody tag like in the following HTML example. You will also need to add the scope attribute to the columns and rows.

   The scope attribute can be added to table cell, which is a table attribute used to ensure that the user either reading or using a screen reader to access the Web page recognizes the cell as a heading. The scope attribute accepts the following values: col, colgroup, row, and rowgroup and is mainly used for accessibility of Web pages.

   ```
   <table border="1" cellpadding="4">
     <caption>2010 Traffic</caption>
     <thead>
       <tr>
   ```

177

```
        <th></th>
        <th scope="col">New Visits</th>
        <th scope="col">Return Visits</th>
      </tr>
    </thead>
    <tbody>
      <tr>
        <td scope="row">Music</td>
        <td>1000</td>
        <td>3500</td>
      </tr>
      <tr>
        <th scope="row">Sports</th>
        <td>1432</td>
        <td>4633</td>
      </tr>
      <tr>
      <th scope="row">Clothing</th>
        <td>1834</td>
          <td>8503</td>
        </tr>
        <tr>
          <td scope="row">Art</td>
          <td>2543</td>
          <td>3472</td>
        </tr>
        <tr>
          <td scope="row">Shoes</td>
          <td>4632</td>
          <td>8493</td>
        </tr>
        </tbody>
      </table>
```

2. When you use a plug-in with jQuery, you always need to include it in the top of your page. You should load plug-ins before any code that references them. Any code that doesn't reference the plug-in can happily be loaded before the plug-in, but always after the jQuery library.

```
<script type="text/javascript" src="js/visualize.jquery.js"></script>
```

3. Set up a document ready handler and, within it, add a statement that selects the .table table and applies the visualize() method to it. Apply the visualize method and pass in the following option: type:'bar'.

```
$(document).ready(function(){
  $('table').visualize({type:'bar'});
});
```

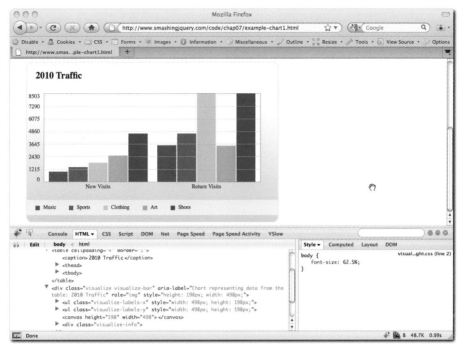

Figure 7-15: The Visualize plug-in has been applied to the table

179

8

CREATING ADVANCED FORMS WITH JQUERY

FORMS ARE COMMONPLACE all over the Internet, whether they are forms for ecommerce and registration or search input fields. Validation ensures that Web forms accept correct data, show clear error messages when faulty data is entered, and that fields are filled out when a form is submitted. Validation is often handled on the server side by Web developers using programming languages such as PHP, JSP or ASP. Validation on the client side using JavaScript is becoming increasingly more common, in addition to server-side validation depending on the security level of the data that is being validated. Web designers who know jQuery and

JavaScript can create a better user interface with forms than can a developer using backend development.

jQuery offers several events (`focus`, `blur`, `change`) specifically to be used in forms, which I review in Chapter 4, about events. These events are not new to JavaScript, but jQuery makes it easier to use these events in conjunction with forms. In this chapter, I review many different scenarios where jQuery can help you do more with your forms. The techniques that you learn from this chapter are necessary when you work with Ajax, which I cover in Chapter 9.

FOCUSING ON AN INPUT BOX AFTER PAGE LOAD

Driving focus to a particular form field on a page is a great way to direct users to perform a specific action on a page, whether it's logging in or filling out a registration. It's a simple script you can add to any page to ensure that the user is focused on the input right away, as shown in Figure 8-1. If you have a conversion-based ecommerce or retail Web site, this could potentially give you a small boost in conversion rates.

1. Set up the HTML form elements. For this example, set up two form `input="text"` elements so that you can demonstrate using the `:first` filter when more than two elements are present on the page.

   ```
   <input type="text1" />
   <input type="text2" />
   ```

2. Add a statement that selects the first input and attaches the focus event to it. This ensures that when the page loads, the first input has focus applied to it:

   ```
   $('input:first').focus();
   ```

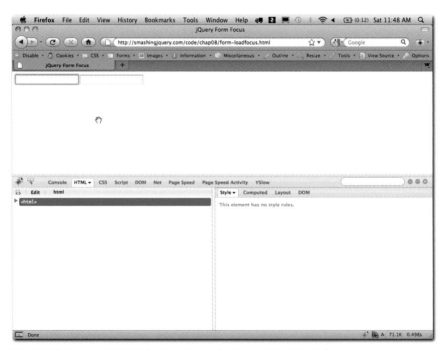

Figure 8-1: The focus is applied to the first input element after the page is loaded in Firefox

DISABLING AND ENABLING FORM ELEMENTS

Disabling and enabling form elements is required in areas of a Web site where you don't want to allow your users to change a field, as shown in Figure 8-2. One scenario that calls for

disabling form elements is a multi-part form. On the first page, say that you collect information such as username, password, and e-mail address. On the second page, you collect billing
addresses and payment information and confirm the information that is passed over from the
first page, but as disabled form fields:

1. Set up the HTML form input element that you wish to disable after the page has loaded.

   ```
   <input type="text" id="name-input" />
   ```

2. Add a statement that selects the `name-input` element and sets the disabled attribute or
   false using the `attr()` method:

   ```
   $("#name-input").attr("disabled", "false");
   ```

If you would like to enable the input field, just change the parameters that you pass into the
`attr` method from `disabled` to `enabled` or `true`.

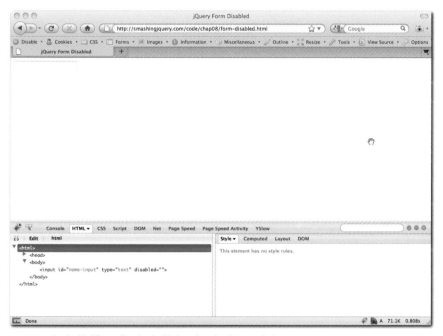

Figure 8-2: The disabled form after the disabled attribute has been applied

HIGHLIGHTING CURRENT FIELDS IN FORMS

In larger forms, you can help users keep track of where they are by highlighting which field
they are currently on. Most browsers have built-in events that highlight the current field, such
as the Firefox example in Figure 8-3.

You can set up a secondary highlight using CSS and the jQuery `focus` event. By adding a
custom highlight, you can ensure that users know how far along they are in any given form.
Using CSS, you can add a highlight as shown on the contact form example from Wufoo
(www.wufoo.com) in Figure 8-4.

A highlighted form field

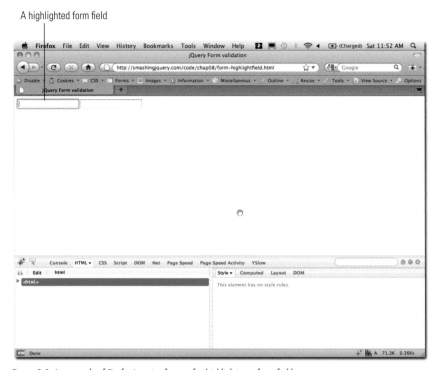

Figure 8-3: An example of Firefox's native feature for highlighting a form field

A highlight

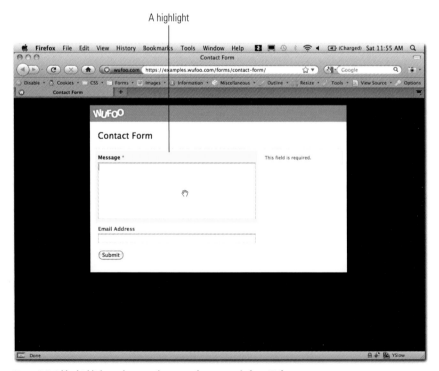

Figure 8-4: Add a highlight as shown on the contact form example from Wufoo

In the following example, you use the focus and blur events to highlight different fields as the user clicks or tabs into them. The final working result is shown in Figure 8-5.

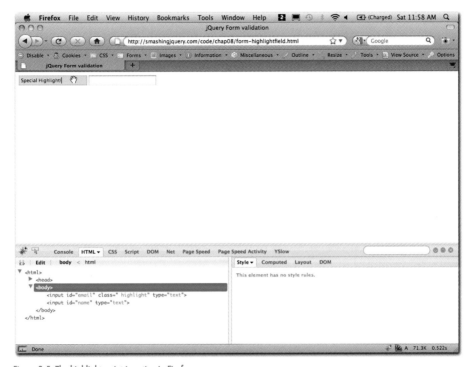

Figure 8-5: The highlight script in action in Firefox

1. Set up the HTML form input element, which you wish to highlight after the page has loaded:

```
<input type="text" id="email-input" />
```

2. Add CSS to control how the highlight will look. In this case, it has a yellow background with 5 pixels of padding:

```
.highlight {background:yellow;padding:5px;}
```

3. Select all input elements and attach a focus event. Inside the event handler function, add a statement that selects the element that was focused into and add a class called highlight. When the input has focus (the user has clicked or tabbed into that field), a highlight class is applied to the input field.

```
$('input').bind('focus', function(){
    $(this).addClass('highlight');
});
```

4. Select all input elements and attach a blur event. Inside the event handler function, add a statement that selects this element and removes the class highlight. When the input has blue (the user has moved out of that field), a highlight class is removed from the input field.

```
$('input').bind('blur', function(){
    $(this).removeClass('highlight');
});
```

CREATING DEFAULT TEXT WITHIN INPUT FIELDS

Setting default text on form fields helps to instruct users on what needs to be entered into the fields. Many Web designers use the default text as form input labels to help save space or change up the design of the forms. You can set a default value using the `value` attribute, but the problem is that if a user clicks into the field, they need to delete what is currently there. In Figure 8-6, the Laithwaites Wine Web site (`www.laithwateswine.com`) has a simple implementation of this: their e-mail newsletter signup field at the bottom left corner of the Web page.

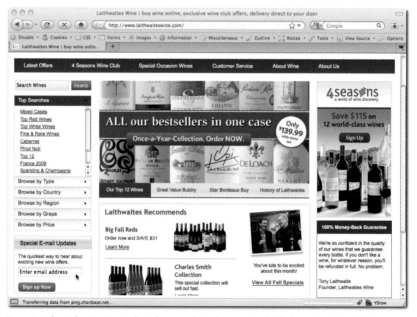

Figure 8-6: The Laithwaites Wine Web site has a simple implementation of default text in an input field

Reproduced from Laithwaiteswine.com

The following script allows you to set default text in a field. If a user clicks into that field, the default text disappears and the user can then enter their own text. If the user doesn't enter any text and then clicks or tabs out of the input field, the default text is added back in. The script uses the `focus` and `blur` events to achieve this effect and an example of the script in action is shown in Figure 8-7.

1. Set up the HTML form input element that should contain the default text:

   ```
   <input type="text" id="email-input" value="Search"/>
   ```

2. Create a variable to hold the value of the default text that will be displayed in the field:

   ```
   var defaultText = "Search";
   ```

Default text

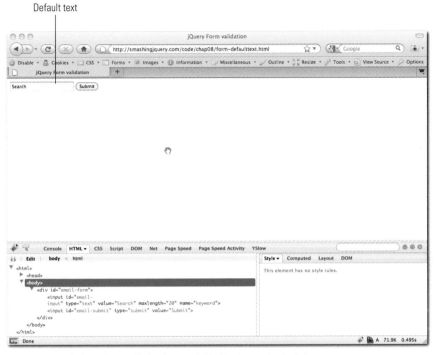

Figure 8-7: The default text being added to the input field after the page has loaded

3. Select the #email-input element and attach a focus event:

```
$("#email-input").bind('focus', function(){
});
```

4. Within the focus event handler function, add an if statement that tests whether the selected input (this) contains any value. If no value is detected, set the value to defaultText. If a value is detected, remove it. Regardless of whether a value exists, the color of the text changes to #333 (dark gray).

```
$("#email-input").bind('focus', function(){
  if ($(this).val() == defaultText) {
    $(this).val('');
  }
  $(this).css('color', '#333')
});
```

5. Next, set up a blur event to fire when the #email-input element loses focus.

```
$("#email-input").bind('blur', function(){
});
```

6. Within the blur event handler function, add a similar if statement that tests whether the selected input (this) contains any value. If no value is detected, set the value to defaultText. Also, change the color of the text to #3333.

```
$("#email-input").bind('blur', function(){
  if ($(this).val() == '') {
    $(this).val(defaultText)
```

```
    }
        $(this).css('color', '#333')
    });
```

LIMITING CHARACTER COUNTS ON INPUT FIELDS

Being able to limit a character count on an input field can be used to restrict how many words are included or how many characters you can include in your status message. The 140-character limit on Twitter (www.twitter.com) has made the limiting character count type of script quite popular in the past year, but it's still always a challenge to keep your message or thought under 140 characters. A character count limit can also display to the user how many characters they have left to work with under the limit.

In this tutorial, I show you how you can make a remaining character script shown in Figure 8-8 and similar to the one used on Twitter.com when creating status updates shorter than 140 characters using the jQuery event `keypress`.

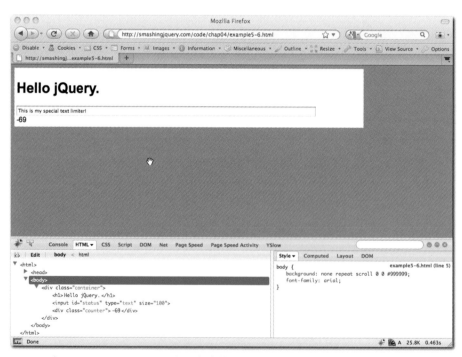

Figure 8-8: The script in action as text is entered into the field and the counter counts down

1. The first step involves setting up the HTML. Set up an input field and give it an ID of `status`. This input is used with the `change` event to detect the characters being added.

   ```
   <textarea cols="50" rows="5" id="status"></textarea>
   ```

2. Add an empty `div` called `counter`, which is where the remaining character number shows up as you type into the input field.

   ```
   <div id="counter"></div>
   ```

3. Set up a variable called maxNum, which will be the maximum amount of characters allowed, and set it to 100.

```
var maxNum = 100;
```

4. Create a selector statement that will match the status element and bind the keypress event to the event handler. The keypress event fires each time a key on the keyboard is depressed and then released, which is the perfect event for testing input on form fields.

```
$('#status').bind({
   keypress : function() {
   });
});
```

5. After the keypress fires, you need to capture the value of the status input field. I have set up a variable called inputText that stores this value. Set up another variable called numChar, which stores the length of the inputText variable. Next, create a variable called charRemain, which holds the result of subtracting numChar from maxNum.

```
$('#status').bind({
   keypress : function() {
      var inputText = $(this).val();
      var numChar = inputText.length;
      var charRemain = numChar - maxNum;
   });
});
```

6. After setting up all the variables, add a conditional statement using a comparison operator to check whether numChar is less than or equal to maxNum. If the expression returns true, select the counter element and change the text within to the variable charRemain, which is the number of remaining characters.

```
$('#status').bind({
   keypress : function() {
      var inputText = $(this).val();
      var numChar = inputText.length;
      var charRemain = numChar - maxNum;
      if (numChar <= maxNum) {
         $('.counter').text(charRemain);
      }
   }
});
```

7. Finally, add an else if statement that checks to see whether the maxNum is greater than or equal to the numChar. If this expression returns true, prevent the user from typing any more letters into the text field using event.preventDefault().

```
$('#status').bind({
   keypress : function() {
      var inputText = $(this).val();
      var numChar = inputText.length;
      var charRemain = numChar - maxNum;
      if (numChar <= maxNum) {
         $('.counter').text(charRemain);
      }
      else if (numChar > maxNum) {
```

189

```
        event.preventDefault();
    }
  });
});
```

CREATING A CHECK ALL CHECK BOXES LINK

You can use jQuery to programmatically select and deselect all of the check boxes on a Web page, a technique that is often used with a preferences section on a Web site. The user sees 20 or so check boxes and a link that lets them select all of the check boxes with a single click. The following tutorial shows you how you can set up a Check All Check Boxes link as shown in Figure 8-9 using the jQuery `click` event and conditional logic.

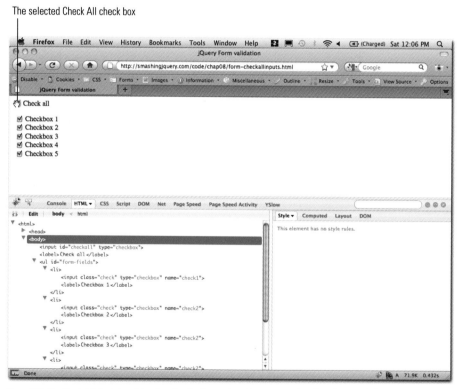

Figure 8-9: The Check All check box link, viewed in Firefox, with Firebug open to show how the input fields are altered on the fly

1. First, set up five check box input elements in an unordered list with an ID of `form-fields` and apply the class `check` to each check box element.

```
<ul id="form-fields">
    <li><input name="check1" class="check" type="checkbox"/> <label>Checkbox 1</
    label></li>
    <li><input name="check2" class="check" type="checkbox"/> <label>Checkbox 2</
    label></li>
```

```
<li><input name="check2" class="check" type="checkbox"/> <label>Checkbox 3</
label></li>
    <li><input name="check2" class="check" type="checkbox"/> <label>Checkbox 4</
label></li>
    <li><input name="check2" class="check" type="checkbox"/> <label>Checkbox 5</
label></li>
    </ul>
```

2. Add an input check box with an ID of `checkall` directly before the list of check boxes. This check box is used to control the checking and un-checking of the inputs.

```
<input type="checkbox" id="checkall" /> <label>Check all</label>
```

3. Select the `#checkall` element and attach a `click` event.

```
$('#checkall').bind('click', function(){
});
```

4. Add a variable called `checkboxes` and a statement that selects all the list items found in the unordered list and searches for all of those with the class check. The variable will hold this matched set:

```
$('#checkall').bind('click', function(){
  var checkboxes = $('#form-fields li').find('.check');
});
```

5. You can optionally add `if` and `else` statements to test if the input `#checkall` element is checked or un-checked, if you want to give the option to check and uncheck all check boxes. If the element is checked, apply the attribute `'checked', 'true'` to all of the check boxes contained in the matched set of the `checkboxes` variable that you set up in the previous step. If the element is not checked, remove the checks from all of the check boxes contained within the variable `checkboxes`.

```
$('#checkall').bind('click', function(){
  var checkboxes = $('#form-fields li').find('.check');
if (this.checked) {
    checkboxes.attr('checked', 'true');
    }
    else {
    checkboxes.attr('checked', 'false');
    };
});
```

When you test the final code in the browser, you should see a smooth, flexible check/uncheck function for managing multiple check boxes.

GETTING THE VALUE OF AN INPUT BOX

Retrieving the value of an input is a very basic form technique, as shown in Figure 8-10, and is useful in many situations. It's incredibly easy to set up and can be used for a number of applications. I commonly use this technique when submitting forms using Ajax when I need to pass over the values from all of the form fields. I review this type of action in Chapter 9.

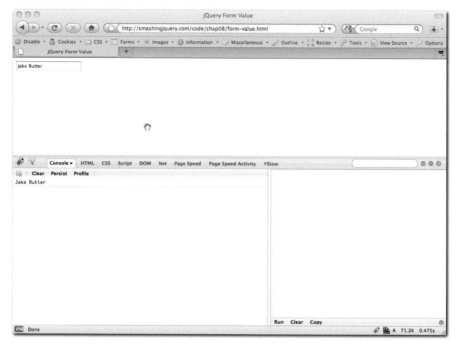

Figure 8-10: The value being captured and displayed through the console in Firebug

1. Set up the HTML form input element that will contain the value that you would like to retrieve from the form element.

   ```
   <input type="text" name="special" id="my-input" value="Very Cool!"/>
   ```

2. Select the #my-input input element and attach the val() method.

   ```
   $("#my-input").val();
   ```

   In order to see if the value is being retrieved, you need to set up a variable and assign it to the value of the my-input field. Then you can set up an alert to test whether this input is passing the value.

3. Add a variable called inputVal and assign as the value of this variable to the statement that you created in step 2.

   ```
   var inputVal = $("#my-input").val();
   ```

   If you would like to get the value of the my-input element as it changes, you can wrap the statement in a change event.

4. Wrap the previous statement in a selector statement that selects the my-input element and attaches a change event to it. This ensures that as data is entered into the field, the value of the variable changes as new data is input.

   ```
   $('#my-input').change(function() {
     var inputVal = $('#my-input').val();
     alert(inputVal);
   });
   ```

In some browsers (including Opera), when the change event is bound to a text input field, the event will only fire on blur, not immediately when the change happens.

RETRIEVING THE VALUE OF A SELECT OPTION

Using jQuery to retrieve the value from a select option is also simple to set up, yet can be very useful in any type of Web site or application. An example of this functionality can be seen on Crutchfield.com, a car and home audio electronics Web site, in the Outfit Your Car section shown in Figure 8-11. Crutchfield allows you to select your car year, model, and make — each time you make a selection, the value of the select option a retrieved and then used to display another option with list items that are filtered by the previous select.

Figure 8-11: The Crutchfield.com Outfit Your Car Wizard

1. Set up the HTML form `select` element that will be used to retrieve the value of the selected option:

```
<select id="my-select" name="question1">
<option value="yes">yes</option>
<option value="no">no</option>
</select>
```

2. Set up a selector statement that selects the `my-select` element and attach a change event to it.

```
$('#my-select').change(function() {
});
```

3. Add a variable to the change event handler called `selectVal` and make it equal to this value (the one that is being selected):

```
$('#my-select').change(function() {
  var selectVal = $(this).val();
  alert(selectVal);
});
```

ADDING SIMPLE E-MAIL VALIDATION TO A FORM

E-mail validation is critical for a newsletter sign-up on a Web site. If users submit a bad e-mail address, it can cost you time and money to get it cleaned out your database. Using jQuery, you can set up simple e-mail validation on a form without having to write a lot of code. This sort of script can be useful on a Web site, such as the Laithwaites Wine special offer email sign-up form in Figure 8-12, where you don't need to validate multiple fields with different types data requiring advanced validation. I demonstrate advanced validation using a popular jQuery validation plug-in at the end of this chapter. It's important to remember that you should never rely solely on client-side JavaScript validation; server-side validation should always be present if client-side is not available.

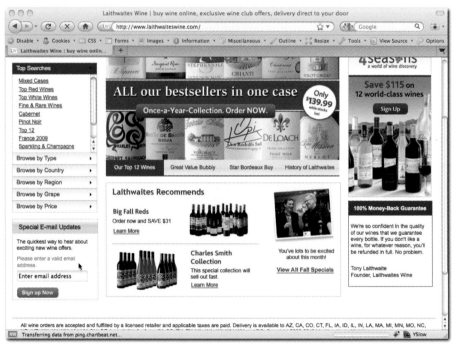

Figure 8-12: The Laithwaites Wine Web site uses simple e-mail validation on their newsletter signup link
Reproduced from Laithwaiteswine.com

The following code uses a regular expression to test that the e-mail address being submitted is in the correct format. The `click` event is attached to the Submit button so that the e-mail address is validated only upon submission. Various error and success messages are shown to the user depending upon whether the e-mail address is invalid or no e-mail address is entered. Upon successful capture of the e-mail address, the form is replaced with a message thanking the user for signing up, as shown in Figure 8-13.

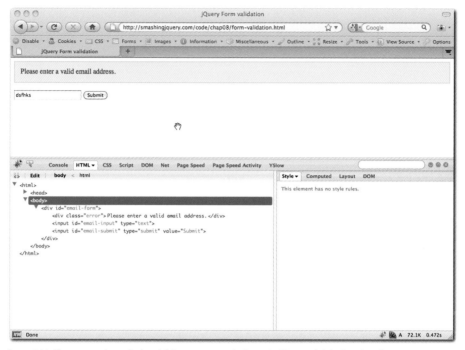

Figure 8-13: The message that is displayed if the user enters a bad e-mail address and clicks the Submit button

Regular expressions are special patterns that can be created to match strings of text and numbers. They are commonly used for matching e-mail addresses, phone numbers, ZIP codes, credit card numbers, and so on. Regular expressions are a standard practice used in most Web programming languages and you can search for specific regular expressions on the Internet to be used in your scripts.

1. Start off by creating a very simple e-mail form with an e-mail input field and a Submit button.

```
<div id="email-form">
  <input type="text" id="email-input" name="email"/>
  <input type="submit" value="Submit" id="email-submit" name="submit"/>
</div>
```

2. Select the #email-submit button and attach a click event to it. Inside of the click event, add a return false statement to ensure that when the button is clicked, the default submission is halted.

```
$("#email-submit").bind('click', function(){
  return false;
});
```

195

3. Create a variable called `emailReg` and set it equal to a regular expression for testing that the e-mail is valid and accurate.

```
$("#email-submit").bind('click', function(){
  var emailReg = /^([a-zA-Z0-9_.-])+@(([a-zA-Z0-9-])+.)+([a-zA-Z0-9]{2,4})+$/;
  return false;
});
```

4. Create a variable called `email` and set the value of `#email-input` using a selector statement.

```
$("#email-submit").bind('click', function(){
  var emailReg = /^([a-zA-Z0-9_.-])+@(([a-zA-Z0-9-])+.)+([a-zA-Z0-9]{2,4})+$/;
  var email = $("#email-input").val();
  return false;
});
```

5. Add a selector statement that selects the `#email-form` element and inserts an error `div` before it. This holds all of the error messaging needed to show the error messages to the user.

```
$("#email-submit").bind('click', function(){
  var emailReg = /^([a-zA-Z0-9_.-])+@(([a-zA-Z0-9-])+.)+([a-zA-Z0-9]{2,4})+$/;
  var email = $("#email-input").val();
  $('#email-form').prepend('<div class="error"></div>');
  return false;
});
```

6. Add an `else if` statement that is used to test whether something has been entered when the Submit button is clicked.

```
$("#email-submit").bind('click', function(){
  var emailReg = /^([a-zA-Z0-9_.-])+@(([a-zA-Z0-9-])+.)+([a-zA-Z0-9]{2,4})+$/;
  var email = $("#email-input").val();
  $('#email-form').prepend('<div class="error"></div>');
  if(email == '') {
  } else if {
  }
  else {
  }
return false;
});
```

7. In the `if` statement, add a `selector` statement to select the `error` `div` and replace it with an `error` element that contains text informing the user that they failed to enter an e-mail address:

```
$("#email-submit").bind('click', function(){
  var emailReg = /^([a-zA-Z0-9_.-])+@(([a-zA-Z0-9-])+.)+([a-zA-Z0-9]{2,4})+$/;
  var email = $("#email-input").val();
  $('#email-form').prepend('<div class="error"></div>');
  if(email == '') {
    $(".error").replaceWith('<div class="error">You forgot to enter an email
  address.</div>');
```

```
  } else if {
  }
  else {
  }
return false;
});
```

8. In the `else if` statement, add a `selector` statement to select the `error div` and replace it with an `error` element that contains text informing the user that they failed to enter an e-mail address. The `else if` statement tests whether the e-mail is valid when compared with the regular expression.

```
$("#email-submit").bind('click', function(){
  var emailReg = /^([\w-\.]+@([\w-]+\.)+[\w-]{2,4})?$/;
          var email = $("#email-input").val();
  $('#email-form').prepend('<div class="error"></div>');
  if(email == '') {
    $(".error").replaceWith('<div class="error">You forgot to enter an email
  address.</div>');
  } else if(!emailReg.test(email)) {
    $(".error").replaceWith('<div class="error">Please enter a valid email
  address.</div>');
  }
  else {
  }
return false;
});
```

9. Finally, add an `else` statement that will replace the e-mail form elements with a message that informs the user that they have subscribed. This message is displayed only if the `if` and `else if` statements pass their tests.

```
$("#email-submit").bind('click', function(){
  var emailReg = /^([\w-\.]+@([\w-]+\.)+[\w-]{2,4})?$/;
  var email = $("#email-input").val();
  $('#email-form').prepend('<div class="error"></div>');
  if(email == '') {
    $(".error").replaceWith('<div class="error">You forgot to enter an email
  address.</div>');
  } else if(!emailReg.test(email)) {
    $(".error").replaceWith('<div class="error">Please enter a valid email
  address.</div>');
  }
  else {
    $("#email-form").html('<div class="success">Thank you, you have been sub-
  scribed.</div>');
  }
return false;
});
```

Here are some ways to improve this script:

- You could change the `click` event to a `change` event and bind it to the input field instead of the button if you wanted to set up a real-time validation that occurs as the user types into the input field. This would require some additional coding to set up the correct message to inform the user of what is required for the field and so on.

- Add an error highlight to the e-mail input field after submitting the form if the wrong data has been entered.

- Use the popular regular expressions in Table 8.1 to add more fields to your form and validate different types of data.

Regular expressions can be found all over the Web. Check out Table 8.1 to see a summary of some of the more popular regular expressions used on the Web today.

Table 8.1   Other Popular Regular Expressions for Form Validation

Usage	Example
Phone Number	(/^[0-9-+]+$/)
Date (dd/mm/yyyy)	(/^\d{1,2}\/\/\d{1,2}\/\/\d{4}$/)
Numbers only	(^[0-9]+$)
Letters only	(^[A-Za-z]+$)

COPYING THE CONTENTS OF ONE FIELD INTO ANOTHER

If you have ever purchased something online, you probably had to fill out a form by entering your billing address and shipping address. For most consumers, this information is the same, so such forms often have a Same As Billing Address check box that says "same as billing" that copies over all the form fields from billing to shipping, preventing the customer from needing to re-enter all of that information. This check box uses a copy field functionality. Not only does it save the customer time, but also reduces the likelihood of them mis-entering data. Figure 8-14 shows an example of a copy field check box on the checkout page of Best Buy's Web site (`www.bestbuy.com`).

The following script shows how to set up a copy field check box, which can be added to any form. It doesn't have to be a billing/shipping form, as it is in the following example. The working script is shown in Figure 8-15.

1. Start off by creating a two sets of address input fields. The first set contains the billing address and the second set contains the shipping address. Add an input check box before the fields to control the copying of the fields from the billing to shipping.

```
<label>Copy Fields</label>
<input type="checkbox" id="copy-fields"/>

<div id="billing-address">
<h2>Billing Address</h2>
<label>First Name</label>
<input type="text" id="b-first-name"/>

<label>Last Name</label>
<input type="text" id="b-last-name"/>
</div>

<div id="shipping-address">
<h2>Shipping Address</h2>
<label>First Name</label>
<input type="text" id="s-first-name"/>

<label>First Name</label>
<input type="text" id="s-last-name"/>
</div>
```

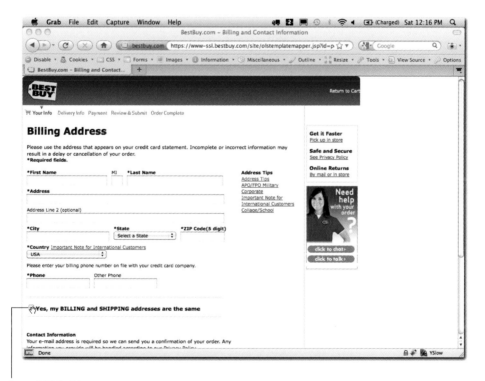

A copy field check box

Figure 8-14: An example of a copy field check box on the checkout page of the Best Buy Web site

2. Select the `#copy-fields` input element and attach a `click` event to it.

```
$('#copy-fields').bind('click', function(){
});
```

3. Add a variable for each field that you would like to copy over. Each variable stores the value for a field located within the billing address.

```
$('#copy-fields').bind('click', function(){
  var billFName = $('#b-first-name').val();
  var billLName = $('#b-last-name').val();
});
```

4. Create an `if else` statement to test whether the copy fields element is checked before performing any actions within the `click` event.

```
$('#copy-fields').bind('click', function(){
  var billFName = $('#b-first-name').val();
  var billLName = $('#b-last-name').val();
  if (this.checked) {
  }
  else {
  };
});
```

5. If the `copy-fields` element is checked, set the values of the corresponding shipping fields equal to their counterparts in the billing fields.

```
$('#copy-fields').bind('click', function(){
  var billFName = $('#b-first-name').val();
  var billLName = $('#b-last-name').val();
  if (this.checked) {
    $('#s-first-name').val(billFName);
    $('#s-last-name').val(billLName);
  }
  else {
  };
});
```

6. You need to set up an alternative option within the `else` statement that clears all the shipping input fields when the `copy fields` input is unchecked.

```
$('#copy-fields').bind('click', function(){
  var billFName = $('#b-first-name').val();
  var billLName = $('#b-last-name').val();
  if (this.checked) {
    $('#s-first-name').val(billFName);
    $('#s-last-name').val(billLName);
  }
  else {
    $('.shipping-address input').val('');
  };
});
```

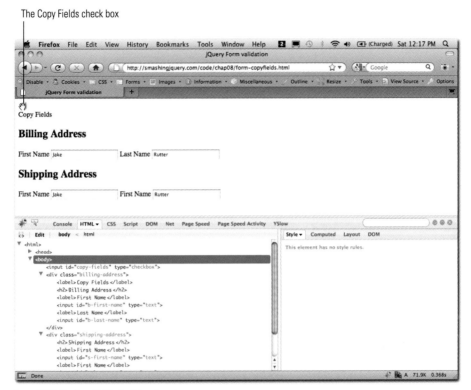

Figure 8-15: The Copy Fields check box in action

ENHANCING FORMS WITH PLUG-INS

Incorporating third-party or open source plug-ins into your Web site or application allows you to code faster and offer better form validation or even interaction. Due to the large community of followers and supporters who work with jQuery, a very wide range of plug-ins exists. You can find plug-ins that do anything from setting default text on a field to validating every field on your form.

I use plug-ins when creating something myself is not an option due to a limited timeframe. In most cases, if someone has already done a good job of creating a plug-in, I find it unnecessary to try to write my own anyway. In this section, I review two plug-ins that I frequently use with forms: qTip and Validate.

INCORPORATING QTIP INTO YOUR WEB SITE

qTip is a jQuery plug-in that allows you to easily set up advanced tooltips on any element. The tooltips can contain both static and dynamic content. qTip has many features that make it an extremely attractive and lightweight plug-in such as cross-browser compatibility with IE, Firefox, Safari, Opera, and Chrome. On those browsers that aren't supported, the tooltip degrades gracefully. qTip can be applied to any element on the page, including paragraph tags, as shown in Figure 8-16.

I like to use tooltips with forms to give the user tips on what he needs to enter. You could very easily create a basic tooltip from scratch and apply it to an element like I explained in Chapter 5, but qTip comes with a complete API of methods, which allow you to change the styling to fit within your Web site, placement on the page, animation effects, and add dynamic content.

The major benefit of qTip is all of the configuration options that you can set up; the documentation on qTip is wonderful. That's why I continue to use it. Some plug-ins have horrible documentation and poor support that make them difficult to use. When I come across a plug-in with bad documentation, I usually just try to write something similar myself instead.

A tooltip created with qTip

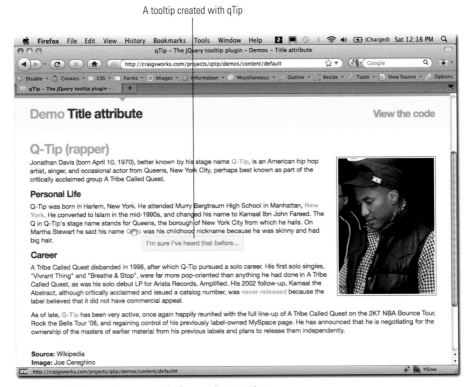

Figure 8-16: qTip being used on a paragraph of text on the qTip Web site

Reproduced from CraigWorks.com

Table 8.2 outlines the various options available for the qTip jQuery plug-in.

Table 8.2   qTip Plug-In Options

Class	Description
content	Allows you to specify what appears in the tooltip
position	Allows you to specify where the tooltip will show up in your DOM
show	Allows you to specify the effects used to show the tooltip
hide	Allows you to specify the effects used to hide the tooltip

Class	Description
style	Allows you to specify how the tooltip is styled
api	Allows you to set up callback functions

For a complete list of options, visit http://craigsworks.com/projects/qtip/docs/reference/

CREATING A BASIC FORM FIELD QTIP USING THE TITLE ATTRIBUTE

In this section, I show you how to incorporate the qTip plug-in on your Web site and set up a tooltip on a form element. The tooltip instructs the user on what data needs to be entered into the field they have clicked on. You use the `title` attribute to set the text that you wish to display. Using the `title` attribute allows users who do not have JavaScript enabled to still see the tooltip if they hover their mouse pointer over the input field, although it won't look as pretty.

1. Set up an input field and give it an ID of `email`.

```
<input type="text" id="email" />
```

2. When using a plug-in with jQuery, you always need to include the path to your plug-in at the top of your page. It should always be included directly after the jQuery library, but before any jQuery code that you have created that references the plug-in.

```
<script type="text/javascript" src="js/jquery.qtip-1.0.0-rc3.min.js"></script>
```

3. Add a `title` attribute to the text input field. The text contained within the `title` attribute is used as part of the tooltip.

```
<input type="text" id="email" title="Please enter your email address."/>
```

4. Create a `selector` statement that selects any and all inputs that contain a `title` attribute and apply the `qtip()` method. If no options are passed into the qTip method, the default configuration is applied.

```
$('input[title]').qtip({});
```

5. Customize the qTip on your page by passing in options from the qTip API. The following code is an example of the options I chose to pass in to achieve the qTip tooltip shown in Figure 8-17:

```
$('input[title]').qtip({
    style: { color: 'black', name: 'blue', tip: true },
    position: { corner: { target: 'bottomMiddle' }},
    show: { when: { event: 'focus' }},
    hide: { when: { event: 'blur' }}
});
```

USING THE JQUERY VALIDATE PLUG-IN TO VALIDATE YOUR FORMS

The jQuery Validate plug-in has been on the scene since July 2006 and is one of the oldest, most well-supported validation plug-ins available. You have a lot of options when it comes to setting up form validation on your Web site or application, as I've discussed throughout this chapter. If you're looking to add simple form validation such as validating a few input fields, I would advise you to write it yourself in jQuery.

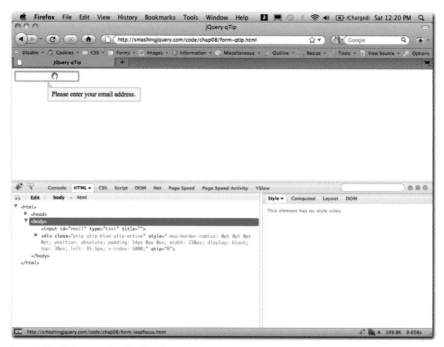

Figure 8-17: qTip being used to show form hints

The Validate plug-in is a robust solution that includes standard regular expressions to validate phone numbers, e-mail addresses, dates, and credit card numbers, just to name a few. It places error and notification messages directly into the DOM via many different types of events such as `submit`, `keypress`, and `focus`. The Validate plug-in has an extensive API that offers full customization of how you validate the data. You can also opt for an out-of-the-box implementation.

The Validate plug-in is perfect for a scenario where you have a registration form that requires first and last name, address, city, state, zip and a unique username and password containing at least five characters with upper and lower case characters. A long form that has multiple rules for each different input field and you want to give your users a helping hand as they work through the fields.

Figure 8-18 shows the Validate plug-in being applied to a form. If the user clicks the Submit button without having properly filled in each field, all of the required form fields have text appended to them outlining the required fields.

ADDING SIMPLE VALIDATION TO A CONTACT FORM

By using the Validate plug-in, you can save yourself a ton of time by setting up each individual input validation script. In the following tutorial, I demonstrate how you can apply default validation to your form with just one line of jQuery and some simple additions to your form.

1. Set up a contact form that contains fields for name, e-mail address, phone number, message, and a Submit button.

```
<form id="contact-form">
```

```html
<ul>
    <li><label>Name</label>
    <input type="text" id="name" name="name"/>
    </li>
    <li><label>Email</label>
    <input type="text" id="email" name="email"/>
    </li>
    <li><label>Phone</label>
    <input type="text" id="phone" name="phone"/>
    </li>
    <li><label>Message</label>
    <textarea name="message" id="message"></textarea>
    </li>
    <li><input type="submit"/></li>
</ul>
</form>
```

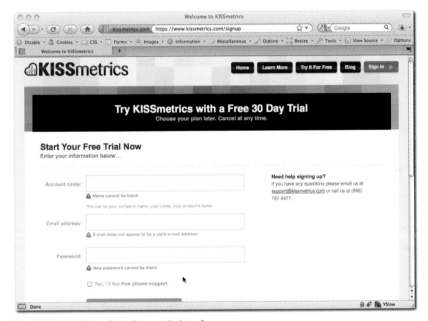

Figure 8-18: The Validate plug-in being applied to a form

Reproduced from KissMetrics.com

2. When using a plug-in with jQuery, you always need to include the path to your plug-in at the top of your page. It should always be included directly after the jQuery library, but before any jQuery code that you have created that references the plug-in.

```html
<script src="js/jquery.validate.min.js" type="text/javascript"></script>
```

3. Add a `document.ready` function. Within this function, select the `contact-form` element and apply the `validate()` method to it.

```javascript
$(document).(function() {
    $("#contact-form").validate();
});
```

It's that easy! The validate plug-in has now been applied to your Web site. If you bring up the Web page in Firefox and click the Submit button, however, you won't see any validation occurring because you have not set any up yet, as shown in Figure 8-19.

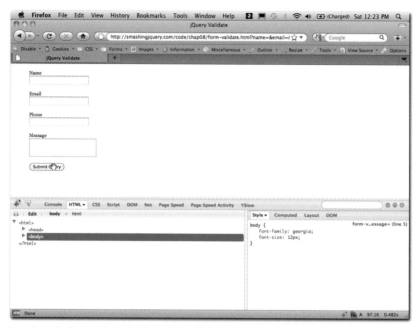

Figure 8-19: The form is submitted with no validation firing

You can quite easily add validation to the form using various classes. This is the quickest and simplest way to do it, but you cannot control the message or setup any advanced rules such as an input field needs to have a minimum of five characters and a maximum of ten characters and so on. It's pretty much out-of-the-box functionality. I review advanced options in greater detail in the next tutorial.

- Add `class="required"` to any field that is mandatory
- Add `class="email"` to validate for an email address
- Add `class="digits"` to validate that only numbers were entered into the field

4. Adjust the form fields to include the validation classes.

```
<form id="contact-form">
    <ul>
        <li><label>Name</label>
        <input type="text" id="name" name="name" class="required"/>
        </li>
        <li><label>Email</label>
        <input type="text" id="email" name="email" class="required email"/>
        </li>
        <li><label>Phone</label>
```

```
          <input type="text" id="phone" name="phone" class="required digits"/>
          </li>
          <li><label>Message</label>
          <textarea name="message" id="message" class="required"></textarea>
          </li>
          <li><input type="submit"/></li>
      </ul>
  </form>
```

After adding the required and `email/digit` classes to the input elements within the form and after submitting it, you see an error validation message appear, as shown in Figure 8-20. If you start to enter an e-mail address, the message changes from `This field is required` to `Please enter a valid email address`. The message changes as you type, so as soon as it accepts that the e-mail address you've entered is correct, it stops displaying messages.

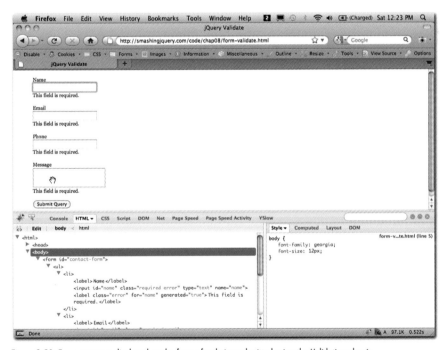

Figure 8-20: Error messages displayed on the form after being submitted using the Validation plug-in

Refer to the Table 8.3 for the full list of options that you can apply with the validate plug-in.

Table 8.3   Validate Options

Class	Description
required	Requires a value
minlength	Requires a minimum length

continued

Table 8.3   (continued)

Class	Description
maxlength	Requires a maximum length
email	Requires a valid e-mail address
url	Requires a valid URL
date	Requires a valid date
number	Requires a valid decimal number
digits	Requires a valid digit
creditcard	Requires a valid credit card
accept	Requires a certain file extension
equalTo	Requires two elements to be equal to each other, often used with password and confirm password

For complete documentation, visit: http://docs.jquery.com/Plugins/Validation

Here are two ways in which you can set up these options with the `validate` plug-in:

- Embed the options into the form using classes:

```
<input type="text" id="email" name="email" class="required email"/>
```

- Pass the options into the `validate` method using JavaScript Object Notation (JSON):

```
rules: {
  email : {
    required:true
  }
}
```

ADDING ADVANCED VALIDATION RULES AND MESSAGES TO A CONTACT FORM

The Validate plug-in has many extremely flexible options that can be added to any form to ensure all of the data is validated and that the user is being notified when information is not correct. Using the HTML from the previous form, in this section, I show you how you can use the advanced options from the Validate API to set up validation on fields and to display custom messages as shown in Figure 8-21.

1. Add CSS to style the form and error messages that are created from the Validate plug-in.

```
body{font-family:georgia; font-size:12px}
label{display:block}
ul{list-style-type:none}
ul li{margin:15px 0}
.error, .notice, .success{padding:.8em; margin-bottom:1em; border:2px solid
  #ddd}
.error{background:#FBE3E4; color:#8a1f11; border-color:#FBC2C4}
.notice{background:#FFF6BF; color:#514721; border-color:#FFD324}
```

```
.success{background:#E6EFC2; color:#264409; border-color:#C6D880}
#contact-form{width:400px}
```

2. Set up a contact form that contains fields for name, e-mail address, phone number, a message, and a Submit button.

```
<form id="contact-form">
    <ul>
        <li><label>Name</label>
        <input type="text" id="name" name="name"/>
        </li>
        <li><label>Email</label>
        <input type="text" id="email" name="email"/>
        </li>
        <li><label>Phone</label>
        <input type="text" id="phone" name="phone"/>
        </li>
        <li><label>Message</label>
        <textarea name="message" id="message"></textarea>
        </li>
        <li><input type="submit"/></li>
    </ul>
</form>
```

3. When using a plug-in with jQuery, you always need to include the path to your plug-in at the top of your page. It should always be included directly after the jQuery library, but before any jQuery code that you have created that references the plug-in.

```
<script src="js/jquery.validate.min.js" type="text/javascript"></script>
```

4. Select the `contact-form` element and apply the `validate()` method to it.

```
$("#contact-form").validate();
```

5. First, set up the advanced rules for the form elements that need to be validated. The rules are passed into the `validate` method using JavaScript Object Notation (JSON). The input elements are referenced using their `name` attribute. Name, e-mail address, and phone numbers are required. E-mail addresses are validated for being real addresses.

```
$("#contact-form").validate({
  rules: {
    name: "required",
    email: {
      required: true,
      email: true
    },
    phone: "required"
  }
});
```

6. Next, add the custom messages that you want to display. You can set up as many or as few as you want. If you don't declare a custom error message for a field, the default message `This field is required` is used. In the same format as the rules, set up a messages branch. Within the curly brackets, add each message using the `name` attribute followed by a colon and the text string of the message.

```
$("#contact-form").validate({
  rules: {
    name: "required",
    email: {
      required: true,
      email: true
    },
    phone: "required"
  },
  messages: {
    name: "Name is required.",
    email: "Email is required.",
    phone: "Phone is required."
  }
});
```

Voila! If you load this page in Firefox and submit the form, all of the fields are validated and the custom messages you have created are displayed. It's that easy. The beauty of the Validate plug-in is that it's client-side, so no page refresh is necessary. After the errors have fired, if you re-enter the data, the field validates as you type, which is an added bonus to this already amazing plug-in.

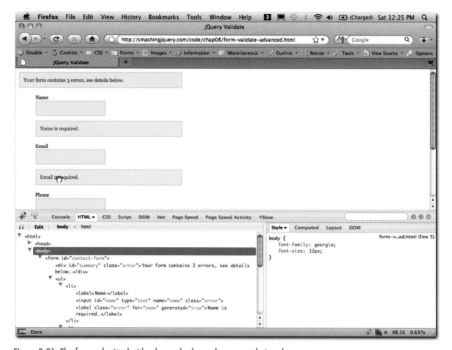

Figure 8-21: The form submitted with advanced rules and messages being shown

If you spend some time playing around with this plug-in, you can achieve great results. If you run into any issues with the setup of the plug-in, refer to the documentation or search Google for an answer. Chances are that someone has run into a similar issue, especially because this plug-in has been around for almost five years now and is still supported.

IV

EXPLORING ADVANCED JQUERY

Chapter 9: Working with Dynamic Data and Ajax

Chapter 10: Creating and Using jQuery Plug-Ins

Chapter 11: Developing for the Mobile Web with jQuery

Chapter 12: Finding jQuery Resources

9

WORKING WITH DYNAMIC DATA AND AJAX

JQUERY IS CAPABLE of DOM manipulation and does it really well. What you might not be aware of is that jQuery has various methods that allow for Ajax-type interactions. Many people have misconceptions about what Ajax is and what it isn't. The acronym *Ajax* became a big buzzword around the dawn of Web 2.0. Web designers, developers, and marketers all claimed they could do Ajax, but what does that mean? It means being able to design, build, and market Web sites and applications that transmit data back and forth behind the scenes — letting you present a much richer user experience to your customers.

In this chapter, I review how you can use jQuery to perform Ajax-type requests with server-side data. I use code examples that I built in previous chapters and show you how you can add dynamic content to create self-updating widgets. I won't instruct you on how to set up the server-side component, which requires knowledge of a backend programming language such as PHP or ASP.net and is beyond the scope of the book. I do show you how to interact with a few popular server-side third-party APIs (application programming interfaces) to build dynamic integrations that can pull data from their API's and present it on a Web site using jQuery.

DISCOVERING AJAX

Ajax stands for Asynchronous JavaScript and XML. The lesser-known buzzword is XHR, which stands for XML HTTP Request. If you use Firebug for Firefox a lot, you've probably seen Ajax requests labeled XHR, a type of Ajax request, as shown in Figure 9-1.

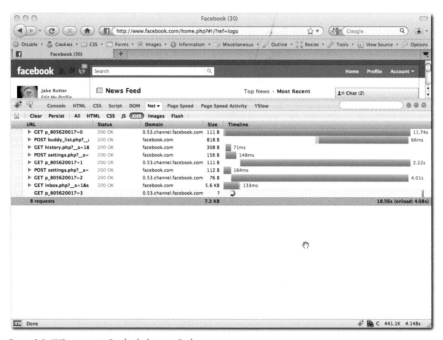

Figure 9-1: XHR requests in Facebook shown in Firebug

Ajax is a group of patterns and techniques that allow client-side applications to pass data back and forth with server-side applications without requiring a page refresh or reload. Ajax creates a seemingly seamless flow of data behind the scenes, which is why *asynchronous* is part of its name. It passes data back and forth asynchronously. Ajax requests are performed via POST or GET requests.

Ajax requests can be done synchronously and sometimes *must* be. (Say, for example, you are loading an external configuration file and you do not want the rest of the script to proceed until you are sure that the config file has been loaded successfully.) I focus on asynchronous requests only throughout this chapter.

Facebook offers a great example of Ajax in action. When you log on to Facebook, you typically see your news feed of your friends' status updates and latest activities. On the left is a list of your friends who are currently online. This is controlled through an Ajax request to the server that constantly checks to see whether any of your friends are online. Perhaps one of your friends notices you are online and opens a chat session — that's another Ajax request. While you are chatting with your friend, two other friends update their statuses, so a message appears at the top of your news feed notifying you of the new news feed items. All of these events are occurring through Ajax requests; you haven't had to refresh/reload the page once. Quite amazing!

Gmail incorporates a lot of Ajax functionality with such features as a built-in real-time chat client, the ability to make phone calls through your Gmail account, drag-and-drop functionality for moving messages around, and auto-completion for the To field of an e-mail message. Gmail is another great example of Ajax being used to its fullest capacity as shown in Figure 9-2.

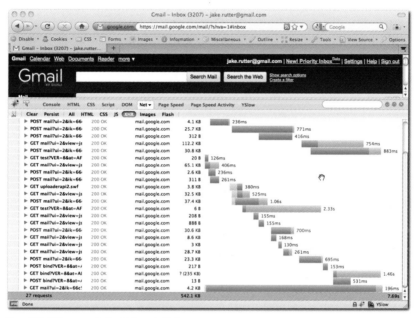

Figure 9-2: XHR requests in Gmail shown in Firebug

Reproduced from 2010 © Google

LOADING DYNAMIC CONTENT FROM A WEB PAGE

You can use the jQuery `load` method to include HTML content from another location on your Web server into your current Web page. The `load` method takes the URL of the content as an argument passed into the method. The URL needs to be set up as relative path from the page where you are referencing it. The `load` method only allows you to include content that lives on the same server or domain.

If you would like to include content from another domain, you need to set up a JSON-P request with a Web service, API, or Web server that can support JSON-P, which I review later in the chapter.

```
$(selector).load(URL)
```

If you would like something to occur after or only if the content has been loaded, you can provide a callback function to the `load` method either as an anonymous function or a function name:

```
$(selector).load(URL, function(){
alert('The content was loaded');
})
```

If the document does not contain the selector that you are trying to match, the content won't load.

LOADING ALL OF THE CONTENT

If you would like to include all of the content from a separate HTML file, you need to set up a `selector` statement, attach the `load` method, and pass in the URL of the HTML file as a relative path.

In the following example, I have set up an external HTML page with some dummy content using `H2` and `P` tags. I have another HTML Web page set up with an empty `#content` div that I want to load the content into. I use a `load()` statement to pull in the content and display it on the page, as shown in Figure 9-3.

1. Create the HTML content that you would like to load. If you do not add any CSS styling to this content, it inherits the styling from the parent page. Save this file as `ajax-content.html`.

```
<!doctype html>
  <head>
    <title>jQuery Content</title>
    <style>
    body {font-family:georgia;font-size:12px;}
    </style>
  </head>
  <body>
  <h1>Dolor Neque Placerat Sem Lacus Senectus</h1>

  <h2>Posuere Eleifend Amet</h2>
  <p>Scelerisque. Vivamus at interdum aliquam turpis euismod adipiscing dolor
  nec fusce nulla amet facilisis fusce montes donec enim integer  habitant
  euismod dignissim sodales eu dui Lacus <em>potenti</em> gravida gravida. Amet
  cum. Accumsan hac.</p>

  <p>Ligula. Sodales, suscipit elementum. Faucibus tincidunt feugiat con-
  sectetuer cum accumsan platea mauris augue <strong>curae;</strong> semper
  risus. Dapibus Scelerisque. Ante proin leo. Dolor, arcu sociis mattis conubia
  nisi mi venenatis montes molestie mi, per. Fermentum enim iaculis magnis
  nonummy.</p>

  <p>Rutrum <em>tortor</em> aptent vestibulum aliquet. Sollicitudin, mattis cras
  ac accumsan bibendum pellentesque platea sociosqu parturient ad ligula. Sociis
  nisi mus venenatis maecenas vel quisque. Volutpat turpis praesent tempus
  nulla.</p>
  </body>
</html>
```

2. Create a `#content` element on the current Web page. This is where the content will be loaded into. You can also load the content into a specific tag such as `body`.

```
<div id="content"></div>
```

3. Create a `document.ready` handler and add a statement inside of it that selects the `#content` element and loads the `ajax-content.html` file into the page.

```
$(document).ready(function() {
  $('#content').load('ajax-content.html');
});
```

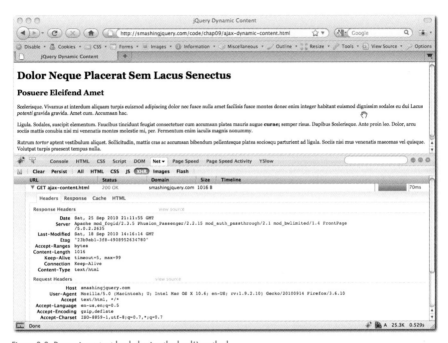

Figure 9-3: Dynamic content loaded using the load() method

HANDLING ERRORS IF THE CONTENT YOU LOAD IS MISSING

What happens if the content you are including on the page is missing? Your users won't see the content and might end up leaving the site having had a bad experience. To further improve upon the preceding script, you could pass in a callback function that checks to see if the file exists. If the file doesn't exist or if some other issue prevents it from being loaded, you can display a message to the user. Error-handling is a good practice that should always be built into any script that you create.

The `load` method can handle a callback function with three XHR properties that can be passed into it as referenced in Table 9.1. Use the `XMLHttpRequest` object to look for different response codes and perform different actions based on the response.

```
$(selector).load(URL, function(responseText, textStatus, XMLHttpRequest){
// test for different response codes
})
```

Table 9.1   XHR Request Properties

Metho.d	Description
responseText	Returns the response data as a string
textStatus	Returns the response data as XML data
XMLHttpRequest	Returns the status-number (for example, "404" for "Not Found" or "200" for "OK")

Source: www.w3schools.com/dom/dom_http.asp

Using the preceding code, I review how to add some additional jQuery to the function to look for and catch any errors using server response codes from Table 9.2 and the example shown in Figure 9-3. Server response codes are passed from the Web server to the browser through the HTTP protocol. The response codes are communicated through the XMLHttpRequest. status property. You can also find these response codes in the XHR pane of Firebug: Refer to Figure 9-2, which shows Gmail Ajax requests in Firebug.

Table 9.2   Common Server Error Response Codes

Code	Definition
200	Success
301	Moved permanently
302	Moved temporarily
400	Bad request
401	Unauthorized
403	Forbidden
404	Not found
500	Server error

1. Add a callback function to the end of the `load` method and pass in the three properties that the method can accept.

```
$('#content').load('ajax-content-1.html',
  function(responseText, textStatus, XMLHttpRequest){
});
```

2. Inside of the callback function, create an `if/else` conditional statement that looks for any 404 or 500 errors. If an error is encountered, a message is displayed to the user, as shown in Figure 9-4. Otherwise, the content is loaded and no messages are shown.

```
$('#content').load('ajax-content-1.html', function(responseText, textStatus,
  XMLHttpRequest){
    if (XMLHttpRequest.status == 404 || XMLHttpRequest.status == 500) {
      $('#content').html('There has been an error, please try again later.');
    }
    else {
    // do nothing
    }
        });
```

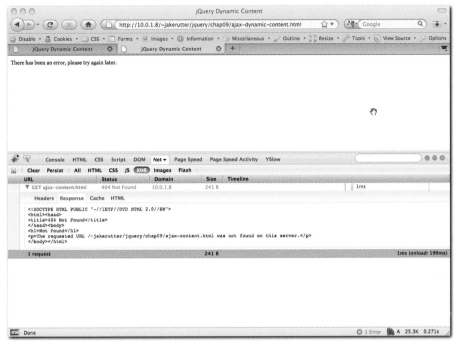

Figure 9-4: A 404 error message appears when requested content is not available

219

If you are loading a large amount of content, consider showing a loading animation to let them know that content is being loaded. You can add a statement preceding the `load` method that adds a loading graphic to the `#content` element before the element is replaced with the loaded content. If the user is loading a small external content file, she may never even see the loading graphic, but it's a good precautionary measure for larger files or slower network connections.

```
$('#content').html('<img src="images/loading.gif" alt=""/>');
$('#content').load('ajax-content-1.html', function(responseText, textStatus,
 XMLHttpRequest)
  {
  if (XMLHttpRequest.status == 404 || XMLHttpRequest.status == 500) {
    $('#content').html('There has been an error, please try again later.');
  }
  else {
  // do nothing
  }
});
```

LOADING SECTIONS OF THE CONTENT

If you would like to load only specific sections of the content from an external HTML file, you can do so by passing in the `ID`, class, or tag name into the selector statement.

```
$(selector).load(URL class or id or tag name)
```

In the following example, I use the same external HTML page with some dummy content using H2 and P tags. One of the paragraphs has a .special class applied to the paragraph tag. I have another HTML Web page set up with an empty #content div to which I want to load the content. In this case, I load in only the content contained within the paragraph tag with a class of .special, as shown in Figure 9-5.

1. Create the HTML content that you would like to load in. Add class="special" to the second paragraph. This is used to grab only this content in the next step. Resave this file as ajax-content.html.

```html
<!doctype html>
  <head>
    <title>jQuery Content</title>
    <style>
    body {font-family:georgia;font-size:12px;}
    </style>
  </head>
  <body>
  <h1>Dolor Neque Placerat Sem Lacus Senectus</h1>

  <h2>Posuere Eleifend Amet</h2>
  <p>Scelerisque. Vivamus at interdum aliquam turpis euismod adipiscing dolor
  nec fusce nulla amet facilisis fusce montes donec enim integer habitant euismod
  dignissim sodales eu dui Lacus <em>potenti</em> gravida gravida. Amet cum.
  Accumsan hac.</p>

  <p class="special">Ligula. Sodales, suscipit elementum. Faucibus tincidunt
  feugiat consectetuer cum accumsan platea mauris augue <strong>curae;</strong>
  semper risus. Dapibus Scelerisque. Ante proin leo. Dolor, arcu sociis mattis
  conubia nisi mi venenatis montes molestie mi, per. Fermentum enim iaculis
  magnis nonummy.</p>

  <p>Rutrum <em>tortor</em> aptent vestibulum aliquet. Sollicitudin, mattis cras
  ac accumsan bibendum pellentesque platea sociosqu parturient ad ligula. Sociis
  nisi mus venenatis maecenas vel quisque. Volutpat turpis praesent tempus
  nulla.</p>
  </body>
</html>
```

2. Create a #content element on the current Web page. If the document that you are loading does not contain the selector that you are trying to match, the content loads but nothing is inserted into the #content element.

```html
<div id="content"></div>
```

3. Create a document.ready statement and add a statement inside of it that selects the #content element and loads the ajax-content.html file into the page. Notice that the .special class has been added into the load statement. This ensures that only this content is added to the page.

```javascript
$(document).ready(function() {
    $('#content').load('ajax-content.html .special');
});
```

Figure 9-5: Only the content wrapped with the .special class is included on the page

SUBMITTING FORMS USING GET AND POST

GET and POST requests are very similar; they can both transmit data from forms to a server-side process. Either type of request has its pros and cons, but usually the backend developer defines the type of request and the Web developer or designer is required to interface with it.

Understanding GET Requests

GET requests submit data to a server-side process by passing parameters in the query string. A query string is used to pass form data along from one Web page or application to another Web page or application. The server-side process always picks up the key:value pairs from the URL and the content of the page may be altered based on the query string in the URL directly.

Here's an example of a query string:

```
http://www.website.com?keyword=product&page=5&size=5&color=brown
```

By passing parameters in the query string, the risk is that the query string can be easily changed by a user. If the proper security precautions are not set up on the server-side script, hackers can infiltrate and cause havoc to your Web site or application. Using GET requests is not recommended for unsafe data such as financial information or passwords or data you wish to be passed around or shown to users. GET requests can be bookmarked and shared, as shown in Figure 9-6, a Google search results page.

Figure 9-6: Google search results that use a GET request

Reproduced from 2010© Google

Understanding POST Requests

POST requests are different from GET requests in that they post the data to the server-side process behind the scenes, which makes them safer, especially for transmitting sensitive data. POST requests can also handle long requests when passing lots of data to the server-side program better than GET requests can.

If you have ever submitted a POST request and tried to refresh the page, you got a notice about how the page needs to resend the data to the server. This is a result of the way POST requests are structured.

POST and GET requests are handled in jQuery using the ajax() method. This method can be passed many different settings to control what is sent to the server and what is received.

```
$.ajax ({
type: 'POST',
url: url,
data: data,
success: success,
dataType: datatype
});
```

If you were to write this method in native JavaScript, you would end up with something similar to the following code. You need to write different XMLHttpRequest methods for different browsers. jQuery handles all of this in one nice, clean function.

```
function loadXMLDoc()
{
if (window.XMLHttpRequest)
{
  // code for IE7+, Firefox, Chrome, Opera, Safari
  xmlhttp=new XMLHttpRequest();
}
else
{
  // code for IE6, IE5
  xmlhttp=new ActiveXObject("Microsoft.XMLHTTP");
}
  xmlhttp.onreadystatechange=function()
{
  if (xmlhttp.readyState==4 && xmlhttp.status==200)
  {
  document.getElementById("myDiv").innerHTML=xmlhttp.responseText;
  }
}
  xmlhttp.open("GET","ajax_info.txt",true);
  xmlhttp.send();
}
```

USING POST TO SUBMIT CONTACT FORMS WITHOUT PAGE RELOAD

The POST request is perfectly suited for submitting contact forms because they usually contain personal and confidential information that you need to keep secure. POST requests are also common in login and registration forms, as seen on the Mint.com registration screen, shown in Figure 9-7.

Setting up a POST submission with jQuery is incredibly easy. As with most jQuery methods, you have a choice of longhand and shorthand ways of setting up the POST submission. In the following two code examples, the first piece of code uses the POST method, which is the longhand way. The second piece of code uses the Ajax method, which is the shorthand and preferred way because it can handle multiple types of requests.

```
$.post(url, [data], [success], dataType);

$.ajax({
  url: url,
  data: data,
  success: success,
  dataType: dataType
});
```

Testing POST submissions in the browser can be challenging because you cannot see the parameters being passed in the query string. Using Firebug, you can monitor XHR requests and view the parameters that are being passed behind the scenes, as shown in Figure 9-8.

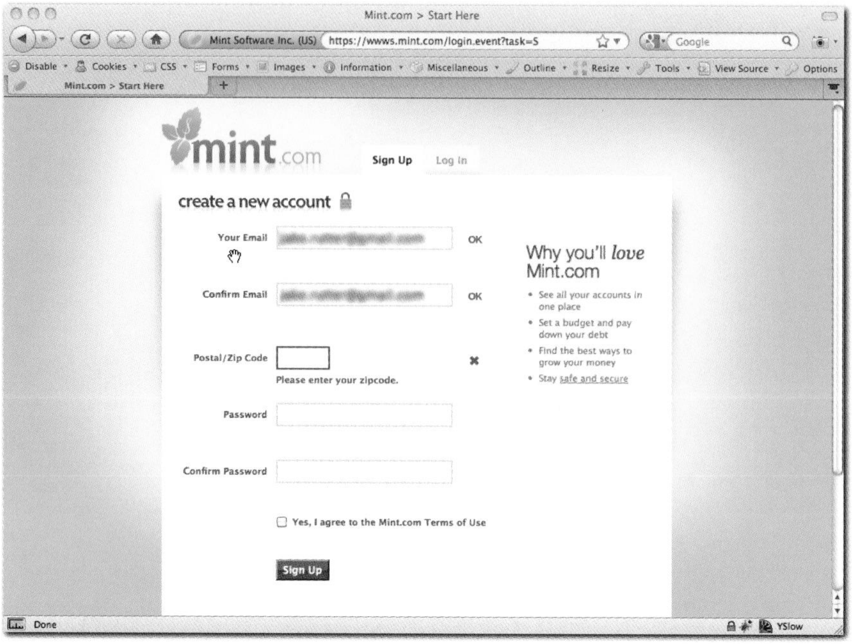

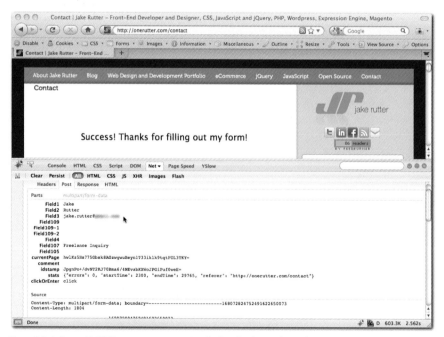

Figure 9-7: Mint.com uses a post request for new account sign-up

Reproduced from Mint.com

Figure 9-8: A Contact Us POST request parameter after the form has been submitted

Reproduced from onerutter.com

1. Set up the HTML form that will be used to submit the data to the server-side process. It's very important that you set up unique IDs for each input because those are used to select each input in the next step.

```
<form id="contact-form">
    <ul>
        <li><label>Name</label>

        <input type="text" id="name" name="name"/>
        </li>
        <li><label>Email</label>
        <input type="text" id="email" name="email"/>
        </li>
        <li><label>Phone</label>
        <input type="text" id="phone" name="phone"/>
        </li>
        <li><label>Message</label>
        <textarea name="message" id="message"></textarea>
        </li>
        <li><input type="submit" id="submit"/></li>
    </ul>
</form>
```

Imagine the following steps in a scenario where a user visits your Web site and fills out a form, which is submitted behind the scenes as an Ajax request:

2. Create a `selector` statement that selects the `#submit` input button and binds the `click` event. Add a return `false` statement so that if the button is clicked, the default form action doesn't take place.

```
$('#submit').bind('click', function(){
  return false;
});
```

3. Next, set up four variables inside of the statement: `nameVal`, `emailVal`, `phoneVal`, and `msgVal`. Each variable is set equal to the value of the input element. This is how you grab all the values from the form fields to pass to the server.

```
$('#submit').bind('click', function(){
  var nameVal = $('#name').val();
  var emailVal = $('#email').val();
  var phoneVal = $('#phone').val();
  var msgVal = $('#message').val();
  return false;
});
```

4. Add the `POST` method after the variables. When setting up the `POST` method, you have to pass in all of the form parameters in order for the post to work correctly. The form parameters are matched up with each value from the form that were set up in the previous step and passed into the `POST` method as `key:value` pairs.

```
$('#submit').bind('click', function(){
  var nameVal = $('#name').val();
  var emailVal = $('#email').val();
  var phoneVal = $('#phone').val();
```

```
    var msgVal = $('#message').val();
    $.post("form.php",
    {name:nameVal,
    phone:phoneVal,
    email:emailVal,
    message:msgVal}
    );
    return false;
});
```

5. Lastly, you should always include a callback function, whether it be used to check for error handling or to show error messages to the user if the submission fails. Add a callback function to the POST method after the form values are passed along. Figure 9-9 shows the following code in a Web browser with a view of the parameters that have been passed.

```
$('#submit').bind('click', function(){
    var nameVal = $('#name').val();
    var emailVal = $('#email').val();
    var phoneVal = $('#phone').val();
    var msgVal = $('#message').val();
    $.post("form.php",
    {name:nameVal,
    phone:phoneVal,
    email:emailVal,
    message:msgVal}, function(data) {
        alert('Successful Submission');
    }
    );
});
```

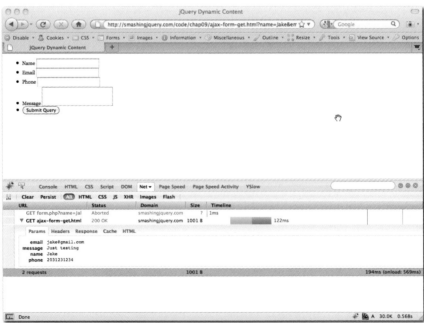

Figure 9-9: After the form has been submitted and the parameters have been posted

WORKING WITH XML DATA

XML stands for eXtensible Markup Language and was first introduced on the scene in 1996, so it's by no means new technology. XML allows you to define a custom data structure based on a common standard, which is platform-independent. XML is used in many different applications for anything from submitting bank data to creating RSS (Really Simple Syndication) feeds. XML is everywhere and is a reliable way of transmitting data. Figure 9-10 shows an example of an RSS feed from Smashing Magazine (www.smashingmagazine.com).

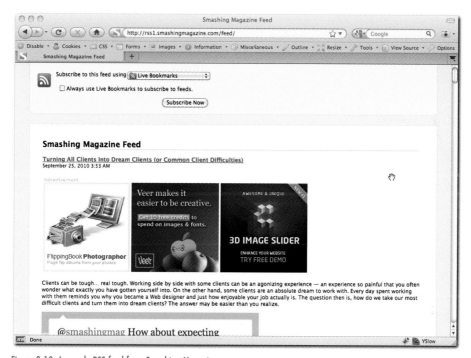

Figure 9-10: A sample RSS feed from Smashing Magazine

Smashing Media GmbH. Created by Sven Lennartz & Vitaly Friedman

Think about this scenario: You have a home page with a carousel of images. These images are maintained by a business user who uploads the images and adds a title, description, and URL for where a click should take the user. You could work with a developer to create an XML feed of the image data, which is updated on a daily basis. You could then take the path to the XML feed and use it in a jQuery GET request to build the home page carousel. The upside to using an XML feed is that it can be used with other front-end platforms like Flash, Mobile Apps, and so on. In a way, you have one data structure that can feed many different types of applications and you only need to involve a developer to initially get the XML feed set up.

The downsides to working with XML are that you can only use XML data if it is coming from the same Web site domain that you are currently working on, and that the code is bloated. If you want to work with data on other domains, you need to use JSON-P from the client side, which I cover in the next tutorial.

227

I have created the following XML file, which I use in the following XML tutorial. I have saved the file as `favoritebooks.xml` and placed it in the same directory as all of the other files. Back-end developers can set up processes to create XML from data that lives on the server and, in turn, you can pick up that data and do things with it.

XML is set up using a hierarchy and can be described as a family tree with parents and children. Each item can also be referred to as a node. The following code is an example of XML. Figure 9-11 shows this XML as viewed in a Web browser.

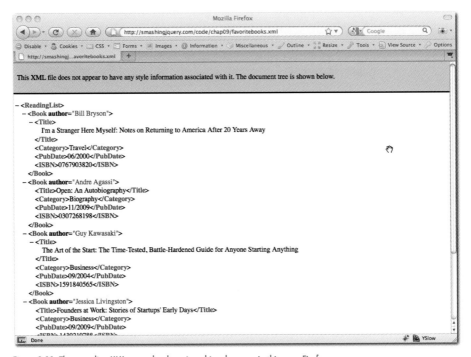

Figure 9-11: The preceding XML example when viewed in a browser; in this case, Firefox

```xml
<?xml version="1.0" encoding="utf-8" ?>
<ReadingList>
  <Book author="Bill Bryson">
    <Title>I'm a Stranger Here Myself: Notes on Returning to America After 20 Years
  Away</Title>
    <Category>Travel</Category>
    <PubDate>06/2000</PubDate>
    <ISBN>0767903820</ISBN>
  </Book>
  <Book author="Andre Agassi">
    <Title>Open: An Autobiography</Title>
    <Category>Biography</Category>
    <PubDate>11/2009</PubDate>
    <ISBN>0307268198</ISBN>
  </Book>
```

```
  <Book author="Guy Kawasaki">
    <Title>The Art of the Start: The Time-Tested, Battle-Hardened Guide for Anyone
  Starting Anything</Title>
    <Category>Business</Category>
    <PubDate>09/2004</PubDate>
    <ISBN>1591840565</ISBN>
  </Book>
  <Book author="Jessica Livingston">
    <Title>Founders at Work: Stories of Startups' Early Days</Title>
    <Category>Business</Category>
    <PubDate>09/2009</PubDate>
    <ISBN>1430210788</ISBN>
  </Book>
  <Book author="Jason Fried">
    <Title>Getting Real: The smarter, faster, easier way to build a successful web
  application</Title>
    <Category>Business</Category>
    <PubDate>09/2009</PubDate>
    <ISBN>0578012810</ISBN>
  </Book>
</ReadingList>
```

PARSING INTERNAL XML DATA AND CREATING HTML

Using the XML from the preceding example, I'm going to show you how to use jQuery to load the XML using an Ajax request and then parse the XML as HTML content on your page. You will be using the `ajax()` method, but you could also use the shorthand GET() method. Loading XML is fast and easy to set up; it only takes a few lines of jQuery code to get going. It can be thought of as a two-step process: First, load the XML. Second, parse it using a callback function, which fires only if the XML is successfully loaded.

The end result of this script is an unordered list of five of my favorite books, as shown in Figure 9-12:

1. First, you need to set up the HTML that will contain the unordered list of books. Create an unordered list with the ID #books.

   ```
   <ul id="books">
   <h1>My Favorite Books</h1>
   </ul>
   ```

2. Set up the `ajax()` method and include four parameters. The `type` is a GET request. The `dataType` is XML. The `url` is `favoritebooks.xml` and the callback function is called `parseXML`.

   ```
   $.ajax({
   type: "GET",
   dataType: "XML",
   url: "favoritebooks.xml",
   success: parseXML
   });
   ```

3. Create an empty callback function called `parseXML` that will be used to accept the `xml` as a data argument. jQuery on callback automatically passes arguments to the callback, whether it's set up to receive them or not. The arguments passed depend on whether it's the success or error callback that has been set up.

```
function parseXML(xml) {

}
```

4. Add a `selector` statement within the `parseXML` function, which uses the `find()` and `each()` methods to find each book node.

```
function parseXML(xml) {
  $(xml).find("Book").each(function(){
  });
}
```

5. Set up four variables: `author`, `title`, `category`, and `pubdate`. Each variable is assigned a value using different `selector` statements. Because `author` is an attribute of the `book` node, you can use the `attribute` filter to select it. The remaining values can all be obtained by using the `find()` method to search for each node and grab the text out of it.

```
function parseXML(xml) {
  $(xml).find("Book").each(function(){
    var author = $(this).attr('author');
    var title = $(this).find('title').text();
    var category = $(this).find('category').text();
    var pubdate = $(this).find('pubdate').text();
  });
}
```

6. After you have set up all the variables, it's time to create the HTML that will dynamically show up on the page. Create a `selector` statement that sets up a list item (`<li></li>`) and, using the `HTML()` method, adds all of the variables that we have set up mixed with some HTML tags for formatting. As each list item is created, it is appended to the `#books` unordered list.

```
function parseXML(xml) {
  $(xml).find("Book").each(function(){
    var author = $(this).attr('author');
    var title = $(this).find('title').text();
    var category = $(this).find('category').text();
    var pubdate = $(this).find('pubdate').text();
    $('<li></li>').html('<b>Title:</b> '+title +'</br><b>Author</b>: '+ author
  +'</br>'+category +' - '+pubdate).appendTo('#books');
  });
        }
```

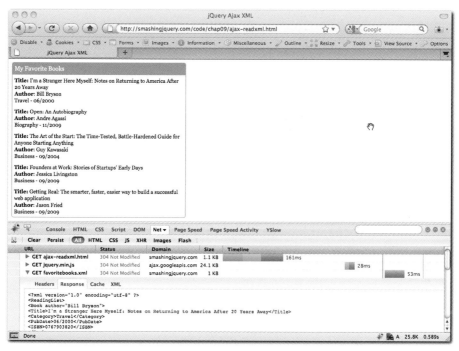

Figure 9-12: The XML being pulled in and loaded to display My Favorite Books widget

WORKING WITH JSON DATA

JSON stands for JavaScript Object Notation, which is similar to XML, but was created only for JavaScript. JSON allows you to create your own data structures in the form of name/value pairs. JSON and XML are alike in they are both hierarchical and can be processed with Ajax.

JSON has some advantages over XML; I personally find that JSON is easier to read. You don't have tags to define the structure; the structure is defined by the data. This cleaner approach leads to code that is much more concise than XML and easier to work with and understand. Debates continue to rage online about whether JSON or XML is better, so it comes down to personal opinion.

The following code is an example of JSON code also shown in Figure 9-13. I have used the same data from the preceding XML example so you can see how the two types of data compare. At a quick glance, you can see that the JSON is much easier to read. Whether that's a big advantage is debatable — most of the time, your scripts, not a human, will be reading the JSON code.

```
{"books":[
    {
    "title": "I'm a Stranger Here Myself: Notes on Returning to America After 20
Years Away",
```

```
         "author": "Bill Bryson",
         "category": "Travel",
         "pubdate": "06/2000",
         "isbn": "0767903820"
         },
         {
         "title": "Open: An Autobiography",
         "author": "Andre Agassi",
         "category": "Biography",
         "pubdate": "11/2009",
         "isbn": "0307268198"
         },
         {
         "title": "The Art of the Start: The Time-Tested, Battle-Hardened Guide for
Anyone Starting Anything",
         "author": "Guy Kawasaki",
         "category": "Business",
         "pubdate":"09/2004",
         "isbn": "1591840565"
         },
         {
         "title": "Founders at Work: Stories of Startups' Early Days",
         "author": "Jessica Livingston",
         "category": "Business",
         "pubdate": "09/2009",
         "isbn": "1430210788"
         },
         {
         "title": "Getting Real: The smarter, faster, easier way to build a success-
ful web application",
         "author": "Jason Fried",
         "category": "Business",
         "pubdate": "09/2009",
         "isbn": "0578012810"
         }
    ]
}
```

When you're writing JSON code yourself, you should use a validator to make sure the JSON is valid with no mistakes. If it's not valid, when you try to pull it into a page using GET, you end up with no content and an error message. Douglas Crockford created a JSON validator called JSONLint (www.jsonlint.com/), shown in Figure 9-14, that accepts raw JSON or the URL where the JSON code is located. If you pass JSON into this tool that does not validate, you receive an error message that helps you to solve any issues. Figure 9-14 shows the preceding JSON code after it has been processed in the JSONLint tool and passed as valid.

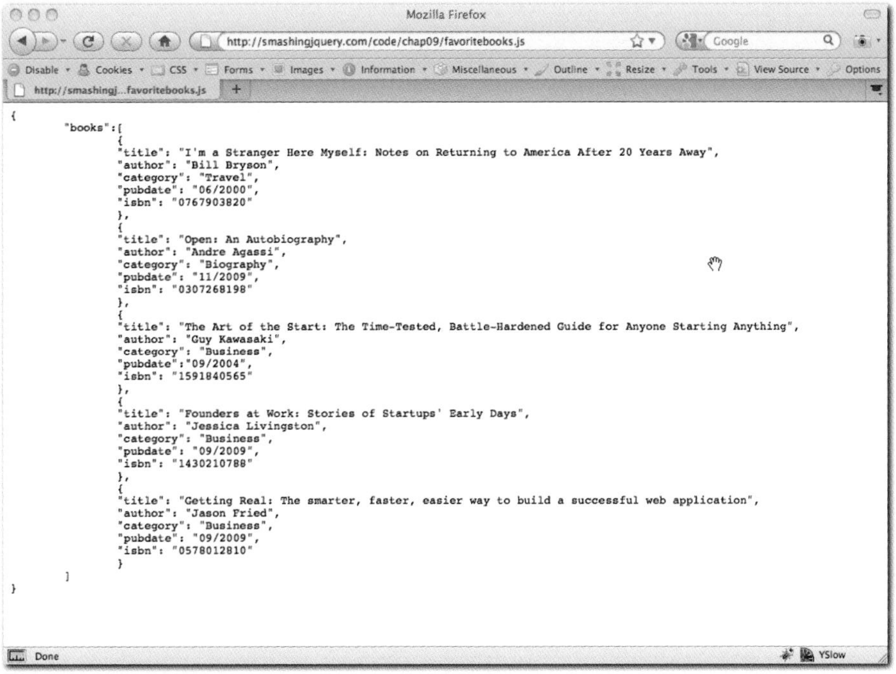

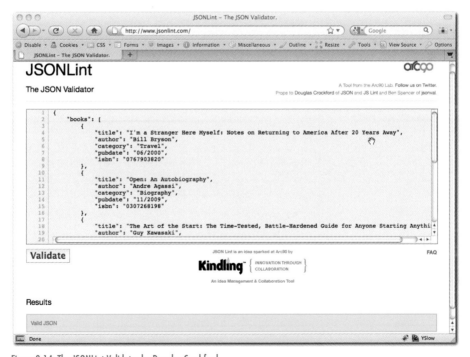

Figure 9-13: The preceding JSON example when viewed in the browser

233

Figure 9-14: The JSONLint Validator by Douglas Crockford

RETRIEVING INTERNAL JSON
DATA AND CREATING HTML

Using the JSON code from the preceding example, I'm going to show you how to use jQuery to load JSON using an Ajax request and then parse the JSON as HTML content on your page as shown in Figure 9-15. I use the `ajax()` method, but could also use the shorthand `get JSON()` method.

Retrieving JSON data using jQuery is very similar to retrieving XML data. Fewer steps are involved because the data is already in JavaScript format, which makes it a faster alternative to XML.

The end result of this script is an unordered list of all five of my favorite books, as shown in Figure 9-12.

1. First, you need to set up the HTML that will contain the unordered list of books. Create an unordered list with the ID of #books.

```
<h1>My Favorite Books</h1>
<ul id="books">
</ul>
```

2. Set up the `ajax()` method and include four parameters. The type will be a GET request. The `dataType` is JSON. The `url` is `favoritebooks.json` and the callback function is called `processJSON`, which you set up in the next step.

```
$.ajax({
type: "GET",
dataType: "JSON",
url: "favoritebooks.json",
success: processJSON
});
```

3. Create an empty callback function called `processJSON` and pass in the JSON as the data.

```
function processJSON(data) {

}
```

4. Create a loop using the `each` method, which loops through all of the data in the `data. books` object literal. The array index is `i` and the corresponding value is `item`.

```
function processJSON(data){
  $.each(data.books, function(i,item){
  });
}
```

5. Within the `each` method, create a `selector` statement that sets up a list item (`<li></li>`) and, using the `html()` method, adds the data mixed with some HTML tags for formatting. As each list item is created, it is appended to the #books unordered list. Each data item is accessed by using item and the name; `Title` is accessed by using `item.title`. This is the big benefit compared to XML: You can access the items directly without first having to assign variables to pull the values out.

```
function processJSON(data){
  $.each(data.books, function(i,item){
```

```
    $('<li></li>').html('<b>Title:</b> '+item.title +'</br><b>Author</b>: '+
  item.author +'</br>'+item.category +' - '+item.pubdate).appendTo('#books');
    });
}
```

Both tutorials have the same end result, but JSON can process data from another Web server faster and using one less step, which equals less code. Creating the JSON code can be a little tricky, however, because of its strict nature: If you leave in an extra comma or add an extra bracket, it can throw off everything.

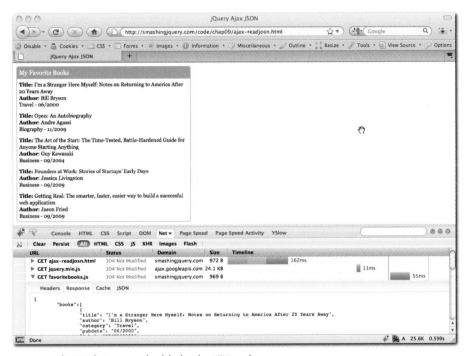

Figure 9-15: The JSON being retrieved and displayed as HTML on the page

CREATING A DELICIOUS USER WIDGET BY RECEIVING JSONP DATA FROM API REQUESTS

Delicious (www.delicious.com), shown in Figure 9-16, is a social bookmarking site for sharing and discovering Web bookmarks. It lets you bookmark your own favorite sites and see what others are bookmarking. Delicious was started in September 2003 and was sold to Yahoo! in 2005. The Web site has more than 5.3 million users and more than 180 million bookmarked URLs. I have been using Delicious for a few years to keep track of favorite and useful links. It lets you access your bookmarks from any computer with Internet access, and it's also a good place to post your own projects to gain access to more traffic and popularity. Delicious offers various browser plug-ins that make it incredibly easy to save favorite bookmarks without having to visit the Delicious Web site. This is one of the reasons the application is so popular.

235

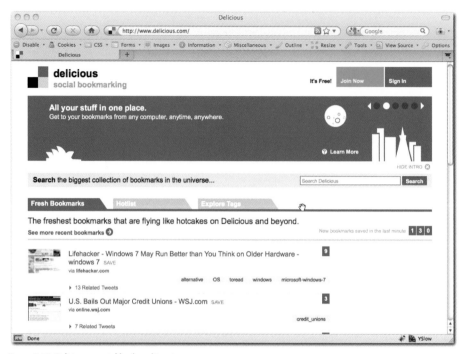

Figure 9-16: Delicious, a social bookmarking site

Like many online social applications and Web sites, Delicious has a great developer community and API (application programming interface). Delicious offers RSS (Really Simple Syndication) feeds of every page as shown in Figure 9-17, including the most popular bookmarks and bookmarks organized by the specific user who created them. RSS is created using the XML standard used for Web feeds.

Delicious also offers an API interface for more advanced users who wish to build Web and mobile apps that interface with the Delicious API, as shown in Figure 9-18. The API allows you to post content to and display content from Delicious. This requires authentication in the form of an API key.

For the following tutorial, I use the Delicious feeds that are RSS (XML) and JSON feeds of data that already resides on the site. You can pass parameters into the query string to display specific content, but you can't do add any content to Delicious via these feeds. Refer to the documentation on the Delicious Web site for a complete list of all available query string variables, also shown in Figure 9-19.

By adding my username `"jakerutter"` into the query string of the URL (`http://feeds.delicious.com/v2/json/jakerutter?count=10`), I can retrieve the last ten bookmarks that I have added to Delicious, as shown in Figure 9-20. This feed is available to every user and can be used to follow a friend's feed to see all of the bookmarks they have been creating.

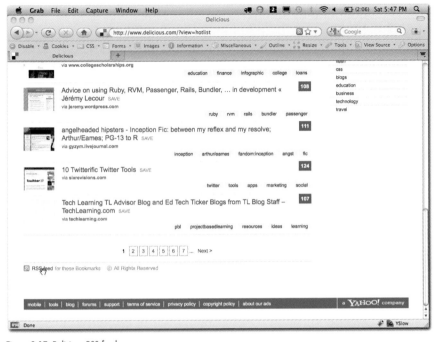

Figure 9-17: Delicious RSS feeds

237

Figure 9-18: Delicious API documentation

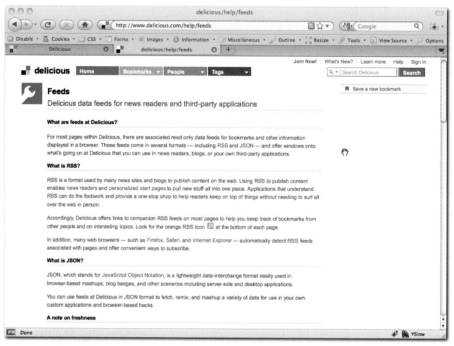

Figure 9-19: Delicious feeds documentation

Figure 9-20: My Bookmarks JSON feed

In this tutorial, I show you how you can set up a Delicious personal favorites widget that you can place on your own Web site or any other Web site using jQuery, as shown in Figure 9-21. This tutorial involves setting up JSONP, (JSON with Padding), which is a required step when working with cross-domain Ajax calls. JSONP allows you to perform cross-domain calls by wrapping the returned JSON in a callback function that is specified by you. Without JSONP, your cross-domain calls fail. You cannot use JSONP with an API that is not set up to receive JSONP requests.

1. The CSS controls how the widget is laid out on the page. You can either build all the CSS before starting the jQuery, or create the foundation for how it will look and work as you go. In the following CSS sample code, there are some references to browser-specific rounded corners for Mozilla Firefox and Safari WebKit. The remaining browsers just see straight corners using the border property.

```
body{
font-family:georgia;
font-size:12px;
}
.widget{
border:1px solid #1179CB;
-moz-border-radius:5px;
-webkit-border-radius:5px;
width:200px;
}
.widget h1{
font:14px georgia;
padding:5px;
color:#fff;
background:#1179CB url(images/delicious_32.png) 2px 5px no-repeat;
text-indent:20px;
height:20px;
margin:0;
}
#user-feed{
list-style-type:none;
margin:0;
padding:0;}
#user-feed li{
padding:5px;
}
a{
color:#1179CB;
}
```

2. Set up the HTML widget that contains the unordered list of bookmarks. Create an unordered list with the ID #news-feed.

```
<div class="widget">
  <h1>My Delicious Feed</h1>
  <ul id="news-feed"></ul>
</div>
```

239

3. Create a variable named `query` and set it equal to the URL of my Delicious feed.

```
var query = "http://feeds.delicious.com/v2/json/jakerutter?count=10";
```

4. Set up the `ajax()` method and include the following parameters. The `type` is a `GET` request. The `dataType` is `JSONP`. The `url` is set to my variable `query` and the callback function is called `processData`.

```
$.ajax({
    type: "GET",
    dataType: "jsonp",
    url: query,
    success: processData
});
```

5. Create an empty callback function called `processData` that is used to accept the `JSON` as a data argument.

```
function processData(data) {

}
```

6. Create a loop using the `each` method, which loops through all of the data in the `data.books` object literal. The index will be accessed as `item`.

```
function processData(data) {
$.each(data, function(i, item) {
    });
}
```

7. Within the `each` method, create a selector statement that sets up a list item (`<li></li>`) and, using the `html()` method, adds an anchor tag. As each list item is created, it is appended to the `#user-feed` unordered list. In each anchor tag, the URL and title is added using the index to access each item and its JSON object name. In this case `.u` is the URL and `.d` is the title.

```
function processData(data) {
    $.each(data, function(i, item) {
        $('<li></li>').html("<a href='"+item.u+"'>"+item.d+"</a>").
    appendTo('#user-feed');
    });
}
```

8. Set up two variables. `newsLength` is set to the length of the `newsArray`. `newsInterval` holds the numeric value for how often to grab a new headline and insert it into the news ticker.

```
var newsLength = 5;
var newsInterval = 2000;
```

9. Next, I set up a function called `slideArticle()` that contains all of the effects to make the Delicious user feed widget work. The first statement inside of the function selects the last item in the `news-feed` unordered list, clones it, and adds it back into the list, but at the top using the `prependTo` method. The second statement added to the function selects the first item in the news feed and adds the `slideDown` effect to it. Not only do I want to slide down the first item at a duration of 500 milliseconds, but also I would like to fade the item at a duration of 1,000 milliseconds before it slides into place. I accomplish this by chaining the `fadeIn` method into the same statement that contains the `slideDown` method. One last statement is added to the `slideArticle` function, which removes the last item in the list. These three statements all occur one after the other, which simulates a nice fade and sliding effect.

240

```
function slideArticle() {
    $('#user-feed li:last').clone().prependTo('#news-feed').css('display','none');
    $('#user-feed li:first').fadeIn(1000).slideDown(500);
    $('#user-feed li:last').fadeOut().remove();
}
```

10. This last piece of JavaScript is probably the most important. I need to set up the set Interval function to execute the slideArticle function at the newsInterval rate (2,000 milliseconds). This function continuously loops the news ticker. Without this function, the Delicious user feed widget won't run.

```
setInterval(slideArticle, newsInterval);
```

Figure 9-21: The animated Delicious user feed widget

CREATING A YELP TOP REVIEWS WIDGET USING JSONP VIA THE YELP API

Yelp (www.yelp.com) is an online local search and reviews service that was founded in 2004. The Web site offers local business reviews and ratings for everything from restaurants to bookstores, as shown in Figure 9-22. Local customers who have visited the establishments and leave feedback power the online community. In 2007, Yelp improved their site by providing an API for developers to create applications based on Yelp data: This has greatly increased the reach of the Yelp reviews.

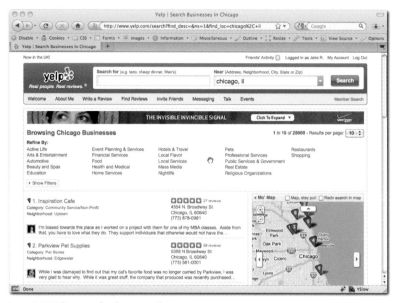

Figure 9-22: Yelp reviews for Chicago area businesses

Reproduced by permission of yelp.com

Yelp for Developers (www.yelp.com/developers/documentation) is a portal for the development community with links to applications built on the API, code samples, API documentation, and so on, as shown in Figure 9-23. It's a great example of how companies should structure their API documentation to ensure that developers have the right tools to get started in building their own applications using the company's API.

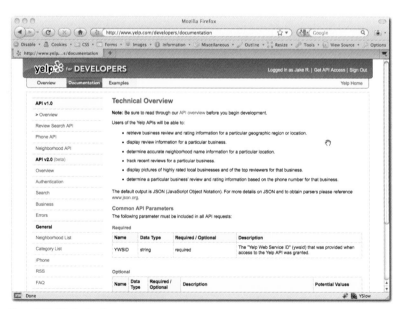

Figure 9-23: Yelp for Developers

Reproduced by permission of yelp.com

GETTING APPROVED FOR A YELP API KEY

Before you can work with any third-party APIs, you typically need to apply for an API key except in some cases as you experienced with the previous Delicious API. The API key allows the third party to monitor your activity: By using their API, you access their servers and they need to monitor your traffic and requests. Most APIs allow 100 requests per day; anything more than that needs approval. Sometimes fees are involved. You should always check the API before starting any development.

The Yelp API limits requests to 100 per day for development projects, which can be extended to 10,000 requests per day for live implementations after approval from Yelp. The API allows you to search businesses by business type, location, and neighborhood using three different methods: review search, phone search, and neighborhood.

The approval process involves submitting a simple form outlining the intention of your application and how you plan to utilize the Yelp API. After submitting the application, you receive an e-mail from Yelp and are assigned an account manager, who reviews your application and approves or disapproves your project. When integrating the Yelp API into your project, it is important that you give proper credit to the Yelp reviews by displaying the Yelp logo. This also helps to ensure that your project implementation is approved by Yelp. I review this process in the following tutorial.

1. Before you can apply for a Yelp API key, you need a basic Yelp account. Navigate to `www.yelp.com/signup`, shown in Figure 9-24, and provide the requested information request (basics like your birth date, e-mail address, and so on).
2. After you have created a basic Yelp account, you need to login to Yelp through the developer portal shown in Figure 9-25, or at `www.yelp.com/login?return_url=%2Fdevelopers%2Fgetting_started%2Fapi_access`.
3. After you successfully log into the developers portal, you need to navigate to the API access section shown in Figure 9-26 or at `www.yelp.com/developers/getting_started/api_access`.

When you sign up for API access, you are asked for the URL of your Web site and how you plan to use the API. After you are granted access, you receive a few e-mails from Yelp with instructions on how to use the API, and so on. After you have set up your application, you need to show it to the account manager at Yelp that you have been assigned to have it approved for production usage. They usually make sure that you are using the Yelp logo and also displaying the necessary information as spelled out in the Terms and Conditions you agreed to when you signed up for API access.

USING THE YELP API TO SHOW REVIEWS BASED ON TELEPHONE NUMBERS

I originally created this project for a Web site I manage called StamfordCTGuide.com. The site is a local online guide to Stamford, Connecticut with more than 350 pages of content managed by my wife and I.

Figure 9-24: The Yelp account creation page

Reproduced by permission of yelp.com

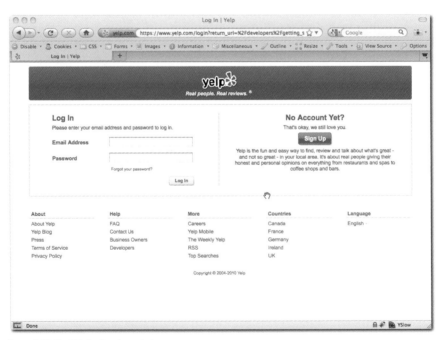

Figure 9-25: The Yelp for Developers login page

Reproduced by permission of yelp.com

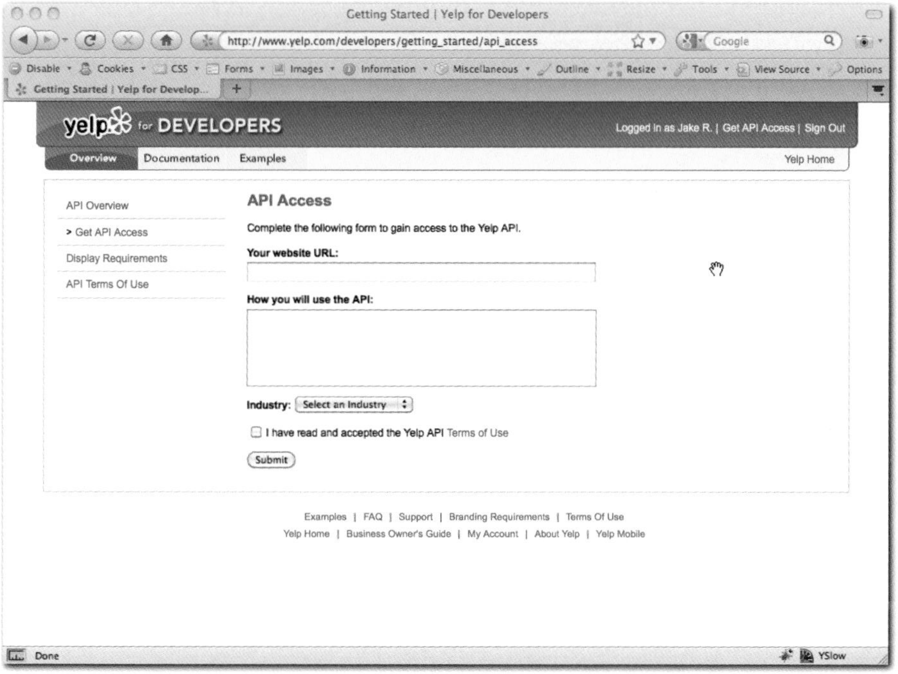

Figure 9-26: The Yelp API access application

Reproduced by permission of yelp.com

StamfordCTGuide.com is run on top of WordPress (a blogging and content management service platform) and I have a WordPress plug-in set up to allow users to create reviews on restaurants. Our small site doesn't draw enough reviewers yet, however, and Yelp has a lot of credibility in terms of reviews and ratings. After reading through the Yelp documentation, I decided to set up an integration between Yelp and StamfordCTGuide.com to include reviews from Yelp for every restaurant listing on my site, as shown in Figure 9-27.

As I stated previously, Yelp has a few APIs: Review Search, Phone, and Neighborhood. Review Search and Phone interest me the most. All of the restaurants on StamfordCTGuide.com are listed with a street address and phone number. Using the Review Search API first, I tried passing restaurant address data into the method to match up local restaurants with listing on Yelp for reviews using this URL: `http://api.yelp.com/business_review_search?location=650%20Mission%20St%2ASan%20Francisco%2A%20CA&ywsid=XXXXXXXXXXXXXXXX`. The problem I encountered is that the Review Search API didn't always return one result. Most times, multiple results were returned, as shown in Figure 9-28.

After a bit of testing, I learned that this was because of the inconsistency with which I had entered the addresses into the site, I didn't always add the ZIP code or correct street address. The API uses the address to match a review. If a full address isn't provided, the API has a harder time making an exact match. Some API calls returned one result, whereas others returned five. This option was not going to work.

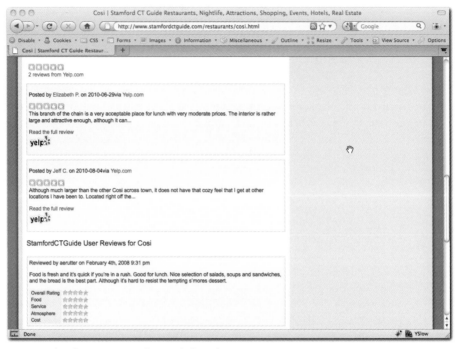

Figure 9-27: The Yelp reviews integrated on StamfordCTGuide.com

Reproduced by permission of yelp.com

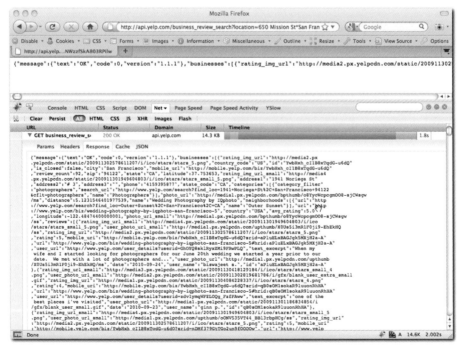

Figure 9-28: Review search results

The only alternative left is to use the Phone Search API to try to match up restaurants from my Web site with listing on Yelp. Upon looking at my database of restaurants, I found that there were more listings with phone numbers set up than full address information. Using Phone Search would offer more consistent data matchups from Yelp.

Before setting up any code, I began playing around with a few requests using some phone numbers from some local restaurants and found that the API only returned the restaurant listing for the phone number that I had supplied, as shown in Figure 9-29. If no restaurant was found using the phone number supplied, nothing was returned. Here is an example of the URL structure used with the Phone Search API: `http://api.yelp.com/phone_search?phone=1234567890&ywsid=XXXXXXXXXXXXXXXXXX`.

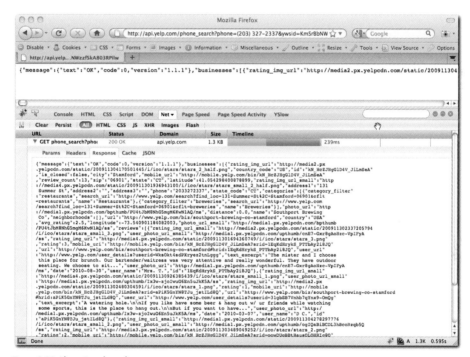

Figure 9-29: Phone Search results

After completing the preceding research on how best to integrate the Yelp reviews and ratings API into StamfordCTGuide, I can move onto the next step of setting up the actual implementation by using jQuery to pull Yelp reviews into my Web site.

Because the integration between the Yelp API and StamfordCTGuide.com will be a cross-domain request, I need to set up a callback using JSONP, but there is another problem: The Yelp API v1.0 doesn't support JSONP. You can work your way around this issue, however. The workaround only works for retrieving data from JSON. You won't be able to add reviews, ratings, and so on, but that's okay — I don't need that functionality for this implementation.

The workaround involves setting up a `script` tag with the API request link being called in the source, which is then evaluated. I use this technique to get around the cross-domain issue purely because I only need to pull content from Yelp. It's a one-way communication. After the page has loaded, there will be no more calls the API. The API is only called when the page initially loads to pull in Yelp content.

The solution involves interfacing with HTML, CSS, jQuery, and PHP. I use PHP to pull the location's phone number and assign it to a JavaScript variable, `locPhone`.

1. Add the HTML to the page that will hold all of the review content from Yelp. Create a `div` with an ID of #yelpReviews.

```
<div id="yelpReviews" style="margin:5px;"></div>
```

2. Set up a `document.ready` handler and, inside of it, add a call to the function `write ScriptTag`, which you define in the next step. You pass in the URL that contains the phone number, API key, limit of number of results returned, and callback to the function.

```
$(document).ready(function(){
  writeScriptTag( "http://api.yelp.com/phone_search?"+
  "&phone="+locPhone+
  "&ywsid=KmSrBbNWzzfSkA803RPilw"+
  "&limit=1"+
  "&callback=showData"); // <- callback
});
```

3. Next, set up the `writeScriptTag` function. Inside of the function. add a variable called `script` to build a script tag when the document is ready. Make sure the type is `text/javascript` and the source is set to the path that you passed in from the previous step. The final statement appends the script the body of the document.

```
function writeScriptTag(path) {
  var yelpScript=document.createElement('script');
  yelpScript.type='text/javascript';
  yelpScript.src=path;
  $("body").append(yelpScript);
}
```

4. Create an empty callback function called `showData` that will be used to accept the JSON as a data argument.

```
function showData(data) {
}
```

5. You need to create two loops using the `each` method. The first one loops through all of the data in the `data.businesses` object literal. The array index is `i` and the corresponding value is `business`. The second loop is nested inside of the first one and loops through all of the data in the `data.reviews` branch. The array index is `i` and the corresponding value is `reviews`.

```
function showData(data) {
  $.each(data.businesses, function(i,business){
    $.each(business.reviews, function(i,review){
    });
  });
}
```

6. In the first loop, you access the total review count for the business and insert it into the `#yelpReviews` element on the page. This is a requirement from Yelp to always display the total number of reviews with a link back to the business on the Yelp Web site. Figure 9-30 shows all of the data that can be pulled out of Yelp via the Phone Search API.

```
function showData(data) {
  $.each(data.businesses, function(i,business){
    var bizContent = '<p><img src="' + business.rating_img_url + '" alt=""/><br><a
    href="'+ business.url +'">'+ business.review_count + ' reviews from Yelp.com</
    a></p>';
    $(bizContent).appendTo('#yelpReviews');

      $.each(business.reviews, function(i,review){
    });
  });
}
```

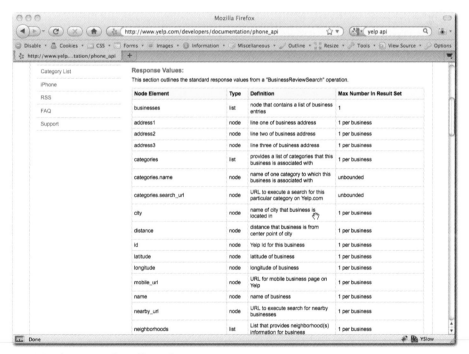

Figure 9-30: The response values table on Yelp

7. In the second loop, you will be accessing each individual review from the review's object literal. You can pull out each user, their user review URL, review date, rating image, and rating excerpt using the index to call each one out. You are also required to display the Yelp logo beside any Yelp reviews so that proper attribution is set up. Each review is inserted after the `#yelpReviews` element, each contained within their own `.comments-block` element.

```
function showData(data) {

  $.each(data.businesses, function(i,business){
  // extra loop
  var bizContent = '<p><img src="' + business.rating_img_url + '" img=""/><br><a
  href="'+ business.url +'">'+ business.review_count + ' reviews from Yelp.com</
  a></p>';
  $(bizContent).appendTo('#yelpAVG');

    $.each(business.reviews, function(i,review){
    var content = '<div class="comments-block"><p>Posted by <a href="'+review.
  user_url+'">' +review.user_name + ' </a> on ' + review.date + 'via <a
  href="'+review.url+'">Yelp.com</a>';
    content += '<p><img src="' + review.rating_img_url + '" img=""/><br>';
    content += review.text_excerpt  + '</p>';
    content += '<p><a href="'+review.url + '">Read the full review</a><br>';
    content += '<img src="http://media3.px.yelpcdn.com/
  static/200911302846157596/i/developers/yelp_logo_50x25.png"></div>';
    $(content).insertAfter('#yelpReviews');
    });
  });
}
```

The implementation is simple and fun! Think of the possibilities: So many companies now offer APIs for their Web site data. Now, on Web sites that allow the JSON-P request, you can tap into the APIs and easily include content from other sites without having to create tons and tons of backend code, all with the power of jQuery.

10

CREATING AND USING JQUERY PLUG-INS

JQUERY ALLOWS WEB DESIGNERS and developers to write powerful plug-ins that extend the core functionality of the jQuery library. Developers can also incorporate plug-ins created by the open-source community into any Web site or application. Any Web designer or developer can implement a jQuery plug-in, but building a custom plug-in requires intermediate to expert knowledge of JavaScript.

In the following chapter, I walk you through how to set up popular jQuery plug-ins such as jQuery UI, jQuery Tools, and Fancybox, a lightbox alternative. The last part of the chapter focuses on building and distributing custom jQuery plug-ins.

GETTING TO KNOW PLUG-INS

jQuery plug-ins are very widely used; for example, most lightbox windows on Web sites are done with a jQuery plug-in. A lightbox shows larger images (such as zoom images in a product catalog Web site) without the user having to leave the current Web page. This is done with a `div` layer with the larger image appearing over a semi-transparent background that covers the page. The blogging platform WordPress (`www.wordpress.com`) uses a lightbox-type plug-in within the admin interface to add media to a blog post, as shown in Figure 10-1.

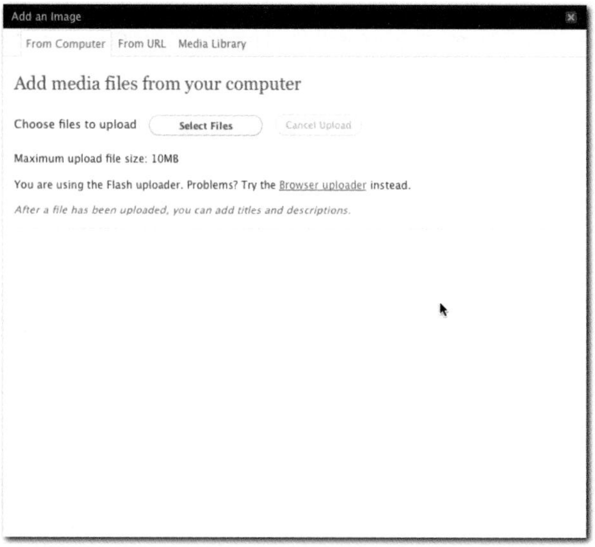

Figure 10-1: WordPress uses a lightbox-type plug-in within the admin interface to add media to a blog post

jQuery has an enormous community of plug-in developers who create great plug-ins for commonly used stuff like image galleries, forms, and form elements. Writing jQuery plug-ins requires advanced knowledge of JavaScript: You have to be able to write a script that can be adapted and applied to a wide range of situations.

Here are some tips you should consider before using a plug-in:

- Check that it is compatible with the version of jQuery that you are currently using.
- Check that the plug-in is cross-browser compatible (Internet Explorer, Firefox, Safari, Chrome, and Opera).
- Check the date of the last release. If the date is a few years back, you can assume that the plug-in is no longer supported.
- Read the documentation provided with the plug-in to find out how easy the plug-in is to implement and whether it can be extended.
- Check to see what the community response to the plug-in has been. Have most people had success with the plug-in?

- If you run into issues or bugs and the plug-in is listed on the jQuery Plug-in Web site (http://plugins.jquery.com/) or on the Google Code Project Hosting Web site (http://code.google.com/hosting/), you can file a bug report to notify the creator of the issue.

- If the plug-in looks out of date, search for something newer.

INCORPORATING A JQUERY PLUG-IN INTO YOUR WEB SITE

Including a jQuery plug-in on your Web site is incredible easy. Think of it the same way as how you have to include the jQuery library before you can write any jQuery. You have to do the same for the jQuery plug-in that you are looking to apply to your site. Always make sure the jQuery plug-in file is included directly after the jQuery library file or the plug-in won't work.

You can include as many plug-ins as you would like. The only downside to adding multiple plug-ins with separate file includes is an increase in requests to the Web server as the page loads, which could create slower response and longer loading times. Figure 10-2 shows multiple jQuery includes being loaded on a Web page in Firebug. An easy way to avoid having multiple requests is to combine all of your jQuery plug-ins into one file called jquery.plugins.js and only include that file.

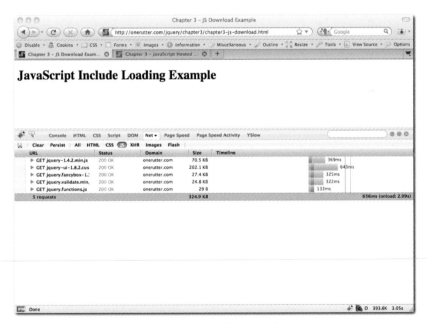

Figure 10-2: Multiple jQuery includes being loaded on a Web page in Firebug

INCORPORATING JQUERY UI INTO YOUR WEB SITE

jQuery has an official user interface library called jQuery UI, as shown in Figure 10-3, which you can access by navigating to jqueryui.com. The jQuery UI library is separate from the jQuery library, but is dependent upon the jQuery library's presence.

Figure 10-3: The jQuery UI home page

© 2010 The jQuery Project and the jQuery UI Team

The jQuery UI library is made up mainly of interactions and widgets. Interactions are functional scripts that you can incorporate into your Web site applications to help achieve a task. For example, one interaction, called Droppable, can be used in any application that performs drag and drop.

Table 10.1 outlines all of the feature components that are included within the jQuery UI library. I review the most common components in the next few sections of this chapter.

Table 10.1   jQuery UI Components

Interactions	Widgets	Utilities	Effects
Draggable	Accordion	Position	Show
Droppable	Autocomplete		Hide
Resizable	Button		Toggle
Selectable	Date Picker		
Sortable	Dialog		
	Progress Bar (forms)		
	Slider (forms)		
	Tabs (forms)		

Widgets are self-contained components such as the Accordion widget, which can be embedded directly into a Web application to offer a level of interaction for those engaging with your user interface. I mainly focus on how to implement a few of the widgets into your Web sites.

jQuery UI also offers methods to extend the jQuery core event methods, such as being able to animate background and border colors. The jQuery Easing plug-in is now included in the jQuery UI core to allow anyone to add powerful easing effects to their existing animations.

jQuery UI is often used in conjunction with Rich Internet Applications (RIA) where a lot of interaction takes place within the browser and all of the UI components can be utilized.

DOWNLOADING JQUERY UI

You can download the jQuery UI library, as shown in Figure 10-4, by pointing your browser to `http://jqueryui.com/download`. You can download the entire UI library or split it up into smaller chunks with the Build Your Download page to download just the jQuery UI components that you will be using. This is a nice option to have: jQuery UI is considerably larger than jQuery and you probably won't use all of the components wrapped into the full library.

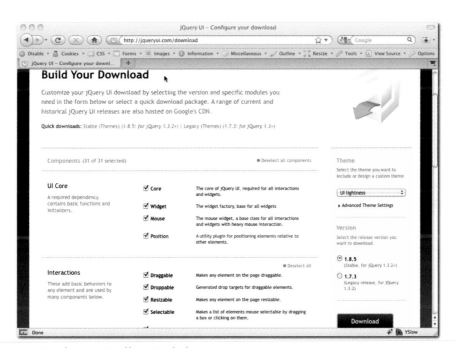

Figure 10-4: The jQuery UI Build Your Download page
© 2010 The jQuery Project and the jQuery UI Team

ADDING JQUERY UI TO YOUR SITE

Similar to the jQuery library, jQuery UI is included as a standalone JavaScript file that is uploaded to your Web server and inserted into the head of your page directly after the jQuery library. jQuery UI is also available through the Google CDN (content delivery network).

```
<script src="http://ajax.googleapis.com/ajax/libs/jqueryui/1.8.5/jquery-ui.min.js
"></script>
```

255

The downside to including the library through the Google CDN is that you will be accessing the entire library with all the components included, which could be unnecessary. The benefits of using the Google CDN are improved performance and caching for your Web site.

The jQuery UI and jQuery library header lines should look like the following:

```
<script type="text/javascript" src="js/jquery-1.4.2.min.js"></script>
<script type="text/javascript" src="js/jquery-ui-1.8.4.custom.min.js"></script>
```

UNDERSTANDING HOW JQUERY UI WIDGETS WORK

Each widget has an extensive API comprised of options, events, and methods that can be applied to create customized components on your site and easily used in other places on the Tabs widget page, as shown in Figure 10-5. The component drives the functionality either through the default setup or through options from the API.

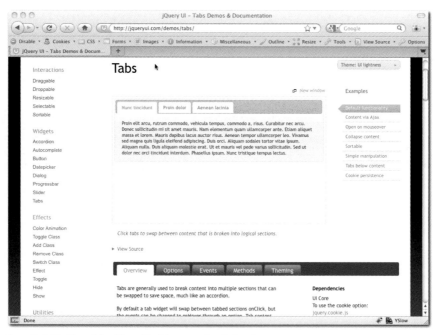

Figure 10-5: The jQuery Tabs widget with all documentation displayed
© 2010 The jQuery Project and the jQuery UI Team

CUSTOMIZING THE DESIGN OF JQUERY UI

The jQuery UI library is built on top of a CSS framework, which means you can easily customize it either by creating your own styles or by creating a theme using ThemeRoller. I get into more detail on ThemeRoller later in this chapter in the section called "Creating a UI Theme with ThemeRoller." A theme is a collection of CSS styles and images that can be applied to all of the components in the jQuery UI Library. By using the jQuery UI CSS framework, you can assure that any design work applies to current and future UI components.

The beauty of using the CSS framework is that all of the components use the same classes, so if you set up a style for an active state, it is set up across all of the components.

The CSS framework is made up of two external style sheets:

- ui.core.css
- ui.theme.css

Here's an example of the rendered HTML from a jQuery UI widget:

```
<div role="tablist" class="ui-accordion ui-widget ui-helper-reset ui-accordion-
icons" id="accordion">
<h3 tabindex="0" aria-expanded="true" role="tab" class="ui-accordion-header ui-
helper-reset ui-state-default ui-state-active ui-corner-top">
<span class="ui-icon ui-icon-triangle-1-s">
</span>
<a tabindex="-1" href="#">
NY Mets
</a>
</h3>
<div role="tabpanel" style="height: 93px;" class="ui-accordion-content ui-helper-
reset ui-widget-content ui-corner-bottom ui-accordion-content-active">
<p>
The New York Mets are a professional baseball team based in the borough of Queens
in New York City. The Mets are a member of the East Division of Major League
Baseball's National League. The Mets are also often referred to as the "Amazins" by
fan and media alike.
</p>
<p>One of baseball's first expansion teams in 1962, the Mets won the 1969 World
Series. They have played in a total of four World Series, the most of any MLB
expansion team, including a second dramatic win in 1986.</p>
</div>
<h3 tabindex="-1" aria-expanded="false" role="tab" class="ui-accordion-header
ui-helper-reset ui-state-default ui-corner-all">
<span class="ui-icon ui-icon-triangle-1-e">
</span>
<a tabindex="-1" href="#">
NY Jets
</a>
</h3>
<div role="tabpanel" style="height: 93px; display: none;" class="ui-accordion-con-
tent ui-helper-reset ui-widget-content ui-corner-bottom">
<p>
The New York Jets are a professional Football team based in East Rutherford, New
Jersey, representing the New York metropolitan area. They are members of the
Eastern Division of the American Football Conference (AFC) in the National Football
League (NFL). In a unique arrangement, the Jets share New Meadowlands Stadium
(located in East Rutherford, New Jersey) with the New York Giants.
</p>
</div>
```

257

```
<h3 tabindex="-1" aria-expanded="false" role="tab" class="ui-accordion-header
ui-helper-reset ui-state-default ui-corner-all">
<span class="ui-icon ui-icon-triangle-1-e">
</span>
<a tabindex="-1" href="#">
Manchester United
</a>
</h3>
<div role="tabpanel" style="height: 93px; display: none;" class="ui-accordion-con-
tent ui-helper-reset ui-widget-content ui-corner-bottom">
<p>
Manchester United Football Club is an English professional football club, based in
Old Trafford, Greater Manchester, that plays in the Premier League. Founded as
Newton Heath LYR Football Club in 1878, the club changed its name to Manchester
United in 1902 and moved to Old Trafford in 1910.
</p>
</div>
</div>
```

When you're customizing the look and feel of the components, all of your changes should be executed in the ui.theme.css style sheet. You also have the option of using ThemeRoller, an online Web application created by the jQuery UI team, to set up your own theme. As you change the different style settings, the changes are reflected instantly onscreen in a demo of all the jQuery UI components.

CREATING A UI THEME WITH THEMEROLLER

ThemeRoller (http://jqueryui.com/themeroller/) has an online wizard interface that makes it extremely easy to select fonts, colors, and borders and apply these options to a theme that you can download to use in all of your projects, as shown in Figure 10-6. If you don't have the time to create a full theme from scratch, ThemeRoller has 24 themes that you can use and adapt for your project.

1. Set up the various options in ThemeRoller. When you're creating a theme, you have control over the following options in the theme:
   - Font settings
   - Corner radius
   - Header/toolbar
   - Content
   - Clickable areas: active, hover, default states
   - Highlight
   - Error
   - Modal screen for overlays
   - Drop shadows

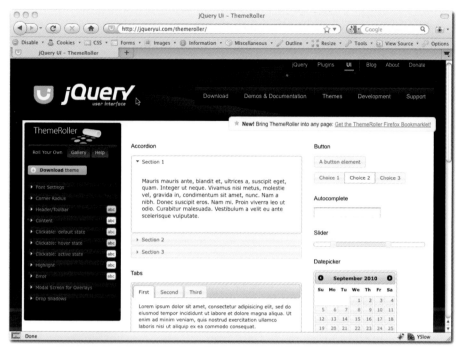

Figure 10-6: The jQuery UI ThemeRoller

© 2010 The jQuery Project and the jQuery UI Team

2. Each option is configured in the ThemeRoller on the left side of the page using a form. As you update the values, an example of the output as it is being applied to all of the jQuery UI components is shown on the right side of the page. You can update as little or as much as you wish.

3. You have the opportunity to download the theme that you've just created. Click the Download Theme button, as shown in Figure 10-7.

4. The theme is available to download as standalone files or grouped into a jQuery UI downloadable package, as shown in Figure 10-8. In this case, deselect all of the jQuery UI files and just download the theme.

5. The theme is delivered in a .zip file that is bundled with the following directory structure and files. The theme files are located in the CSS directory. If you have already downloaded jQuery UI JavaScript files, you can disregard the /js directory:

- /css/custom-theme/jquery-ui-1.8.5.custom.css
- /css/custom-theme/images/
- /development-bundle/
- /js/

Click the Download Theme button

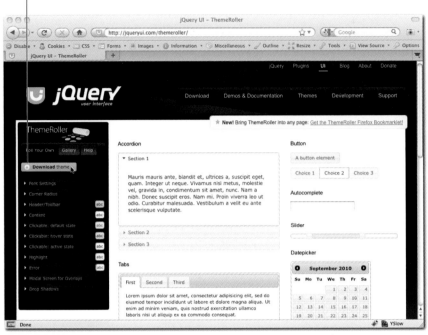

Figure 10-7: The Download Theme button in ThemeRoller app
© 2010 The jQuery Project and the jQuery UI Team

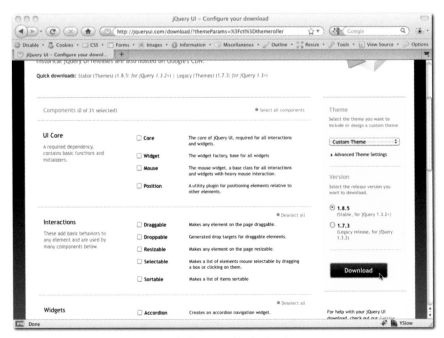

Figure 10-8: The Build Your Download page with all jQuery UI files deselected
© 2010 The jQuery Project and the jQuery UI Team

USING JQUERY UI THEMES

If you decide to create a custom theme through ThemeRoller or to create your own custom theme from scratch, you need to include it in the head of the Web page where you would like to apply it, like this:

```
<link type="text/css" href="../themes/base/jquery.ui.all.css" rel="stylesheet" />
```

INCORPORATING JQUERY UI FEATURES INTO YOUR WEB SITE

After you understand the basics of the jQuery UI plug-in, you can begin incorporating different components into your site with ease. In the following section, I introduce to you how to set up the tabs, accordion, autocomplete, and datepicker components.

Tabs

The jQuery UI tabs is a widget that, when applied to DOM elements, creates dynamic tabs that can be used in a number of ways to add interactivity to your Web site. I recently used the tabs to build an interactive slideshow for the home page of a Web site as shown in Figure 10-9. It was incredibly easy to set up using jQuery UI and saved me a lot of time by using code that is tried and true. The tabs in this example are situated along the bottom of the images. Each tab correlates to an image. As the tabs animate, the images change using a fade transition.

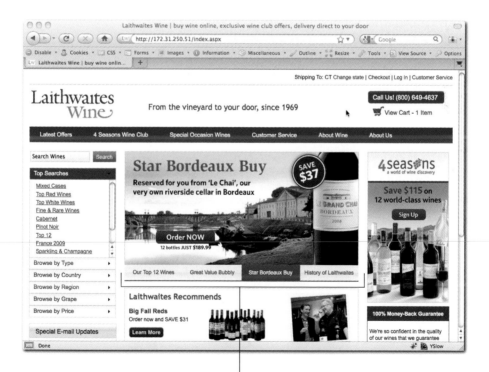

261

A tabbed slideshow

Figure 10-9: The tabbed slideshow on the Laithwaites Wine Web site

Reproduced from Laithwaiteswine.com

In the following tutorial, I show you how you can set up an animated tabbed slideshow just like the one I built for the Laithwaites Wine Web site:

1. Download the tabs component in a jQuery UI bundle using the Build Your Download page (`http://jqueryui.com/download`) and set up the jQuery UI as a JavaScript `include` in the head of your Web page:

```
<link type="text/css" href="../themes/base/jquery.ui.all.css" rel="stylesheet"
 />
```

2. Include the custom theme CSS file:

```
<link type="text/css" href="../themes/base/jquery.ui.all.css" rel="stylesheet"
 />
```

3. Set up the HTML. When you're using jQuery UI components, the HTML is required to be set up in specific way or the component won't render correctly. Wrap all of the HTML within a `div` called `#tabs`. This is used to reference the HTML when the tabs component is applied. Each tab should be given an ID of `#tab` followed by a sequential number (`#tab-1`, `#tab-2`, `#tab-3`).

```
<div id="tabs">
    <div id="tabs-1">
    <a href="#"> <img src="../images/homepage/4s_tab_offer1_july2010.jpg"
 alt="History of Laithwaites Wine" alt=""/></a>
    </div>
    <div id="tabs-2">
    <a href="#"><img src="/images/homepage/4s_tab_offer2_sep2010.jpg" alt="Kings
 of Cabernet" alt=""/></a>
    </div>
    <div id="tabs-3">
    <a href="#"><img src="/images/homepage/4s_tab_offer3_sep2010.jpg"
 alt="Discover Chile" alt=""/></a>
    </div>
    <div id="tabs-4">
    <a href="#"><img src="/images/homepage/4s_tab_offer4_sep2010.
jpg"  alt="World-class Rosé" alt=""/></a>
    </div>
    <ul>
      <li><a href="#tabs-1">History of Laithwaites </a></li>
      <li><a href="#tabs-2">Kings of Cabernet </a></li>
      <li><a href="#tabs-3">Discover Chile </a></li>
      <li><a href="#tabs-4">World-class Rose</a></li>
    </ul>
</div>
```

4. Create a selector statement that selects the `#tabs` element and applies the jQuery UI tabs method. In order to make the tabs animate, pass in the property `rotate` and give it a duration of 7,000, which makes it rotate slides every 7 seconds.

```
$("#tabs").tabs({ fx: { opacity: 'toggle' } }).tabs('rotate', 7000);
```

The accordion

The accordion is a great way to show content or even navigation tools in a small space and has become very popular on the Internet. When it's used for navigation, the accordion condenses a lot of menu options into a small menu, making it easier for users trying to navigate around your site. Sometimes, the various folds of the accordion — like the slides of a slideshow — are populated by Ajax and therefore you don't need to reload the page to get the new content.

In Chapter 6, I review how to create your own accordion menu or content: It amounts to about ten lines of code. jQuery UI can achieve the same end result but with only one line of code for the default settings, as shown in Figure 10-10. Pretty impressive!

An accordion menu

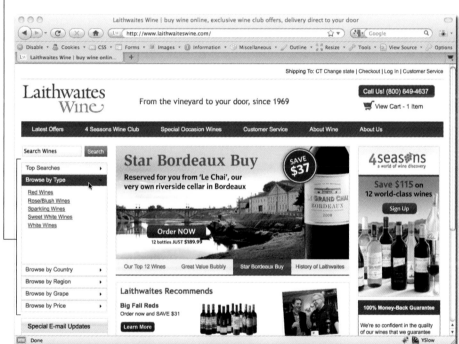

Figure 10-10: An accordion menu on the Laithwaites Wine Web site

Reproduced from Laithwaiteswine.com

1. Download the Accordion component in a jQuery UI bundle using the Build Your Download page (`http://jqueryui.com/download`) and set up the jQuery UI as a JavaScript `include` in the head of your Web page:

   ```
   <script type="text/javascript" src="js/jquery-ui-1.8.4.custom.min.js"></script>
   ```

2. Include the custom theme CSS file.

   ```
   <link type="text/css" href="../themes/base/jquery.ui.all.css" rel="stylesheet" />
   ```

3. Set up the HTML. When you're using jQuery UI components, the HTML must be set up in a certain manner or the component won't render correctly. Each jQuery UI component has a dedicated Web page of documentation. You should always refer to this when setting up components. The documentation for the accordion widget can be found at `http://jqueryui.com/demos/accordion/`. Set up the accordion HTML by wrapping all of the elements within a `div` called `#accordion`, which is then used to apply the accordion component to the HTML. Each accordion fold needs to have an h3 element for the title and a `div` element directly after it to contain the content.

```html
<div id="accordion">
    <h3><a href="#">NY Mets</a></h3>
    <div><p>The New York Mets are a professional baseball team based in the
    borough of Queens in New York City. The Mets are a member of the East Division
    of Major League Baseball's National League. The Mets are also often referred to
    as the "Amazins" by fan and media alike.</p>
    One of baseball's first expansion teams in 1962, the Mets won the 1969 World
    Series. They have played in a total of four World Series, the most of any MLB
    expansion team, including a second dramatic win in 1986.</p>
    </div>
    <h3><a href="#">NY Jets</a></h3>
    <div><p>The New York Jets are a professional Football team based in East
    Rutherford, New Jersey, representing the New York metropolitan area. They are
    members of the Eastern Division of the American Football Conference (AFC) in
    the National Football League (NFL). In a unique arrangement, the Jets share New
    Meadowlands Stadium (located in East Rutherford, New Jersey) with the New York
    Giants.</p>
    </div>
    <h3><a href="#">Manchester United</a></h3>
    <div><p>Manchester United Football Club is an English professional football
    club, based in Old Trafford, Greater Manchester, that plays in the Premier
    League. Founded as Newton Heath LYR Football Club in 1878, the club changed its
    name to Manchester United in 1902 and moved to Old Trafford in 1910.</p>
    </div>
</div>
```

4. Create a statement that selects the `#accordion` element and applies the `accordion()` method to it. The final result of this tutorial is shown in Figure 10-11.

```
$("#accordion").accordion();
```

If you would like to further customize the accordion, the jQuery UI Web site has documentation (`http://jqueryui.com/demos/accordion/`) about all of the available options.

Autocomplete

Google has made autocomplete functionality commonplace in its search engine — see Figure 10-12. When I type **jquery UI**, Google responds with a drop-down menu full of suggestions that I can select. Autocomplete, also known as suggestive search, is often set up on search input fields and many other types of field look-ups. As you start typing, each letter is matched and options are displayed directly below the input field, which makes it much easier to find what you're looking for, especially if you are unsure of the spelling.

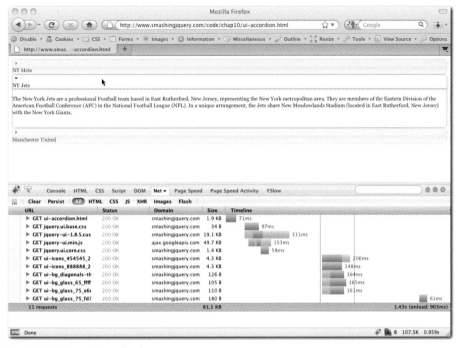

Figure 10-11: A jQuery UI accordion demo

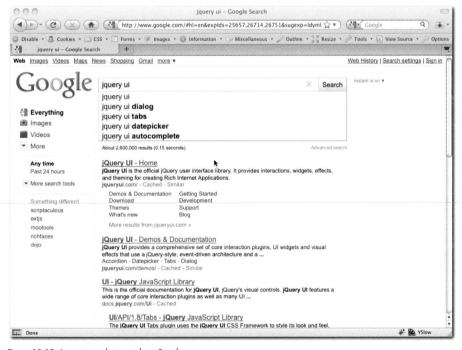

Figure 10-12: An autocomplete search on Google

Reproduced from 2010© Google

jQuery UI includes an autocomplete component that is incredibly easy to set up, requiring only a few lines of JavaScript. In the following example, I review how to set up the basic autocomplete component shown in Figure 10-13.

1. Download the Autocomplete component in a jQuery UI bundle using the Build Your Download page (http://jqueryui.com/download) and set up the jQuery UI as a JavaScript include in the head of your Web page:

   ```
   <script type="text/javascript" src="js/jquery-ui-1.8.4.custom.min.js"></script>
   ```

2. Include the custom theme CSS file:

   ```
   <link type="text/css" href="../themes/base/jquery.ui.all.css" rel="stylesheet"
    />
   ```

3. Create an input field with an ID of #search. Attach the autocomplete component to it.

   ```
   <label>Search</label>
     <input type="text" id="search" />
   ```

4. The autocomplete method contains an option called source. This is the source of the values that are matched against the characters that you type into the input field. You can set the source to be a remote script, an XML file, or, in this case, an array with set tags. Please refer to the jQuery UI documentation for further information about setting different types of sources.

   ```
   var availableTags = [
     "Nike",
     "Puma",
     "Aldo",
     "Tiger",
     "Cole Haan",
     ];
   ```

5. Create a statement that selects the #search element, attaches the autocomplete method, and passes in the source option set to the availableTags variable that was set up in the previous step.

   ```
   $("#search").autocomplete({source: availableTags});
   ```

Datepicker

jQuery UI also includes a very slick datepicker component that applies a date picker (a little pop-up calendar that allows you to select a date) to any input field that it is applied to, similar to the date picker shown on the TripAdvisor Web site in Figure 10-14. Date pickers have become commonplace; I can't think of the last time I had to manually enter a date.

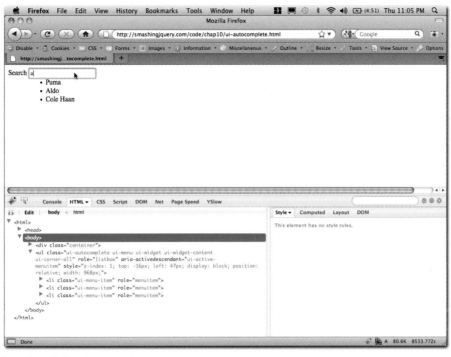

Figure 10-13: A jQuery UI autocomplete demo

267

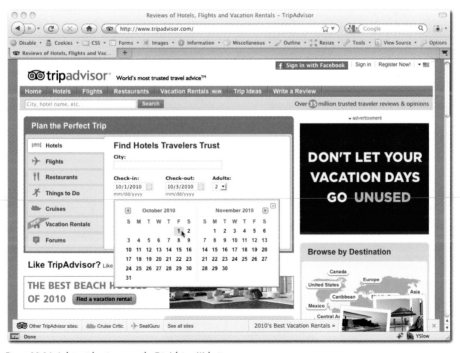

Figure 10-14: A date picker in use on the TripAdvisor Web site

The date picker is a UI component that is hard to live without, and jQuery UI makes it very easy to implement. A working example based on this tutorial can be seen in Figure 10-15:

1. Download the Datepicker component in a jQuery UI bundle using the Build Your Download page (http://jqueryui.com/download) and set up the jQuery UI as a JavaScript `include` in the head of your Web page:

```
<script type="text/javascript" src="js/jquery-ui-1.8.4.custom.min.js"></script>
```

2. Include the custom theme CSS file.

```
<link type="text/css" href="../themes/base/jquery.ui.all.css" rel="stylesheet" />
```

3. Create an input field with an ID of #date. This is used to attach the datepicker component to.

```
<label>Date</label>
  <input type="text" id="date" />
  </div>
```

4. Create a statement that selects the #date element and attach the `datepicker` method. Refer to the jQuery UI documentation if you would like further information on customizing the date picker. It's located at http://jqueryui.com/demos/datepicker/.

```
$('#datepicker').datepicker();
```

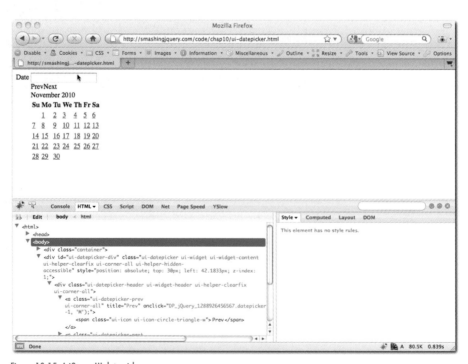

Figure 10-15: A jQuery UI date picker

INCORPORATING POPULAR JQUERY PLUG-INS INTO YOUR WEB SITE

jQuery has a huge audience of Web designers and developers who contribute great plug-ins. The plug-ins have a wide range of applications from Ajax to image galleries. If you are looking to do something, the chances are good that someone has already created a plug-in for that purpose.

The jQuery Web site has a section (`http://plugins.jquery.com/`) dedicated to plug-ins that allows you to submit your own plug-ins as well as bug reports and so on for third-party plug-ins that you are using on your site, as shown in Figure 10-16.

Plug-ins can really speed up your development time. The documentation for plug-ins is usually pretty good, but if you get stuck and can't find the author to ask for help, the jQuery forum (`http://forum.jquery.com/`) is a great place to go for support and advice.

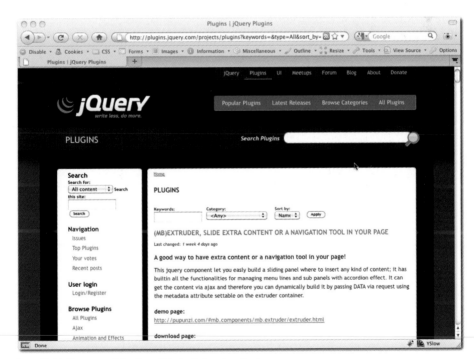

Figure 10-16: The section of the jQuery Web site dedicated to plug-ins

© 2010 The jQuery Project

USING JQUERY TOOLS

Similar to jQuery UI, jQuery Tools (`http://flowplayer.org/tools/index.html`), shown in Figure 10-17, is a UI library with six components: tabs, tooltips, overlays, scrolling functionality, forms, and toolboxes. This library is a great alternative to jQuery UI because of its small size, around 16 KB. jQuery UI has a lot of great features, but it also comes with a lot of features that you might not use. That means you have to include a really large library, which affects page load speed and Web site performance. That gets annoying if you're not even using all of the components in the first place.

Figure 10-17: The jQuery Tools home page

Reproduced by permission of Flowplayer Ltd

jQuery Tools allows you to download only the components that you plan to use, keeping the overall file size of the library to a minimum. jQuery Tools is a much more slimmed-down UI library because it only offers six components, with no theme library or CSS framework.

Adding a design around jQuery Tools components is not as streamlined as using jQuery UI. With no CSS framework or fancy theme library, you are left to define your own HTML and CSS. Depending upon on the Web site or application that you are working with, using jQuery Tools instead of jQuery UI can offer benefits such as a much smaller library footprint (about 4 KB), the ability to use existing HTML code because you don't have to conform to a set HTML structure, and a usable set of components without extra features that you won't use. I have found that if your site has some existing design and functionality, it's much easier to work with jQuery Tools and retrofit some functionality such as tabs or overlay into your code.

Setting Up jQuery Tools

jQuery Tools can be set up in much the same way as jQuery UI. You can either download the entire package plug-in with all of the components already included, or you can pick and choose which components you want and download just those pieces.

When it's time to set up the plug-in with your page, just upload the jQuery Tools JavaScript file to your Web server and place the following `script` tag in your Web page with a path to the location of the plug-in directly after the jQuery Library:

```
<script type="text/javascript" src="js/jquery-1.4.2.min.js"></script>
<script src="js/jquery.tools.min.js"></script>
```

Using the Tabs Tool to Create Dynamic Tabs

I recently used the Tabs tool to set up an in-page tabbed content area for the product details page of a Web site, as shown in Figure 10-18. The jQuery Tabs tool allowed me to use the existing HTML structure already in place on the Web site and instantly add tabs using this tool.

In the following tutorial, I walk you through how to use the tabs tools in jQuery tools to create dynamic tabs similar to the jQuery UI example, but with much less rendered HTML code that you have more control over. When I say more control, I mean that you don't have to adapt to a specific CSS framework such as with jQuery UI to style the tabs.

1. Create the HTML structure for your tabs. In this example, I use an unordered list for the tabs navigation and nested `div` elements to store the content, but anything can be adapted to work with jQuery Tools because it's not as strict when it comes to setting up the HTML as jQuery UI is. You can define the HTML structure.

```
<ul class="product-tabs">
   <li class="t-desc"><a href="#">Description</a></li>
   <li class="t-rev" ><a href="#">Customer Reviews</a></li>
 </ul>


 <div class="tab-panes">

   <div class="description">
     <p>Perfect with food, two presidents and the Queen of England.</p>
     <p>The "Rhône Rangers" are an elite group of California winemakers,
 centered around Paso Robles, whose holy grail is the dark, rich, black fruit
 magic of the best Rhône wines. Don Brady, elected 2006 Paso Robles Winemaker of
 the Year by his peers, has combined the keystone Rhône grapes of Syrah,
 Grenache and Cinsault to conjure his Cuvée de Robles 2006, exclusively for
 WSJwine. After 14 months in oak, with fresh cherry and cranberry aromas and
 rich, silky tannins, this is perfect wine to complement food and honor company.
 Which is why Don's wines were on the table at the White House dinner when the
 company was Queen Elizabeth II.</p>
   </div>

   <div class="customer-reviews" style="display:none;">
     <p>No Reviews Yet.</p>
   </div>

 </div>
```

2. Create a statement that selects the unordered list with a class `.product-tabs` and applies the `tabs` method. Within the parentheses of the `tabs` method, you need to pass in the structure of how the tabbed content is set up. In this case, the content of the tabs is wrapped in an element with the class `tab-panes`, so within the `tabs` method pass, add a parent-child selector that selects all the `div` elements found within the `tab-panes` element. Basically, this statement says, select the `product-tabs` element (tabs navigation) and apply the tabs tool with the content being located within the `div` elements contained within `tab-panes`.

```
$(".product-tabs").tabs(".tab-panes > div");
```

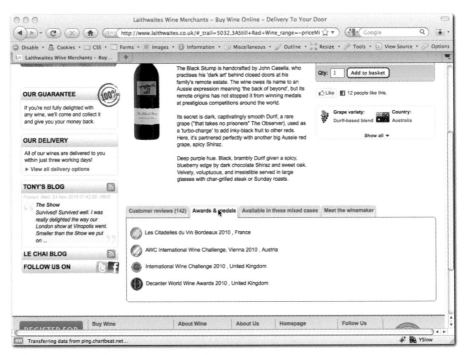

Figure 10-18: The Laithwaites Wine page, which uses tabs

Reproduced by permission of Laithwaites Wine

The tabs component in the jQuery tools plug-in has a wide range of options that can be applied to create more advanced tab implementations such as animated slideshows, fading effects, dynamic content, and so on. Please refer to the jQuery Tools Web site (`http://flowplayer.org/tools/documentation/index.html`) for the full documentation.

FANCYBOX

Fancybox (`http://fancybox.net/`) is lightweight lightbox plug-in based on the jQuery library. A lightbox is a way to display images in an overlay on a page without forcing a user to navigate to a separate page. Instead, a dark semi-transparent background covers the whole screen while an image is displayed in the foreground, usually in a white-bordered container. Figure 10-19 shows a lightbox from the Netflix Web site (`www.netflix.com`).

A lightbox

Figure 10-19: The Netflix Web site uses a lightbox window overlay to show quick info about products

Reproduced by permission of Netflix

273

The story of Fancybox begins with the original Lightbox plug-in. I began using the original Lightbox plug-in (`www.lokeshdhakar.com/projects/lightbox2/`) in 2006. Since then, many new versions have been released, with the last update coming in 2008. Because of the limited support for Lightbox 2, I switched to Thickbox (`http://jquery.com/demo/thickbox/`) by Cody Lindley. Thickbox pushed the envelope with lightbox functionality by allowing not only images, but also videos and even dynamic content loaded from other sources to be displayed in the lightboxes. I used Thickbox for about three years on various project, until the creators of Thickbox stopped supporting it. It was time to move on, so I chose Fancybox, shown in Figure 10-20, and have been quite happy with it.

The lesson behind my history with the Lightbox plug-in is that plug-ins are great, but when the person or company behind that plug-in stops supporting it, you either continue using it with the hopes that future versions of jQuery don't break the plug-in when you upgrade, or you scrap the plug-in and find something else that is supported. Each time this scenario happens, I usually switch to a new plug-in, one that is often better and has more features.

1. When using a plug-in with jQuery, you always need to include it in the top of your page. It should always be included directly after the jQuery library, but before any jQuery code that you have created:

```
<script src="js/fancybox.js"></script>
```

2. When setting up the HTML, add a class to the anchor tags that you want to set up using Fancybox. The class can be anything — I just created one called .fancybox.

```
<a class="fancybox" href="http://farm5.static.flickr.com/4058/4252054277_
  f0fa91e026.jpg"><img alt="example1" src="http://farm5.static.flickr.
  com/4058/4252054277_f0fa91e026_m.jpg" /></a>
```

3. Create a statement that selects the .fancybox element and applies the fancybox method. If you do not pass in any options to the fancybox method, the default behavior is applied.

```
$(".fancybox").fancybox();
```

Figure 10-20: The Fancybox jQuery plug-in demo

Please refer to the Fancybox Web site (http://fancybox.net/) for the full documentation.

WRITING YOUR FIRST JQUERY PLUG-IN

Writing your own jQuery plug-in is a great way to share code that you have created with the jQuery community in a way that anyone can easily adapt to their own projects. You can also write a jQuery plug-in for your own use, if you are going to be using that same method in a variety of applications within a site.

Most Web site issues or enhancements that you encounter when building and maintaining the DOM or Ajax iterations can be solved with jQuery and in turn can be converted into a plug-in for reuse. But on some occasions, if a plug-in already exists with similar functionality or if this is a small one-time fix, moving your code to a plug-in is unnecessary. It's important to keep in mind some key tips when creating a jQuery plug-in:

- Create a unique plug-in name. Before choosing a plug-in name, check to see if a plug-in with this name already exists.
- Avoid using the $ alias to avoid conflicts with other JavaScript libraries that use a similar alias.
- Use comments to explain the plug-in.
- Make sure the plug-in has an open-source license for distributing.
- Plan/sketch out the plug-in on a scrap piece of paper before you start to code.
- Set up default settings that can be overwritten.
- Check out the jQuery plug-in documentation, shown in Figure 10-21 (`http://docs.jquery.com/Plug-ins/Authoring`).

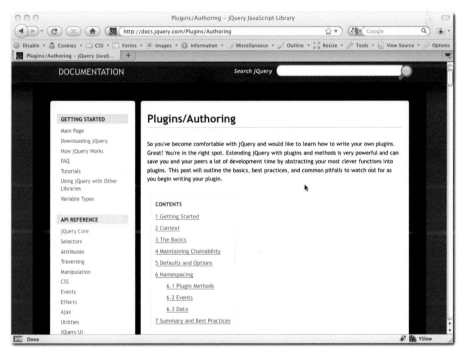

Figure 10-21: The jQuery plug-in documentation

© 2010 The jQuery Project

SKETCHING OUT THE PLUG-IN

For this example plug-in I'd like to create, I want to select an unordered list that is created dynamically and only show the first ten list items and leaving the rest hidden. A simple show and hide type of navigation is displayed to toggle the visibility of the hidden items. I need to be able to change the text in the navigation links and also change the number of links that are shown. This is very basic functionality, but it's perfect for showing how to create a plug-in without getting overcomplicated.

UNDERSTANDING THE PLUG-IN STRUCTURE

Before getting started with how to set up the plug-in, I want to discuss the basic plug-in structure. All jQuery plug-ins are declared in the `jQuery.fn` method.

```
jQuery.fn.showhidePlugin = function() {
   // plug-in stuff goes here
 };
```

The name in bold is where you set up the name of the plug-in; this is how the plug-in will be referenced.

```
$('.selector').showhidePlugin();
```

I also suggest that you save the plug-in file as jquery.pluginname.js for consistency. I always like to add the word jQuery at the beginning of any JavaScript files that are jQuery-related — it's a great organizational tip and helps communicate that it's a jQuery plug-in.

Notice that I'm not using the $ alias; instead, I'm using the jQuery namespace to avoid any potential conflicts. If you want to use the $ alias instead of jQuery, you can do so by wrapping the plug-in function with a self-executing anonymous function. It's almost better to add the self-executing function just to be on the safe side and to be able to use the $ alias without any issues.

```
(function($){
  jQuery.fn.showhidePlugin = function() {
    // plug-in stuff goes here
  };
  })( jQuery );
```

SETTING THE OPTIONS FOR THE PLUG-IN

You can set up options that can be passed into the plug-in method by adding options into parenthesis in the `fn` method. Set up the default settings using JSON (JavaScript Object Notation). This plug-in will have three default settings: `numShown`, `showText`, and `hide-Text`. The default settings are created in the plug-in, but passing these options into the method at runtime can overwrite these settings.

```
(function($){
  jQuery.fn.showhidePlugin = function(options) {

  //Set the default values, use comma to separate the settings
  var defaults = {
    numShown: 10,
     showText : 'Show More Links',
     hideText : 'Hide Links'
  }

  };
  })( jQuery );
```

Next, using `extend`, you merge the defaults and options. If options are passed into the defaults, they overwrite any options that were declared in the function.

.extend() allows you to extend an object with one or more additional objects by merging the right object(s) into the left (first) object.

```
(function($){
  jQuery.fn.showhidePlugin = function(options) {

    //Set the default values, use a comma to separate
    the settings
    var defaults = {
    numShown: 10,
    showText : 'Show More Links',
    hideText : 'Hide Links'
    }

    var options =   $.extend(defaults, options);


  };
})( jQuery );
```

CREATING THE PLUG-IN

After you set up the options for the plug-in in the previous steps, it's time to build in the functionality, using a mixture of jQuery and native JavaScript, that allows you to apply this plug-in to any unordered list of items. You can then truncate the list using the value from the numShown variable and add hide and show links to toggle the visibility of the hidden items.

1. Add an each method that iterates through the matched set from the selector statement that this function is attached to using return this. This is important for any plug-in to function. If you set up the plug-in an unordered list, the each method applies to all of the content contained within the unordered list.

   ```
   return this.each(function() {
     });
   ```

2. Create two variables — o and obj. The purpose of these variables is to make referencing this and options quicker and easier instead of having to write each of them out each time. The selector that the plug-in has been applied to will now be known as obj.

   ```
   return this.each(function() {
     var o = options;
     var obj = $(this);
     });
   ```

3. Next, create three more variables: pLength, numHidden, and pList. The value of pLength is set to the number of children that obj contains. The value of numHidden is equal to pLength minus numShown, which is a default setting. If there are 30 items in pLength and 5 in numShown, numHidden equals 25. The value of pList is set to the children of obj.

277

```
return this.each(function() {
  var o = options;
  var obj = $(this);

  // Determine the length of items here and calculate the number hidden
  var pLength = obj.children().length;
  var numHidden = pLength - o.numShown;
  var pList = obj.children();

});
```

4. Create another variable called `shLink`. This variable is used to display the `anchor` tag for showing and hiding the text. The `anchor` tag is set to the `showText` default setting and has a class `.view` to be referenced later on. This link is used to control the show/hide effect.

```
return this.each(function() {
  var o = options;
  var obj = $(this);

  // Determine the length of items here and calculate the number hidden
  var pLength = obj.children().length;
  var numHidden = pLength - o.numShown;
  var pList = obj.children();

  // Set up Show/Hide Link
  var shLink = "<a href='#' class='view'>" + o.showText + "</a>";
});
```

5. Add a conditional statement that tests whether `pLength` is greater than `numShown`. If the statement is true, insert the `shLink` before the `obj`. This places the show/hide link before the start of the matched set.

```
return this.each(function() {
  var o = options;
  var obj = $(this);

  // Determine the length of items here and calculate the number hidden
  var pLength = obj.children().length;
  var numHidden = pLength - o.numShown;
  var pList = obj.children();

  // Set up Show/Hide Link
  var shLink = "<a href='#' class='view'>" + o.showText + "</a>";

  if (pLength > o.numShown) {
    jQuery(shLink).insertBefore(obj);
  }
});
```

6. Create another `each` loop that is assigned to `pList`. This loop iterates through all the children from the matched set.

```
return this.each(function() {
  var o = options;
```

```
var obj = $(this);

// Determine the length of items here and calculate the number hidden
var pLength = obj.children().length;
var numHidden = pLength - o.numShown;
var pList = obj.children();

// Set up Show/Hide Link
var shLink = "<a href='#' class='view'>" + o.showText + "</a>";

if (pLength > o.numShown) {
jQuery(shLink).insertBefore(obj);
}
pList.each(function(index){
});
});
```

7. Inside of the each function that you just created, add a conditional if/else statement.
First you test whether the index is less than (<) the number shown. If that is true, show
all of the elements that are equal to the index. Otherwise, hide the elements and add a
hidden class to them. The index is the loop's iteration variable or the variable that is
incremented by jQuery with each iteration of the loop.

```
return this.each(function() {
  var o = options;
  var obj = $(this);

  // Determine the length of items here and calculate the number hidden
  var pLength = obj.children().length;
  var numHidden = pLength - o.numShown;
  var pList = obj.children();

  // Set up Show/Hide Link
  var shLink = "<a href='#' class='view'>" + o.showText + "</a>";

  if (pLength > o.numShown) {
  jQuery(shLink).insertBefore(obj);
  }
  pList.each(function(index){
    if (index < o.numShown) {
      jQuery(pList[index]).show();
  }
  else {
    jQuery(pList[index]).hide();
    jQuery(pList[index]).addClass('hidden');
  }
  });
});
```

8. Set up a click handler function that uses the live event handler attachment to bind the
click event to the anchor tag a.view. Add a return false to prevent the default
behavior of the click from occurring. Also add a statement that select all elements with
the class .hidden and toggles their display from show to hide or vice-versa.

```
return this.each(function() {
  var o = options;
  var obj = $(this);

  // Determine the length of items here and calculate the number hidden
  var pLength = obj.children().length;
  var numHidden = pLength - o.numShown;
  var pList = obj.children();

  // Set up Show/Hide Link
  var shLink = "<a href='#' class='view'>" + o.showText + "</a>";

  if (pLength > o.numShown) {
    jQuery(shLink).insertBefore(obj);
  }
  pList.each(function(index){
    if (index < o.numShown) {
//alert('test');
      jQuery(pList[index]).show();
  }
  else {
    jQuery(pList[index]).hide();
    jQuery(pList[index]).addClass('hidden');
  }
  });
  // This is where I toggle the text
  jQuery("a.view").live("click", function(e){
    jQuery('.hidden').toggle();
  return false;
  });
});
```

9. The final step of setting up the plug-in involves adding a conditional statement that toggles the show/hide text within the anchor tag. Use the if statement to test if the a.view link contains the showText. If it does, when it is clicked on, it should change to the hide text. The else condition does the opposite.

```
return this.each(function() {
  var o = options;
  var obj = $(this);

  // Determine the length of items here and calculate the number hidden
  var pLength = obj.children().length;
  var numHidden = pLength - o.numShown;
  var pList = obj.children();

  // Set up Show/Hide Link
  var shLink = "<a href='#' class='view'>" + o.showText + "</a>";

  if (pLength > o.numShown) {
    jQuery(shLink).insertBefore(obj);
  }
```

```
    pList.each(function(index){
       if (index < o.numShown) {
    //alert('test');
          jQuery(pList[index]).show();
    }
    else {
       jQuery(pList[index]).hide();
       jQuery(pList[index]).addClass('hidden');
    }
    });
    // This is where I toggle the text
    jQuery("a.view").live("click", function(e){
    if (jQuery(this).text()==o.showText) {
       jQuery(this).text(o.hideText);
    }
    else {
       jQuery(this).text(o.showText);
    }
    jQuery('.hidden').toggle();
    return false;
    });
    });
```

Here is the complete jQuery plug-in code for jquery.showhide.plugin.js:

```
(function($){
  jQuery.fn.showhidePlugin= function(options) {

  //Set the default values, use comma to separate the settings
  var defaults = {
  numShown: 10,
  showText : 'Show More Links',
  hideText : 'Hide Links'
  }

  var options =  $.extend(defaults, options);

  return this.each(function() {
  var o = options;
  var obj = $(this);

  // Determine the length of items here and calculate the number hidden
  var pLength = obj.children().length;
  var numHidden = pLength - o.numShown;
  var pList = obj.children();

  // Set up Show/Hide Link
  var shLink = "<a href='#' class='view'>" + o.showText + "</a>";

  if (pLength > o.numShown) {
    jQuery(shLink).insertBefore(obj);
```

```
        }

    pList.each(function(index){
        if (index < o.numShown) {
            jQuery(pList[index]).show();
        }
        else {
            jQuery(pList[index]).hide();
            jQuery(pList[index]).addClass('hidden');
        }
    });

    // This is where I toggle the text
    jQuery("a.view").live("click", function(e){

    if (jQuery(this).text()==o.showText) {
        jQuery(this).text(o.hideText);
    }
    else {
        jQuery(this).text(o.showText);
    }
    jQuery('.hidden').toggle();
    return false;
    });

    });
    }
    })(jQuery);
```

The plug-in is now complete. The next step is to test that it works on your Web site by applying it to an element. To do this, I use a simple example of an unordered list that contains more than ten list items.

1. Set up the HTML that you would like to apply the plug-in to. In this example, I use an unordered list with the class .big-list.

```
<ul class="big-list">
    <li>Test 1.</li>
    <li>Test 2.</li>
    <li>Test 3.</li>
    <li>Test 4.</li>
    <li>Test 5.</li>
    <li>Test 6.</li>
    <li>Test 7.</li>
    <li>Test 8.</li>
    <li>Test 9.</li>
    <li>Test 432.</li>
    <li>Test 23.</li>
    <li>Test 0232.</li>
    <li>Test 2002.</li>
    <li>Test 541.</li>
    <li>Test 5432.</li>
```

```
        <li>Test 542.</li>
        <li>Test 542.</li>
        <li>Test 342.</li>
        <li>Test 452.</li>
        <li>Test 42.</li>
        <li>Test 542.</li>
        <li>Test 4542.</li>
        <li>Test 432.</li>
        <li>Test 23.</li>
        <li>Test 0232.</li>
        <li>Test 2002.</li>
    </ul>
```

2. Include the plug-in file directly after the jQuery library in the head of your Web page:

```
<script src="js/jquery.showhidePlugin.js" type="text/javascript"></script>
```

3. Select the `.big-list` element and attach the `showhidePlugin()` method to the end. Because you're not passing any options into the method, the default settings are applied.

```
$(".big-list").showhidePlugin();
```

4. If you would like to change the display of the show/hide plug-in as shown in Figure 10-22, just pass in any of the default settings that you would like to change into the `showHidePlugin()` function inside a single object literal, instead of passing each as a separate arguments.

```
$(".big-list").showhidePlugin({
    numShown:15,
    showText:"Show FTW"
    });
```

283

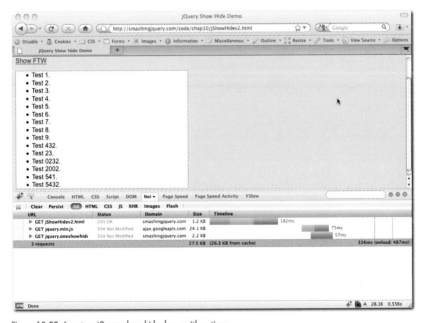

Figure 10-22: A custom jQuery show-hide demo with options

HOW TO DISTRIBUTE A JQUERY PLUG-IN

When you are ready to distribute your plug-in, you have quite a few things to keep in mind. Here is a quick checklist that is useful to go through before releasing your plug-in to the wild!

- Test that the plug-in works on all browsers — IE6, IE7, IE8, Firefox, Safari, Chrome, and Opera.
- Create documentation that explains the options and how the plug-in works.
- Add an open source license from the open source initiative Web site (`www.open source.org/licenses/index.html`) if you wish to make your plug-in open source.

PACKAGING YOUR JQUERY PLUG-IN FOR DISTRIBUTION

Be sure your plug-in code is ready for production environments. To do so, you can use a minification service such as Douglas Crockford's minifier, JavaScript Packer (http://jscompress.com/), shown in Figure 10-23, to compress your plug-in code. *Minification* is a technique used to remove unnecessary characters such as comments, line breaks, white space, and tabs to improve loading times. It's always a good idea to offer both development (uncompressed) and production (minified) versions of your plug-in. If your plug-in is small (under 4 KB uncompressed), you don't have to minify it, but I would get in the habit nonetheless.

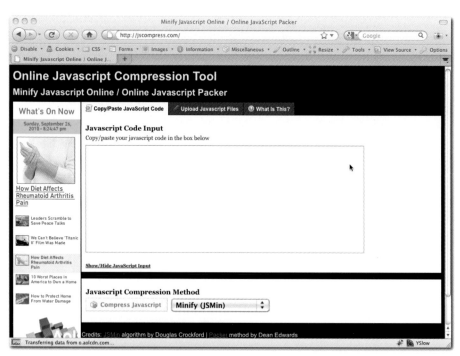

Figure 10-23: Douglas Crockford has created a minifier script

JSMin algoritm by Douglas Crockford | Packer method by Dean Edwards | JavaScript compression tool/service created by Vance Lucas

SUBMITTING YOUR PLUG-IN TO WEB SITES

You can submit your plug-in to a few sites to help ensure its success and distribution to the open source community. If you are releasing your plug-in as open source, I would highly suggest that you post it to these locations:

- **The jQuery Plug-in section** (`http://plugins.jquery.com/`): The jQuery official site offers a wiki where plug-in developers can submit their code. You can upload your code either through the browser or by using version-control software such as Subversion or Git. Here you can add a name and description, respond to bugs, receive ratings from the community, post links to your documentation, and so on.
- **Project Hosting on Google code** (`http://code.google.com/hosting/`): Google project hosting is very similar to the jQuery plug-in section, offering many of the same benefits. The biggest benefit is that it's Google and therefore gets a lot of traffic.

11

DEVELOPING FOR THE MOBILE WEB WITH JQUERY

YOU CAN USE JQUERY on mobile Web applications as you would any other Web site or application. Mobile phones are limited by their screen resolution and bandwidth, which are key factors you should keep in mind when creating mobile Web applications. Mobile Web applications can be either purely online Web applications accessed via a Web browser or on a mobile device, or they can be native Web applications.

In this chapter, I explain the difference between a mobile Web site and a mobile application, discuss the benefits of CSS3 and HTML5 on the mobile Web, and guide you through how to set up and install mobile browser emulators for Google Android and Apple Mobile. Last but not least, I give you a glimpse of what's to come with jQuery Mobile Alpha.

BUILDING FOR THE MOBILE WEB USING JQUERY

You can take a few different routes with mobile Web applications. The mobile Web application market seems to be quite concentrated around two platforms: Apple iPhone/iPad and Google Android.

When you're creating a Web site or application compatible with multiple mobile browsers, you will find it much tougher than doing the same with desktop support for browsers. This is still very new territory for jQuery developers because many popular phones do not have great JavaScript support. Smartphones such as Apple iPhone and Google Android have much more advanced Web browser capabilities, which makes those platforms the easiest to develop for.

Here are a couple of tips for building mobile Web sites and applications:

- Define your audience before starting development. This means you need to determine who you are building the app for. What platform will be they using? Which browser do they use? Will it be Wi-Fi or a cellular network?
- Keep your site or app simple. Mobile devices have limited bandwidth and screen sizes.

The Roanoke College Mobile Web site, shown in Figure 11-1, is a good example of a Web site designed for the iPhone browser that uses jQuery to load content using the Ajax method `load()`. It also uses a jQuery plug-in to offer a slideshow to showcase recent images around the college.

Figure 11-1: The Roanoke College Mobile Web App uses jQuery

MOBILE BROWSERS

Similar to the browser war that has been raging on the desktop for quite a few years now between Internet Explorer, Mozilla Firefox, Apple Safari, Opera, and newcomer Google Chrome, a similar situation is now occurring with the mobile browsers. Each mobile browser can offer different advantages, but as the mobile Web application market advances, you should see more of the same features across the browsers.

You can create a mobile Web browser application without having to touch any native mobile platform code, just by using the tools that you already use: HTML, CSS, and jQuery. The two leading mobile smartphone platforms, Apple iPhone iOS and Google Android, have two very advanced mobile browsers included with them; the HTML5, CSS3, and JavaScript features supported by these devices are outlined in Table 11.1. A *native application* — software that is built for the phone's operating system as opposed to a Web site or Web app that can be viewed on the phone — does offer great benefits, but you can also build something valuable for the browser. This makes even greater sense if you are already developing a Web site for the desktop browser.

Table 11.1   Mobile Browser Features

	HTML5	CSS3	JavaScript
Apple Safari 5	Yes	Yes	Yes
Google Android (Chrome)	Yes	Yes	Yes
Mozilla Firefox Mobile	Yes	Yes	Yes
Opera 10 Mobile	No	Yes	Yes

As you can see from the preceding table, the Safari, Chrome, and Firefox mobile browsers are the best supported with new features currently on the market. Safari and Chrome have a leg up on Firefox because they are the default browsers for iPhone and Android. Opera 10 Mobile is now available as a downloadable application on Google Android and Apple iPhone platforms.

Both platforms support CSS3 and HTML5. If you haven't heard anything about these advances in Web design, you are in for a real treat! CSS3 and HTML5 are usually mentioned in the same sentence because of the nature of what they do, but there are a lot of differences between the two technologies.

UNDERSTANDING CSS3

CSS3 (also known as Cascading Style Sheets 3) has been under development since December 2005. It's just starting to make its way into more advanced browsers such as Apple Safari 4, Google Chrome, Microsoft Internet Explorer 9, Opera 10, and Firefox 4. As these browsers start to gain market share, CSS3 becomes more mainstream. You can create a mobile Web site that utilizes these technologies now using the iPhone and Android platforms. Doing so should help advance your knowledge and career because you gain experience working with the latest and greatest technologies and gain a better understanding of the limitations involved with mobile Web site and application development.

CSS3 offers the following new properties, among others, which you can find out more about at www.css3.info, as shown in Figure 11-2. These properties are beneficial to mobile devices because historically many of these properties would need to be done using images, CSS workarounds and JavaScript, which would increase the size of the pages, therefore decreasing performance. By using CSS properties, the performance of the mobile Web site is not compromised.

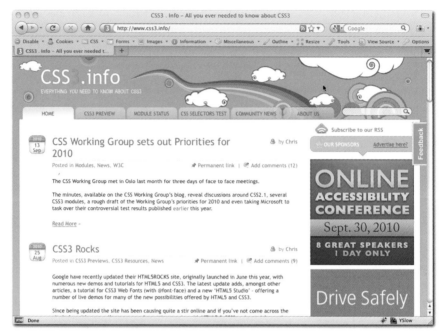

Figure 11-2: A CSS3 resource, CSS3.info

- Border Radius to create rounded corners using CSS, as shown in Figure 11-3
- Border Image to create a border that uses an image
- Box Shadow to create drop shadows using CSS
- Multiple Backgrounds, which lessens the amount of code you need to display different background images and instead declares a different multiple background positioning property in CSS
- New Color Options to support color types other than RGB and hex and offer true opacity to create transparency without resorting to browser hacks
- Text Shadow to create drop shadows on textual elements

For a full list of the new functions and features in CSS3, please visit www.css3.info/preview/. jQuery supports CSS3 selectors.

UNDERSTANDING HTML5

HTML5 has been under development since January 2008 and is just starting to make its way into modern browsers. Among others, HTML5 offers the following features:

- Integrated form validation
- Local storage

The benefits of these features are immense, but HTML5 offers many more that I haven't even mentioned. The future of Web design with browsers supporting both HTML5 and CSS3 is looking hot.

- Header and footer tags for better content organization within HTML files, instead of relying on `div` elements.
- Integrated audio/video tag support
- Canvas tags to create graphics and images on the fly
- Geolocation API (application programming interface)

Figure 11-3: The effects of the CSS3 Border Radius property as viewed on the iPhone Emulator

GETTING SET UP TO START MOBILE WEB DESIGN

The hardest part about designing for mobile Web is testing your work and deciding which mobile platforms to support. I focus on support of Google Android and Apple iPhone. To facilitate this, you could purchase an iPhone and an Android phone, but this would end up costing you a lot of money and effort. Instead, both companies, Apple and Google, have created developer portals and offer a development SDK (Software Development Kit) that includes an emulator. An emulator is a desktop application that you can add to your desktop to simulate iPhone or Android mobile devices and be able to test both native applications and mobile Web applications and Web sites.

Downloading the Apple iPhone Safari desktop emulator

You can access the Apple Safari emulator by pointing your browser to `developer.apple.com/devcenter/ios/index.action`. After you have registered as a developer on the Apple.com developer portal, you can proceed to download and install the iPhone emulator. After you have installed the emulator, you can start it up and browse to any Web site using Safari as you would a real iPhone, as shown in Figure 11-4.

Downloading the Google Android desktop emulator

You can access the Google Android emulator by visiting to `developer.android.com/sdk/index.html`. After you have download and installed the Android Chrome emulator, you can open it up and browse to any Web page using Chrome Mobile as you would on a real Android phone, as shown in Figure 11-5.

Figure 11-4: The Apple iPhone Safari desktop emulator

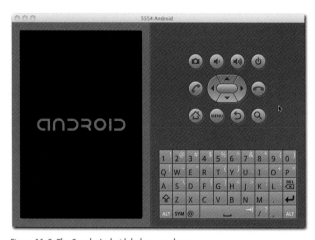

Figure 11-5: The Google Android desktop emulator

292

WORKING WITH THE APPLE IPHONE SAFARI MOBILE BROWSER

Building a Web site or application for the iPhone Safari browser is really exciting because of how advanced the browser is, as shown in Figure 11-6. Safari supports CSS3 and HTML5, so you can probably understand my excitement. The downside is that only a few other browsers, Safari Mobile being one of them, support CSS3 and HTML5, so you have to make a plan of which features and mobile devices to support.

Before native iPhone apps existed, when the first Apple iPhone was released in June 2007, the big thing was Web applications. Apple supported this by adding a section on their iPhone Web site dedicated to showcasing Web apps created specifically for the iPhone, as shown in Figure 11-7.

Apple has put a lot of effort into creating development portals for both the native applications and Safari Web applications. Before you start any development, I highly recommend that you visit the Safari Dev Center (refer to Figure 11-8). The Dev Center offers videos, technical documentation, and sample code to help you get started when you're developing your first Web application for Apple Safari on iPhone.

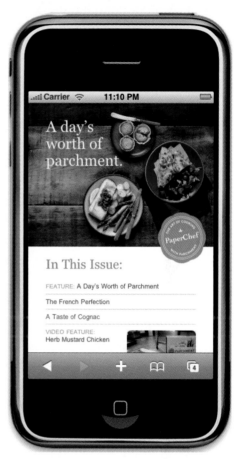

Figure 11-6: The Apple iPhone Safari browser with a mobile Web app

WORKING WITH THE GOOGLE ANDROID BROWSER

Google Chrome, as shown in Figure 11-9, on Android is also exciting to build Web applications for because of its support for new technologies like CSS3 and HTML5. jQuery is also supported on Android, so essentially any work you do for desktop Web sites and applications can be easily transferred to mobile.

Google has devoted a lot of effort to creating an excellent portal for developers. Similar to the iOS Dev Center, Google offers videos, technical documentation, code examples, and discussion forums. The Google Android development center, as shown in Figure 11-10 (http://developer.android.com/index.html), offers a wealth of information and should definitely be checked out before starting any work on a Web application.

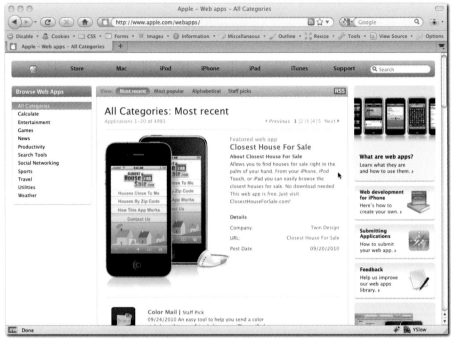

Figure 11-7: The Apple iPhone Web Apps showcase

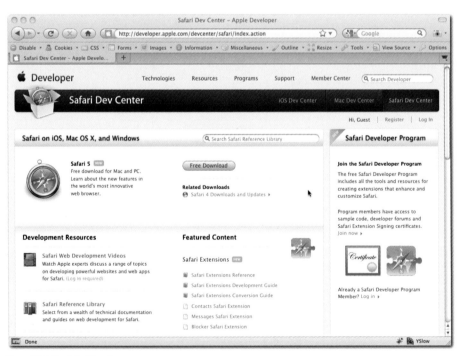

Figure 11-8: The Safari Dev Center

Figure 11-9: The Google Android Chrome browser

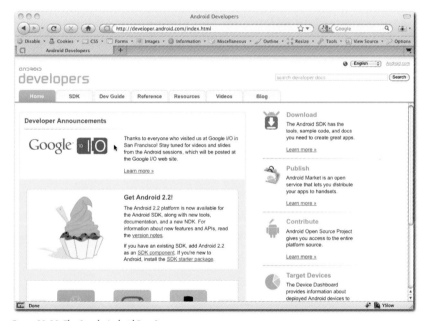

Figure 11-10: The Google Android Dev Center

Reproduced from 2010© Google. www.android.com

DISPLAYING CONTENT BASED ON WHICH SMARTPHONE YOUR USERS HAVE

Using Web server rewrites, you can detect desktop versus mobile browser traffic and show them an appropriate Web site based on their platform. The following code is an example of how you can set up mobile redirects for different mobile platforms. Each line uses a rewrite condition to test if the user agent is an iPhone, BlackBerry, or Android. If it finds a match, the user is redirected to a mobile version of the Web site suited to the mobile device. The rewrites use a regular expression within `Mod_rewrite` to set up the different rules for different mobile platforms.

Before you can use the following code, you need to make sure your Web server is Apache and has `Mod_rewrite` enabled, although there are alternatives if your Web site is hosted on a Windows server that you can find by searching on Google. Ask your Web host and they should be able to point you in the right direction:

```
RewriteCond %{HTTP_USER_AGENT} ^.*iPhone.*$
RewriteRule ^(.*)$ http://iphone.yourdomain.com [R=301]
RewriteCond %{HTTP_USER_AGENT} ^.*BlackBerry.*$
RewriteRule ^(.*)$ http://bb.yourdomain.com [R=301]
RewriteCond %{HTTP_USER_AGENT} ^.*Android.*$
RewriteRule ^(.*)$ http://android.yourdomain.com [R=301]
```

DEVELOPING MOBILE WEB SITES AND APPLICATIONS WITH JQUERY

When you finally start development of a Web site or application for mobile, you can integrate jQuery as you would with a desktop Web site or application. Everything I have reviewed up until this point in previous chapters works on a mobile phone as long as JavaScript is supported.

INTRODUCING JQUERY MOBILE PREVIEW

The jQuery team has announced the release of the jQuery Mobile (http://jquerymobile.com/) plug-in as an alpha version, as shown in Figure 11-11. Discussions and rumors have been circulating on the online jQuery community for some time. Will there be a separate library for jQuery Mobile? Yes, it is a separate plug-in weighing in at 6 KB, which needs to be included after the jQuery library. Which platforms will be supported? Apple iOS, Google Android, Blackberry, bada, Windows Phone, Symbian, Palm webOS, and MeeGo. A full compatibility chart can be viewed at http://jquerymobile.com/gbs/. How big will the download be? The development plug-in is 86KB and the minified plug-in is 12 KB.

Because jQuery Mobile has been released as an alpha version, bugs and issues will occur, but the plug-in looks very promising as far as its level of support and the features that it brings to the table.

MOBILE FRAMEWORKS

Mobile frameworks are similar to JavaScript libraries; they offer a range of APIs that interface with the mobile device that you're developing for. Currently, Appcelerator Titanium and jQTouch are the only mobile frameworks that boast jQuery support.

WORKING WITH APPCELERATOR TITANIUM MOBILE

Appcelerator is a development framework for creating mobile and desktop applications that was introduced in December 2008, as shown in Figure 11-12. Using it, you can create mobile applications for Apple iPhone, Apple iPad, Google Android, and BlackBerry phones using HTML, CSS, and JavaScript/jQuery.

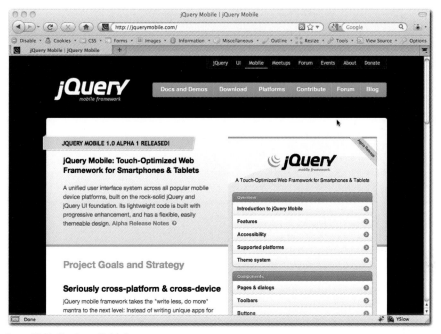

Figure 11-11: The jQuery Mobile home page

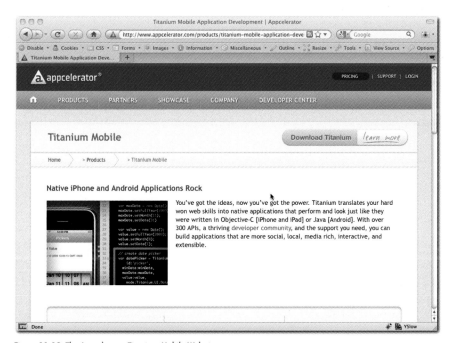

Figure 11-12: The Appcelerator Titanium Mobile Web site

Appcelerator Titanium Mobile has the following features:

- Lets you match the native user interface to create an application that feels familiar to your users
- Multimedia support for photo, music, and video streaming on the actual device
- Local file storage to access and store files on the device to speed up the performance of the application and offer an application that can be used without an Internet connection
- Access a mobile device's camera and video camera to create interactive applications
- Geolocation to create applications that use your location through GPS on the mobile phone to offer an extended user experience
- HTML5 and CSS3 support

You can obtain the full list by going to `www.appcelerator.com/products/titanium-mobile-application-development/`. At the time of this writing (fall of 2010), Appcelerator is personally responsible for 4,900 apps and boasts a support community of more than 75,000 developers. Part of the reason behind Appcelerator's success is that it's an open-source project, which makes it really easy for Web designers with no hardcore programming knowledge to create applications using technology that they use every day.

Appcelerator Titanium Mobile is not meant for absolute beginners, but Appcelerator does offer support and has great online documentation to help you get started.

WORKING WITH THE JQTOUCH PLUG-IN

jQTouch is an open-source jQuery plug-in that allows you to create an iPhone Web application that mimics native functionality such as animations, navigation, and themes as shown in Figure 11-13. jQTouch allows for this functionality by way of HTML, CSS, and jQuery.

jQTouch was recently purchased by Sencha and has since been rolled into an application called Sencha Touch (shown in Figure 11-14), which is a HTML5 mobile app framework that allows you to build Web apps for Apple iOS and Google Android.

Figure 11-13: The jQTouch home page

© 2009–2010 David Kaneda

Figure 11-14: The Sencha Touch home page

© 2006–2010 Sencha Inc.

299

12

FINDING JQUERY RESOURCES

JQUERY HAS A LARGE NUMBER of official and unofficial Web sites and online resources dedicated to it. The official jQuery Web site offers some useful things such as the API, a download area, and bug tracker, but falls short in other areas. On the other hand, the jQuery community is an extremely valuable resource and picks up where the jQuery Web site leaves off by offering tutorials, code examples, plug-ins, and more. In this chapter, I review all of the official and unofficial resources available to the jQuery community.

The process of learning about jQuery should not stop after you finish reading this book. The jQuery community is a very large one that is continually growing every day. If you do a Google search on *jQuery*, 18 million results are returned, and that number increases daily. Every morning, I read Popurls (`popurls.com`), which aggregates the best of sites such as Digg (`www.digg.com`), Delicious (`www.delicious.com`), RedDit (`www.reddit.com`), Twitter (`www.twitter.com`), and many other social communities. Nearly every day, I see at least one top news story that features something about jQuery. It's a hot topic.

WATCHING JQUERY GROW

The growth of jQuery is impressive — not long ago, it was used by only a small network of people. Now with support from companies such as Google and Microsoft, among many others as seen in Figure 12-1, support for jQuery has exploded. Companies that once didn't want to support jQuery are now totally invested in the library.

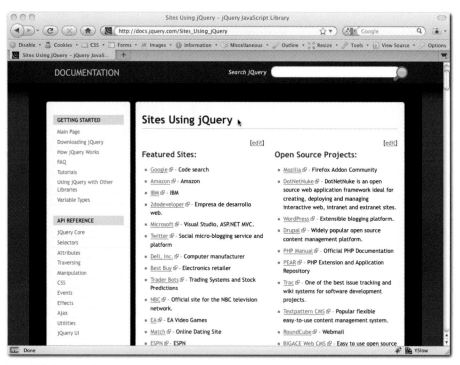

Figure 12-1: Sites using jQuery

The success of jQuery is a product not only of its great creator, John Resig, and his team, but also the massive community that supports jQuery. I encourage everyone who reads this book to donate to the jQuery Project. It doesn't have to be a massive amount — even $5 makes a difference. The jQuery Project is non-profit. Most of the people who work on the project are non-paid volunteers and their goal is to make something great, not to make money.

When you think about all of the time and effort jQuery has probably saved you, donating a few bucks is a great way of saying thanks. To ensure that the people behind jQuery can continue creating such a great product, donate at `http://jquery.org/donate`, shown in Figure 12-2.

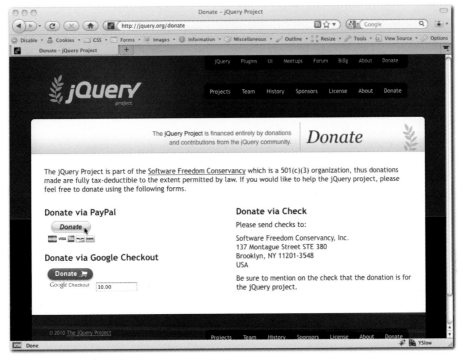

Figure 12-2: Donate to the jQuery Project

© 2010 The jQuery Project

303

USING THE JQUERY WEB SITE

The official jQuery Web site (`jquery.com`) offers great documentation on how to use the API, but some of the other areas are lacking in usability and consistency. The Web site is organized into five sections:

- Download
- Documentation
- Tutorials
- Bug Tracker
- Discussion

The download section offers different ways of accessing the jQuery library for download and also through a CDN (content delivery network).

WORKING WITH JQUERY API DOCUMENTATION

The team behind jQuery has spent an enormous amount of time building incredible online documentation — it's available for everyone to use. The Web site contains information about all of the methods available in current and past versions of jQuery, as shown in Figure 12-3. Access the jQuery API documentation by navigating to `api.jquery.com`.

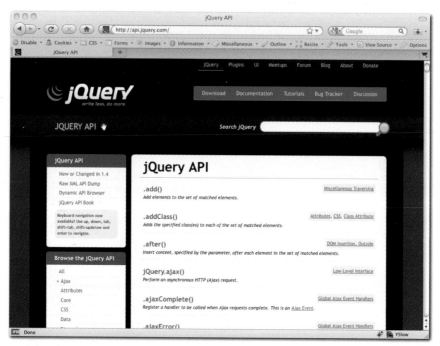

Figure 12-3: The jQuery API documentation

© 2010 The jQuery Project

The jQuery team has also implemented an impressive search feature that makes it easy to find what you are looking for. I've personally never run into any problems trying to find something. The jQuery Web site is also nicely indexed in search engines, which is another way to find information on different methods throughout the API.

Each function or method has its own dedicated page complete with a description, code examples, and a comments section. Figure 12-4 shows the `css()` method dedicated page.

FINDING JQUERY TUTORIALS

The jQuery Web site also houses a section consisting of tutorials created by members of the jQuery community and posted by the jQuery team, as seen in Figure 12-5. There are tutorials on every part of the API, plus tutorials created in other languages. This is a great place to start if you want to learn how to do something new with jQuery. The jQuery tutorials section is accessed by navigating to `docs.jquery.com/Tutorials`.

ATTENDING A JQUERY MEETUP OR CONFERENCE

The jQuery meetups section is accessed by navigating to `http://meetups.jquery.com/`. Version 1.3.2 contains a new section called Meetups, shown in Figure 12-6, which is powered by the Web site Meetup (`www.meetup.com`). Meetups are unofficial clubs or gatherings for jQuery enthusiasts. They are great ways to network and learn more about jQuery. I highly recommend joining a jQuery meetup in a location near you.

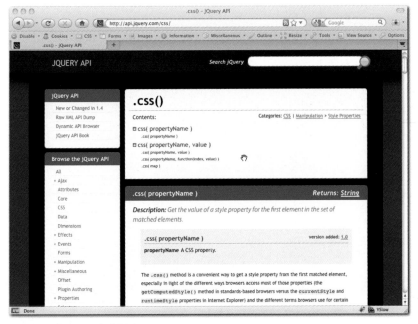

Figure 12-4: The css() method API documentation

© 2010 The jQuery Project

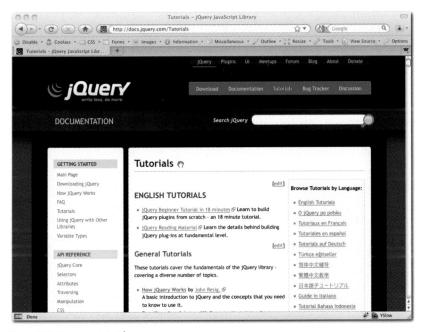

Figure 12-5: jQuery.com tutorials

© 2010 The jQuery Project

Figure 12-6: jQuery.com meetups

© 2010 The jQuery Project

In addition to jQuery meetups that are organized by the jQuery community, the developers behind jQuery also schedule one or two official jQuery conferences a year in locations such as San Francisco and Boston. The jQuery conferences draw small and intimate crowds of about 250-300 attendees who focus solely on jQuery-related topics with great speakers from the core jQuery team and the outside community. The jQuery conferences are a great way to network with other professionals who work with jQuery on a daily basis in their careers as well as people who are new to jQuery. The jQuery team dedicates a section of their Web site to information on the conference, as shown in Figure 12-7.

A few other conferences have been started in support of the JavaScript professional community, but the jQuery Conference is the only one to place full emphasis on jQuery.

SUBMITTING BUGS TO THE BUG TRACKER

As you work with the jQuery library, you may come across a bug in the programming. The jQuery team has created a Bug Tracker, shown in Figure 12-8, to enable users of the library to add bugs to the tracker so that they can be fixed in future versions. Tracking bugs is very important, and with jQuery having such a large community of users, a structured way to submit bugs to the jQuery team is essential. The jQuery bug tracker section is accessed by navigating to `http://bugs.jquery.com/newticket?redirectedfrom=`.

Figure 12-7: The Web site for the official jQuery conference

© 2010 The jQuery Project

Figure 12-8: The jQuery.com Bug Tracker

© 2010 The jQuery Project

GETTING INVOLVED IN THE JQUERY FORUM

The jQuery team runs a forum, shown in Figure 12-9, that you can use to post anything you want about jQuery, whether it be praise, problems, solutions, code examples, and so on. It's a great place for any level of jQuery developer to interact with other developers.

At the time of writing, the forum contains more than 65,000 posts and 143,236 responses, so it's a vibrant and active community. You need to set up a free account before you can participate. The jQuery Forum section is accessed by navigating to `http://forum.jquery.com/`.

OTHER WEB DESIGN AND DEVELOPMENT RESOURCES

These sites, among others, are great places to get help with jQuery and other Web design-related topics:

- Learning jQuery (`www.learningjquery.com`)
- Stack Overflow (`www.stackoverflow.com`)
- jQuery for Designers (`www.jqueryfordesigners.com`)
- Visual jQuery (`www.visualjquery.com`)
- The 14 Days of jQuery (`www.jquery14.com`)
- Nettuts+ (`www.nettuts.com`)
- Ajaxian (`www.ajaxian.com`)
- Forrst (`www.forrst.com`)
- SitePoint (`www.sitepoint.com`)

Figure 12-9: The jQuery.com Forum

© 2010 The jQuery Project

Index

SYMBOLS AND NUMERICS

* (wildcard selector), selecting elements with, 41–42
200 (server error response code), 218
301 (server error response code), 218
302 (server error response code), 218
400 (server error response code), 218
401 (server error response code), 218
403 (server error response code), 218
404 (server error response code), 218
500 (server error response code), 218

A

`<a>` anchor tag, 60
`accept` (validate plug-in option), 208
accordion (jQuery UI), 254, 263–264
accordion menus, creating, 142–147
`.addClass()` method, 69–70
adding
  advanced effects to drop-down menus, 141
  advanced validation rules and messages to forms, 208–210
  classes to DOM elements, 69–70
  content with mouse clicks, 82–84
  CSS to DOM elements, 69
  delay to create timed animations, 114–115
  e-mail validation to forms, 194–198
  `hover` effects to rows, 157–160
  HTML before/after elements in DOM, 66–67
  HTML to DOM, 64
  jQuery UI to Web sites, 255–256
  messages after rows in tables, 162–164, 166
  row colors using filters, 157
  rows based on index value, 165
  text to elements in DOM, 64–65
  validation to forms, 204–208
`after()` method, 66–67
Ajax
  JSON (JavaScript Object Notation) data
    creating Delicious widget, 235–241
    creating Yelp widget, 241–250
    retrieving internal JSON data, 234–235
    working with, 231–233
  loading from Web pages
    handling errors, 217–219
    loading all content, 216–217
    loading sections, 219–221
    overview, 215–216
  overview, 213–215
  submitting forms using GET and POST, 221–226
  XML (eXtensible Markup Language) data
    parsing, 229–231
    working with, 227–229
`Ajax()` method. *See* Ajax
Ajaxian (Web site), 308
alerts, showing, 76–77
Android browser (Google), 293–295
Android desktop emulator (Google), 292
`animate()` method. *See* animations
`:animated` filter, 53
animations
  adding delay to create timed, 114–115
  adding effects to drop-down menus, 141
  creating
    building image galleries, 120–127
    jQuery Easing plug-in, 127–128
    overview, 119
`api` (qTip plug-in option), 203
API documentation, 303–304

API key (Yelp), 243–250

Appcelerator Titanium Mobile, 296–298

`append()` method, 65–66

appending HTML within elements, 65–66

`appendKey` (Visualize configuration option), 177

`appendTitle` (Visualize configuration option), 177

Apple iPhone Safari desktop emulator, 292

Apple iPhone Safari mobile browser, 293

Apple Safari
  compatibility with, 15
  mobile browser features, 289

applications, developing mobile, 296

applying basic filter definitions, 52–53

attributes
  names and functions of, 60–61
  selecting elements in DOM by
    adding, 64–69
    cloning, 64–69
    manipulating HTML and CSS, 63
    overview, 60–61
    replacing, 64–69
    specific text strings, 62–63
    Web site address, 61–62
    working with CSS, 69–70

Autocomplete (jQuery UI), 254, 264–266

B

bar charts, 177–179

`barGroupMargin` (Visualize configuration option), 177

`barMargin` (Visualize configuration option), 177

`before()` method, 66–67

Berkeley Software Distribution (BSD) license, 7

Best Buy (Web site), 198

`bind()` method
  event handler, 78–79
  mouse driven events used with, 81–82

`blur()` event, 94, 95

browsers (mobile)
  Apple iPhone Safari Mobile browser, 293
  CSS3, 289–290
  design setup, 291–292
  developing Web sites and applications, 296
  displaying smartphone specific content, 295–296
  Google Android browser, 293–295
  HTML5, 290–291
  overview, 288–289

BSD (Berkeley Software Distribution) license, 7

Bug Tracker, 306–307

building
  accordion menus, 142–147
  Add to Cart functionality, 89–92
  advanced animations
    building image galleries, 120–127
    overview, 119
    jQuery Easing plug-in, 127–128
  bar charts, 177–179
  charts with Visualize plug-in, 176–177
  check all check box links, 190–191
  default text within input fields, 186–188
  Delicious widget, 235–241
  dynamic tabs with Tabs tool, 271–272
  HTML by parsing XML data, 229–231

HTML by retrieving internal JSON data, 234–235

image galleries with text captions, 120–127

for mobile Web, 288

news feed tickers with effects, 116–119

plug-ins, 277–283

rollover effects on buttons with images, 93

tabbed content, 147–154

tables with plug-ins
  changing default sort order, 175–176
  creating bar charts, 177–179
  overview, 172–173
  tablesorter plug-in, 173–175
  Visualize plug-in, 176–177

tooltips, 85–89

tooltips with `title` attribute, 203

UI themes with Themeroller, 258–260

Yelp widget, 241–250

button (jQuery UI), 254

C

Cascading Style Sheets (CSS)
  adding to DOM elements, 69
  manipulating, 63
  overview, 69
  selectors
    components of, 40
    defined, 39
    descendent, 50–51
    HTML tag, 43
    `ID` selector, 43–45
    multiple elements, 51–52
    overview, 40–41
    `parent-child` selectors, 47–49
    selecting page elements by class, 45–46

selecting page elements
with multiple
classes, 47
wildcard (*), 41–42
styling tables with
hover effect, 157–160
overview, 156–157
row colors, 157
Cascading Style Sheets 3
(CSS3), 289–290
chaining
effects, 115–116
overview, 14
change() event, 94
changing default sort order,
175–176
charts
bar, 177–179
creating with Visualize
plug-in, 176–177
check boxes, creating check all
links, 190–191
Chrome (Google)
compatibility with, 15
mobile browser features, 289
classes
adding to DOM elements,
69–70
removing from DOM
elements, 70
selecting elements by, 45–46
selecting elements with
multiple, 47
toggling on DOM
elements, 70
click event
in Dojo, 9
overview, 82–84
in Prototype, 8
using with bind(), 81
cloning HTML elements, 69
Coda, 20
code editor, choices for, 20
coding options, 14

colors (Visualize configuration option), 177
compatibility (cross-browser),
15
compressed jQuery library, 29
conferences (jQuery), 304–306
console (Firebug), 25–27
:contains filter, 53, 59–60,
166
content (qTip plug-in
option), 202
cookies, using with show()
method, 103–104
copying content between form
fields, 198–201
creating
accordion menus, 142–147
add to cart functionality,
89–92
advanced animations
building image galleries,
120–127
jQuery Easing plug-in,
127–128
overview, 119
bar charts, 177–179
charts with Visualize
plug-in, 176–177
check all check box links,
190–191
default text within input
fields, 186–188
Delicious widget, 235–241
dynamic tabs with Tabs
tool, 271–272
HTML by parsing XML
data, 229–231
HTML by retrieving internal
JSON data, 234–235
image galleries with text
captions, 120–127
for mobile Web, 288
news feed tickers with
effects, 116–119

plug-ins, 277–283
rollover effects on buttons
with images, 93
tabbed content, 147–154
tables with plug-ins
changing default sort
order, 175–176
creating bar charts,
177–179
overview, 172–173
tablesorter plug-in,
173–175
Visualize plug-in, 176–177
tooltips, 85–89
tooltips with title
attribute, 203
UI themes with Themeroller,
258–260
Yelp widget, 241–250
creditcard (validate plug-in
option), 208
cross-browser compatibility, 15
CSS (Cascading Style Sheets)
adding to DOM elements, 69
manipulating, 63
overview, 69
selectors
components of, 40
defined, 39
descendent, 50–51
HTML tag, 43
ID selector, 43–45
multiple elements, 51–52
overview, 40–41
parent-child selectors,
47–49
selecting page elements
by class, 45–46
selecting page elements
with multiple
classes, 47
wildcard (*), 41–42
styling tables with
hover effect, 157–160

CSS (Cascading Style Sheets)
(*continued*)
overview, 156–157
row colors, 157
CSS3 (Cascading Style Sheets
3), 289–290
CSS3-compliance, 15–16
cssAsc (tablesorter
option), 173
.css() method, 69
cssDesc (tablesorter
option), 173
cssHeader (tablesorter
option), 173
customizing jQuery UI
design, 256–258

D

data
JSON (JavaScript Object
Notation)
creating Delicious widget,
235–241
creating Yelp widget,
241–250
retrieving, 234–235
working with, 231–233
manipulating in tables
adding messages after
rows, 162–164, 166
adding rows, 165
overview, 161–162
removing rows, 164–165,
166
XML (eXtensible Markup
Language)
parsing, 229–231
working with, 227–229
date (validate plug-in option),
208
date, as regular expression for
form validation, 198
Datepicker (jQuery UI), 254,
266–268
dblclick event, 81

delay() method, 114–115
delegate() method, 80–81
Delicious (Web site), 301
Delicious widget, 235–241
descendent selectors, 50–51
design (mobile)
downloading Apple
iPhone Safari desktop
emulator, 292
downloading Google
Android desktop
emulator, 292
overview, 291
design, setup of, 291–292
developing mobile Web sites
and applications, 296
development environment,
setting up, 20–27
development resources, 308
Dialog (jQuery UI), 254
Digg (Web site), 301
digits (validate plug-in
option), 208
disabling form elements,
182–183
displaying
alerts, 76–77
backup images, 77
search options with
slideToggle()
method, 107–109
smartphone specific content,
295–296
distributing plug-ins
overview, 284
packaging for distribution,
284
submitting to Web sites, 285
doctype, 30–31
document and window events
error(), 77
load(), 73–76, 215–221
overview, 72–73
ready(), 73
unload(), 76–77

Document Object Model
(DOM)
defined, 6
filtering with selector filters
applying basic definitions,
52–53
:contains filter, 53,
59–60, 166
:empty filter, 57–58
:even filters, 53–55
:first filters, 55–56
:has filter, 56–57
:last filters, 55–56
:odd filters, 53–55
removing classes, 70
selecting elements by
attributes
adding/cloning/replacing,
64–69
manipulating HTML and
CSS, 63
overview, 60–61
specific text strings, 62–63
Web site address, 61–62
working with CSS, 69–70
toggling elements, 70
documentation
API, 303–304
quality, 12–13
Dojo software, 8–9
DOM (Document Object
Model)
defined, 6
filtering with selector filters
applying basic definitions,
52–53
:contains filter, 53,
59–60, 166
:empty filter, 57–58
:even filters, 53–55
:first filters, 55–56
:has filter, 56–57
:last filters, 55–56
:odd filters, 53–55

removing classes, 70
selecting elements by attributes
adding/cloning/replacing, 64–69
manipulating HTML and CSS, 63
overview, 60–61
specific text strings, 62–63
Web site address, 61–62
working with CSS, 69–70
toggling elements, 70
donating to jQuery, 302
double-click event, 85
downloading
Apple iPhone Safari desktop emulator, 292
Google Android desktop emulator, 292
jQuery UI, 255
library (jQuery), 27–30
drop-down menus
adding effects to, 141
creating, 135–141
dynamic content
JSON (JavaScript Object Notation) data
creating Delicious widget, 235–241
creating Yelp widget, 241–250
retrieving internal JSON data, 234–235
working with, 231–233
loading from Web pages
handling errors, 217–219
loading all content, 216–217
loading sections, 219–221
overview, 215–216
submitting forms using GET and POST, 221–226
XML (eXtensible Markup Language) data

parsing, 229–231
working with, 227–229
dynamic tabs, 271–272

E
Easing plug-in (jQuery), 127–128
effects
adding to drop-down menus, 141
chaining, 115–116
creating news feed tickers with, 116–119
creating rollover effects on buttons with images, 93
delay() method, 114–115
fadeIn() method, 101, 109–114
fadeOut() method, 101, 109–114
fadeTo() method, 101, 109–114
hide() method
overview, 101–103
toggling with show(), 104–106
overview, 99, 100
show() method
cookies, 103–104
overview, 101–103
toggling with hide(), 104–106
slideDown() method, 101, 106–107
slideToggle() method, 101, 107–109
slideUp() method, 101, 106–107
toggle() method, 101, 104–106
email (validate plug-in option), 208
e-mail validation, adding to forms, 194–198

:empty filter, 53, 57–58
enabling
Firebug, 23–24
form elements, 182–183
enhancing forms with plug-ins
adding advanced validation rules/messages, 208–210
adding validation, 204–208
overview, 201
qTip, 201–203
tooltips, 203
Validate plug-in, 203–208
:eq() filter, 53, 165
equalTo (validate plug-in option), 208
error handling, 217–219
error() method, 73, 77
error response codes (server), 218
:even filter, 53–55
event delegation
bind event handler, 78–79
delegate method, 80–81
live event handler, 79–80
overview, 77–78
event handling, 71
events and methods
.addClass(), 69–70, 142–147
after(), 66–67
Ajax(). See Ajax
animate()
adding delay to create timed, 114–115
adding effects to drop-down menus, 141
building image galleries, 120–127
jQuery Easing plug-in, 127–128
overview, 119
append(), 65–66
before(), 66–67

events and methods
(continued)
bind()
event handler, 78–79
mouse driven events used
with, 81–82
blur(), 94, 95
change(), 94
click
in Dojo, 9
overview, 82–84
in Prototype, 8
using with bind(), 81
.css(), 69
dblclick, 81
delay(), 114–115
delegate(), 80–81
document and window
error(), 77
load(), 73–76, 215–221
overview, 72–73
ready(), 73
unload(), 76–77
double-click, 85
error(), 73, 77
fadeIn(), 101, 109–114
fadeOut(), 101, 109–114
fadeTo(), 101, 109–114
focus(), 94–95
focusIn(), 94
focusOut(), 94
form
blur event, 95
focus event, 94–95
overview, 94
has(), 53, 56–57
.hasClass(), 69
hide()
overview, 101–103
toggling with show()
method, 104–106
hover, 85–89, 157–160
.html(), 64
keydown(), 95–98
keypress(), 95–98

keyup(), 95–98
load()
loading dynamic content
from Web pages,
215–221
overview, 73–76
mousedown, 81, 89–92
mouseenter, 81
mouseleave, 81
mousemove, 82
mouseout, 82
mouseover, 82
mouseup, 81, 89–92
overview, 72
prepend(), 65–66
ready(), 73
remove()
overview, 67–69
removing rows based on
index value, 166
removing rows in tables,
164–165
.removeClass(), 69, 70
reset(), 94
resize(), 73
responseText, 218
scroll(), 73
select(), 94
show()
cookies, 103–104
overview, 101–103
toggling with hide()
method, 104–106
slideDown(), 101, 106–107
slideToggle(), 101,
107–109
slideUp(), 101, 106–107
submit(), 94
text(), 64–65
textStatus(), 218
toggle(), 101, 104–106
.toggleClass(), 69, 70
unload(), 73, 76–77
XMLHttpRequest, 218

eXtensible Markup Language
(XML) data
parsing, 229–231
working with, 227–229

F
Facebook, 100, 214
fadeIn() method, 101,
109–114
fadeOut() method, 101,
109–114
fadeTo() method, 101,
109–114
Fancybox plug-in, 272–274
fields, highlighting in forms,
183–186
:filter, 52. See also selector
filters
filters
adding row colors using, 157
:animated, 53
applying basic definitions,
52–53
:contains filter, 53, 59–60,
166
defined, 39
:empty filter, 53, 57–58
:eq, 53
:even filters, 53–55
:first filters, 55–56
:first-child, 53
:gt, 53
:has filter, 53, 56–57
:header, 53
:hidden, 53
:last filter, 53–55
:last-child, 53
:lt, 53
:not, 53
:nth- child, 53
:odd filter, 53–55
:only-child, 53
:parent, 53
:visible, 53

Firebug
  console, 25–27
  editing HTML, 25
  enabling, 23–24
  inspecting HTML, 25
  installing, 22–23
  overview, 21–22
  using in Firefox, 21–27
Firefox (Mozilla)
  compatibility with, 15
  mobile browser features, 289
  running JavaScript live in, 27
  using Firebug in, 21–27
:first filter, 55–56
:first-child filter, 53
500 (server error response
  code), 218
focus() event, 94–95
focusin() event, 94
focusout() event, 94
forms
  adding e-mail validation,
    194–198
  copying content between
    fields, 198–201
  creating check all check box
    links, 190–191
  creating default text,
    186–188
  disabling elements, 182–183
  enabling elements, 182–183
  enhancing with plug-ins
    adding advanced
      validation rules/
      messages, 208–210
    adding validation,
      204–208
    overview, 201
    qTip, 201–203
    tooltips, 203
    Validate plug-in, 203–208
  events, 94–95
  highlighting fields in forms,
    183–186

input boxes, 182, 191–192
limiting character counts,
  188–190
overview, 181
retrieving value of select
  options, 193–194
submitting using GET and
  POST, 221–226
value of input boxes,
  191–192
Forrst (Web site), 308
forum (jQuery), 269, 308
400 (server error response
  code), 218
401 (server error response
  code), 218
403 (server error response
  code), 218
404 (server error response
  code), 218
The 14 Days of jQuery (Web
  site), 308
frameworks (mobile)
  Appcelerator Titanium
    Mobile, 296–298
  JQTouch plug-in, 298–299

G

GET requests, submitting forms
  using, 221–226
Gmail, 215
Google Android browser,
  293–295
Google Android desktop
  emulator, 292
Google Chrome
  compatibility with, 15
  mobile browser features, 289
Google project hosting, 285
graceful degradation
  approach, 17
GSGD, 127
:gt filter, 53

H

has() method, 53, 56–57
.hasClass() method, 69
:header filter, 53
height (Visualize configuration option), 177
Hewitt, Joe (Firebug
  creator), 21
:hidden filter, 53
hide (qTip plug-in
  option), 202
hide() method
  overview, 101–103
  toggling with show()
    method, 104–106
highlighting fields in forms,
  183–186
hover effects
  adding to rows, 157–160
  overview, 85–89
HTML (HyperText Markup
  Language)
  adding before/after elements
    in DOM, 66–67
  adding to DOM, 64
  appending within elements,
    65–66
  cloning elements, 69
  creating by parsing XML
    data, 229–231
  creating by retrieving inter-
    nal JSON data, 234–235
  editing, 25
  inspecting, 25
  manipulating, 63
  prepending within elements,
    65–66
  removing elements from
    DOM, 67–69
  tag, 43
HTML5, 290–291
.html() method, 64

315

HyperText Markup Language
(HTML)
adding before/after elements
in DOM, 66–67
adding to DOM, 64
appending within elements,
65–66
cloning elements, 69
creating by parsing XML
data, 229–231
creating by retrieving internal JSON data, 234–235
editing, 25
inspecting, 25
manipulating, 63
prepending within elements,
65–66
removing elements from
DOM, 67–69
tag, 43

I

ID selector, selecting elements
with, 43–45
images
building galleries with text
captions, 120–127
creating rollover effects on
buttons with, 93
displaying backup, 77
preloading with load()
event, 73–76
incorporating
jQuery plug-ins into Web
sites, 253
overview, 269
using Fancybox, 272–274
using jQuery tools,
269–272
jQuery UI into Web sites
adding to site, 255–256
creating theme with
ThemeRoller,
258–260
customizing design,
256–258

downloading, 255
jQuery UI features,
261–268
jQuery UI themes, 261
overview, 253–255
widgets, 256
index value
adding rows based on, 165
removing rows based on,
166
input boxes (forms)
overview, 182
value of, 191–192
input fields
creating default text within,
186–188
limiting character counts
on, 188–190
installing Firebug, 22–23
Internet Explorer
(Microsoft), 15
iPhone Safari desktop emulator
(Apple), 292
iPhone Safari mobile browser
(Apple), 293

J

JavaScript
advanced debugging with
Firebug, 27
libraries
compared with traditional
approach, 6–7
main players, 7–9
overview, 6
obtrusive, 16–17
running live in Firefox, 27
unobtrusive, 16–17
JavaScript Object Notation
(JSON) data
creating
Delicious widget, 235–241
Yelp widget, 241–250
retrieving internal JSON
data, 234–235
working with, 231–233

JQTouch plug-in, 298–299
jQuery. *See also specific topics*
advantages of, 9–17
history of, 10
overview, 5
relationship with Web pages,
11–12
users, 10–11
Web site
API documentation,
303–304
forum, 308
meetup and conferences,
304–306
overview, 9
submitting bugs to Bug
Tracker, 306–307
tutorials, 304
jQuery Easing plug-in,
127–128
jQuery for Designers (Web
site), 308
jQuery forum, 269
jQuery library
downloading, 27–30
including in Web pages,
30–31
jQuery Mobile, 296
jQuery UI, incorporating into
Web sites
adding to sites, 255–256
creating theme with
ThemeRoller, 258–260
customizing design, 256–258
downloading, 255
jQuery UI features, 261–268
jQuery UI themes, 261
overview, 253–255
widgets, 256
jQuery wrapper
overview, 31–33
preventing conflicts with
other libraries, 34–35
running code outside document ready handler, 34
using JavaScript with, 35

JSON (JavaScript Object Notation) data
creating
Delicious widget, 235–241
Yelp widget, 241–250
retrieving internal JSON data, 234–235
working with, 231–233
JSONLint JSON validator, 232–233

K

keyboard events, 95–98
keydown() event, 95–98
keypress() event, 95–98
keyup() event, 95–98

L

:last filter, 55–56
:last-child filter, 53
Learning jQuery (Web site), 308
letters only, as regular expression for form validation, 198
libraries (JavaScript)
compared with traditional approach, 6–7
main players, 7–9
overview, 6
library (jQuery)
downloading, 27–30
including in Web pages, 30–31
lineWeight (Visualize configuration option), 177
links
selecting ones that contain specific Web site addresses, 61–62
setting to open new windows, 132–133
live event handler, 79–80

load() method
loading dynamic content from Web pages, 215–221
overview, 73–76
loading dynamic content from Web pages
handling errors, 217–219
loading all content, 216–217
loading sections, 219–221
overview, 215–216
:lt filter, 53

M

Mac OS X
Apache Web server, 20–21
Coda, 20
MAMP, 20–21
MAMP (Mac/Apache/MySQL/PHP), 20–21
manipulating
CSS, 63
data in tables
adding messages after rows, 162–164, 166
adding rows, 165
overview, 161–162
removing rows, 164–165, 166
HTML, 63
Mashable, 133
maxlength (validate plug-in option), 208
meetups (jQuery), 304–306
menus
accordion, 142–147
drop-down, 135–141
Navigation, 133–135
methods and events
.addClass(), 69–70, 142–147
after(), 66–67
Ajax(). See Ajax

animate()
adding delay to create timed, 114–115
adding effects to drop-down menus, 141
building image galleries, 120–127
jQuery Easing plug-in, 127–128
overview, 119
append(), 65–66
before(), 66–67
bind()
event handler, 78–79
mouse driven events used with, 81–82
blur(), 94, 95
change(), 94
click
in Dojo, 9
overview, 82–84
in Prototype, 8
using with bind(), 81
.css(), 69
dblclick, 81
delay(), 114–115
delegate(), 80–81
document and window
error(), 77
load(), 73–76, 215–221
overview, 72–73
ready(), 73
unload(), 76–77
double-click, 85
error(), 73, 77
fadeIn(), 101, 109–114
fadeOut(), 101, 109–114
fadeTo(), 101, 109–114
focus(), 94–95
focusIn(), 94
focusOut(), 94
form
blur event, 95
focus event, 94–95
overview, 94

methods and events *(continued)*
 has(), 53, 56–57
 .hasClass(), 69
 hide()
  overview, 101–103
  toggling with show()
   method, 104–106
 hover, 85–89, 157–160
 .html(), 64
 keydown(), 95–98
 keypress(), 95–98
 keyup(), 95–98
 load()
  loading dynamic content
   from Web pages,
   215–221
  overview, 73–76
 mousedown, 81, 89–92
 mouseenter, 81
 mouseleave, 81
 mousemove, 82
 mouseout, 82
 mouseover, 82
 mouseup, 81, 89–92
 overview, 72
 prepend(), 65–66
 ready(), 73
 remove()
  overview, 67–69
  removing rows based on
   index value, 166
  removing rows in tables,
   164–165
 .removeClass(), 69, 70
 reset(), 94
 resize(), 73
 responseText, 218
 scroll(), 73
 select(), 94
 show()
  cookies, 103–104
  overview, 101–103
  toggling with hide()
   method, 104–106

slideDown(), 101, 106–107
slideToggle(), 101,
 107–109
slideUp(), 101, 106–107
submit(), 94
text(), 64–65
textStatus(), 218
toggle(), 101, 104–106
.toggleClass(), 69, 70
unload(), 73, 76–77
XMLHttpRequest, 218
Microsoft Internet Explorer, 15
Microsoft software, 7
minlength (validate plug-in
 option), 207
Mobile (jQuery), 296
mobile browsers
 Apple iPhone Safari Mobile
  browser, 293
 CSS3, 289–290
 design setup, 291–292
 developing Web sites and
  applications, 296
 displaying smartphone specific content, 295–296
 Google Android browser,
  293–295
 HTML5, 290–291
 overview, 288–289
mobile frameworks
 Appcelerator Titanium
  Mobile, 296–298
 JQTouch plug-in, 298–299
mobile Web
 building for, 288
 mobile browsers
  Apple iPhone Safari Mo-
   bile browser, 293
  CSS3, 289–290
  design setup, 291–292
  developing Web sites and
   applications, 296
  displaying smartphone
   specific content,
   295–296

Google Android browser,
 293–295
HTML5, 290–291
overview, 288–289
overview, 287
MooTools software, 8
mouse events
 click, 82–84
 creating rollover effects on
  buttons with images, 93
 double-click, 85
 hover, 85–89
 mousedown, 81, 89–92
 mouseenter event, 81
 mouseleave event, 81
 mousemove event, 82
 mouseout event, 82
 mouseover event, 82
 mouseup, 81, 89–92
 overview, 81–82
Mozilla Firefox
 compatibility with, 15
 mobile browser features, 289
 running JavaScript live in, 27
 using Firebug in, 21–27

N
navigation
 creating
  accordion menus, 142–147
  drop-down menus,
   135–141
  tabbed content, 147–154
 overview, 131
 setting
  active items in Navigation
   menu, 133–135
  links to open new win-
   dows, 132–133
Navigation menus, 133–135
Netflix, 272–273
Nettus+ (Web site), 308
nonobtrusive JavaScript, 16–17
:not filter, 53

:nth-child filter, 53
number (validate plug-in
    option), 208
numbers only, as regular
    expression for form
    validation, 198

O

obtrusive JavaScript, 16–17
:odd filter, 53–55
:only-child filter, 53
open source software
    community support, 12
    defined, 7
Opera
    compatibility with, 15
    mobile browser features, 289
options
    coding, 14
    plug-in, 276–277

P

packaging plug-ins for
    distribution, 284
pages (Web)
    including jQuery library in,
        30–31
    loading dynamic content
        from
        handling errors, 217–219
        loading all content,
            216–217
        loading sections, 219–221
        overview, 215–216
pagination (table), 166–172
:parent filter, 53
parent-child selectors,
    47–49
parseDirection (Visualize
    configuration option), 177
parsing XML data, 229–231
phone number, as regular
    expression for form
    validation, 198

pieLabelPos (Visualize con-
    figuration option), 177
pieMargin (Visualize configu-
    ration option), 177
plug-ins
    creating tables with, 277–283
    changing default sort
        order, 175–176
    creating bar charts,
        177–179
    overview, 172–173
    tablesorter plug-in,
        173–175
    Visualize plug-in, 176–177
distributing
    overview, 284
    packaging for
        distribution, 284
    submitting to Web
        sites, 285
enhancing forms with
    adding advanced valida-
        tion rules/messages,
        208–210
    adding validation,
        204–208
    overview, 201
    qTip, 201–203
    tooltips, 203
    Validate plug-in, 203–208
Fancybox, 272–274
incorporating
    jQuery UI into Web sites,
        253–268
    plug-ins into Web sites,
        253, 269–274
JQTouch, 298–299
jQuery Easing, 127
overview, 251–253
Visualize, 176–177
writing
    creating plug-in, 277–283
    overview, 274–275
    setting options, 276–277

sketching it out, 275
structure, 276
Popurls (Web site), 301
position (qTip plug-in
    option), 202
POST requests, submitting
    forms using, 221–226
preloading images with
    load() event, 73–76
prepend() method, 65–66
prepending HTML within
    elements, 65–66
Progress Bar (jQuery UI), 254
progressive enhancement, 17
Prototype software, 8

Q

qTip plug-in, 201–203

R

ready() event, 73
Really Simple Syndication
    (RSS) feeds, 227–229
RedDit (Web site), 301
remove() method
    overview, 67–69
    removing rows based on
        index value, 166
    removing rows in tables,
        164–165
.removeClass() method,
    69, 70
removing
    classes from DOM
        elements, 70
    content with mouse clicks,
        82–84
    HTML elements from DOM,
        67–69
    rows based on content, 166
    rows based on index
        value, 166
    rows using filter selectors,
        164–165

required (validate plug-in option), 207
reset() method, 94
Resig, John (software developer), 10
resize() event, 73
resources
  forum, 308
  jQuery Web site
    API documentation, 303–304
    meetups and conferences, 304–306
    submitting bugs to Bug Tracker, 306–307
    tutorials, 304
  overview, 301
  success of jQuery, 302–303
  Web design and development, 308
responseText method, 218
retrieving
  internal JSON data, 234–235
  value of select options, 193–194
rollover effects, creating, 93
rows (table)
  adding based on index value, 165
  adding hover effects to, 157–160
  adding messages in tables after, 162–164, 166
  removing based on content, 166
  removing based on index value, 166
  removing using filter selectors, 164–165
  sorting using tablesorter plug-in, 173–175
RSS (Really Simple Syndication) feeds, 227–229

Ruby on Rails, 8
running JavaScript live in Firefox, 27

S
Safari (Apple)
  compatibility with, 15
  iPhone Safari desktop emulator, 292
  iPhone Safari mobile browser, 293
  mobile browser features, 289
scroll() event, 73
select() event, 94
selecting
  elements
    with CSS selectors, 41–42
    with descendent selectors, 50–51
    with HTML tag, 43
    with ID selector, 43–45
    multiple, 51–52
    with multiple classes, 47
    with parent-child selectors, 47–49
    with wildcard (*) selector, 41–42
  elements by class, 45–46
  elements in DOM by attributes
    adding, 64–69
    cloning, 64–69
    manipulating HTML and CSS, 63
    overview, 60–61
    replacing, 64–69
    specific text strings, 62–63
    Web site address, 61–62
    working with CSS, 69–70
  links that contain specific Web site addresses, 61–62

selector filters
  applying basic definitions, 52–53
  :contains filter, 53, 59–60, 166
  :empty filter, 57–58
  :even filter, 53–55
  :first filter, 55–56
  has() filter, 56–57
  removing rows using, 164–165
selectors
  components of, 40
  defined, 39
  descendent, 50–51
  overview, 40–41
  selecting page elements with CSS
    by class, 45–46
    descendent selectors, 50–51
    HTML tag, 43
    ID selector, 43–45
    with multiple classes, 47
    multiple elements, 51–52
    overview, 41
    parent-child selectors, 47–49
    wildcard (*), 41–42
server error response codes, 218
setting up
  active items in Navigation menu, 133–135
  development environment, 20–27
  jQuery Tools, 270–271
  links to open new windows, 132–133
  mobile Web design
    downloading Apple iPhone Safari desktop emulator, 292

downloading Google Android desktop emulator, 292

overview, 291

plug-in options, 276–277

table pagination, 166–172

show (qTip plug-in option), 202

show() method

cookies, 103–104

overview, 101–103

toggling with hide() method, 104–106

SitePoint (Web site), 308

sketching out plug-ins, 275

slideDown() method, 101, 106–107

Slider (jQuery UI), 254

slideToggle() method, 101, 107–109

slideUp() method, 101, 106–107

smartphones, 295–296

Smashing Magazine, 227

software

Microsoft, 7

MooTools, 8

open source, 7, 12

Prototype, 8

sortForce (tablesorter option), 173

sorting

changing default sort order, 175–176

rows using tablesorter plug-in, 173–175

sortList (tablesorter option), 173

sortMultiSortKey (tablesorter option), 173

Stack Overflow (Web site), 308

statements (jQuery), anatomy of, 41

Stevenson, Sam (software developer), 8

structure (plug-in), 276

style (qTip plug-in option), 203

styling

items, 55–56

tables with CSS

hover effect, 157–160

overview, 156–157

row colors, 157

submit() event, 94

submitting

bugs to Bug Tracker, 306–307

forms using GET and POST, 221–226

plug-ins to Web sites, 285

T

tabbed content, creating, 147–154

tables

creating with plug-ins

changing default sort order, 175–176

creating bar charts, 177–179

overview, 172–173

tablesorter plug-in, 173–175

Visualize plug-in, 176–177

manipulating data

adding messages after rows, 162–164, 166

adding rows, 165

overview, 161–162

removing rows, 164–165, 166

overview, 155

rows

adding based on index value, 165

adding hover effects to, 157–160

adding messages in tables after, 162–164, 166

removing based on content, 166

removing based on index value, 166

removing using filter selectors, 164–165

sorting using tablesorter plug-in, 173–175

setting up pagination, 166–172

styling with CSS

hover effect, 157–160

overview, 156–157

row colors, 157

zebra striping, 53–55

tablesorter plug-in, 173–175

tabs (jQuery UI), 254, 261–262

Tabs tool, creating dynamic tabs with, 271–272

tags

<a> anchor, 60

HTML, 43

text

adding to elements in DOM, 64–65

building image galleries with captions, 120–127

creating within form input fields, 186–188

text() method, 64–65

textColors (Visualize configuration option), 177

textStatus() method, 218

ThemeRoller, creating UI themes with, 258–260

themes (UI)

creating with ThemeRoller, 258–260

using, 261

third-party extensions, 81–82

301 (server error response code), 218
302 (server error response code), 218
title (Visualize configuration option), 177
title attribute, creating tooltips with, 203
toggle() method, 101, 104–106
.toggleClass() method, 69, 70
toggling classes on DOM elements, 70
tools (jQuery)
    overview, 269–270
    setting up, 270–271
    Tabs tool, 271–272
tooltips
    creating, 85–89
    creating with title attribute, 203
tutorials (jQuery), 304
Twitter (Web site), 106, 188, 301
200 (server error response code), 218
type (Visualize configuration option), 177

U
UI (jQuery), incorporating into Web sites
    adding to sites, 255–256
    creating theme with ThemeRoller, 258–260
    customizing design, 256–258
    downloading, 255
    jQuery UI features, 261–268
    jQuery UI themes, 261
    overview, 253–255
    widgets, 256
uncompressed jQuery library, 29

unload() method, 73, 76–77
unobtrusive JavaScript, 16–17
url (validate plug-in option), 208

V
Validate plug-in
    overview, 204–208
    validating forms with, 203–208
validation
    adding e-mail, 194–198
    adding rules to forms, 208–210
    adding to forms, 204–208
versions (jQuery library), 29
:visible filter, 53
Visual jQuery (Web site), 308
Visualize plug-in, creating charts with, 176–177

W
WampServer (Windows/ Apache/MySQL/PHP Server), 20
Web (mobile)
    building for, 288
    mobile browsers
        Apple iPhone Safari Mobile browser, 293
        CSS3, 289–290
        design setup, 291–292
        developing Web sites and applications, 296
        displaying smartphone specific content, 295–296
        Google Android browser, 293–295
        HTML5, 290–291
        overview, 288–289
    overview, 287

Web design (mobile)
    downloading Apple iPhone Safari desktop emulator, 292
    downloading Google Android desktop emulator, 292
    overview, 291
Web design and development resources, 308
Web pages
    including jQuery library in, 30–31
    loading dynamic content from
        handling errors, 217–219
        loading all content, 216–217
        loading sections, 219–221
        overview, 215–216
Web sites
    developing mobile, 296
    incorporating jQuery plug-ins into
        overview, 253, 269
        using Fancybox, 272–274
        using jQuery tools, 269–272
    incorporating jQuery UI into
        adding to site, 255–256
        creating theme with ThemeRoller, 258–260
        customizing design, 256–258
        downloading, 255
        jQuery UI features, 261–268
        jQuery UI themes, 261
        overview, 253–255
        widgets, 256

jQuery
    API documentation, 303–304
    forum, 308
    meetup and conferences, 304–306
    overview, 9
    submitting bugs to Bug Tracker, 306–307
    tutorials, 304
jQuery plug-in, 253
selecting links that contain specific addresses, 61–62
submitting to Web sites, 285
widgets
    Delicious, 235–241
    jQuery UI, 256
    Yelp, 241–250
width (Visualize configuration option), 177
wildcard (*) selector, selecting elements with, 41–42

window and document events
    error(), 77
    load(), 73–76, 215–221
    overview, 72–73
    ready(), 73
    unload(), 76–77
windows, setting links to open new, 132–133
Windows WampServer, 20
Windows/Apache/MySQL/PHP Server (Wamp-Server), 20
wrapper (jQuery)
    overview, 31–33
    preventing conflicts with other libraries, 34–35
    running code outside document ready handler, 34
    using JavaScript with, 35
writing jQuery plug-ins
    creating plug-in, 277–283
    overview, 274–275
    setting options, 276–277

    sketching it out, 275
    structure, 276
Wufoo, 183–184

X
XHR request properties, 218
XML (eXtensible Markup Language) data
    parsing, 229–231
    working with, 227–229
XMLHttpRequest method, 218

Y
Yahoo! User Interface (YUI), 7–8
Yelp for Developers (Web site), 242
Yelp widget, 241–250
YUI (Yahoo! User Interface), 7–8

Z
zebra striping, 53–55

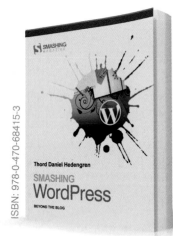